AMC'S **BEST DAY HIKES** IN
VERMONT

W9-BBZ-820

**FOUR-SEASON GUIDE TO 60 OF THE BEST TRAILS
IN THE GREEN MOUNTAIN STATE**

JENNIFER LAMPHERE ROBERTS

Appalachian Mountain Club Books
Boston, Massachusetts

AMC is a nonprofit organization, and sales of AMC Books fund our mission of protecting the Northeast outdoors. If you appreciate our efforts and would like to become a member or make a donation to AMC, visit outdoors.org, call 800-372-1758, or contact us at Appalachian Mountain Club, 5 Joy Street, Boston, MA 02108.

outdoors.org/publications/books

Distributed by The Globe Pequot Press, Guilford, Connecticut.

Front cover photograph © Caleb Kenna
Back cover photographs © Jeb Wallace-Brodeur
Interior photographs © Jennifer Lamphere Roberts, except for pages i © Jerry Monkman,
12 © Gary Lamphere; 59 and 207 © Judy Lamphere; 98 and 178 © Kip Roberts; 112 © Tristan Von
Duntz; 133 © Glenn Suokko; 137 © Julie Roberts; 173 © Stowe Land Trust
Maps by Ken Dumas © Appalachian Mountain Club
Cover design by Gia Giasullo/Studio eg
Interior design by Eric Edstam

Library of Congress Cataloging-in-Publication Data
Roberts, Jennifer Lamphere.
   AMC's best day hikes in Vermont : four-season guide to 60 of the best trails in the Green Mountain State / Jennifer Lamphere Roberts.
      p. cm.
   Includes bibliographical references and index.
   ISBN 978-1-934028-72-8 (alk. paper)
   1. Hiking--Vermont--Guidebooks. 2. Appalachian Trail--Guidebooks. 3. Vermont--Guidebooks. I. Title. II. Title: Appalachian Mountain Club's best day hikes in Vermont.
   GV199.42.V4L35 2013
   796.5109743--dc23
                            2012039256

For Indy Rae. May you grow strong in the mountains.

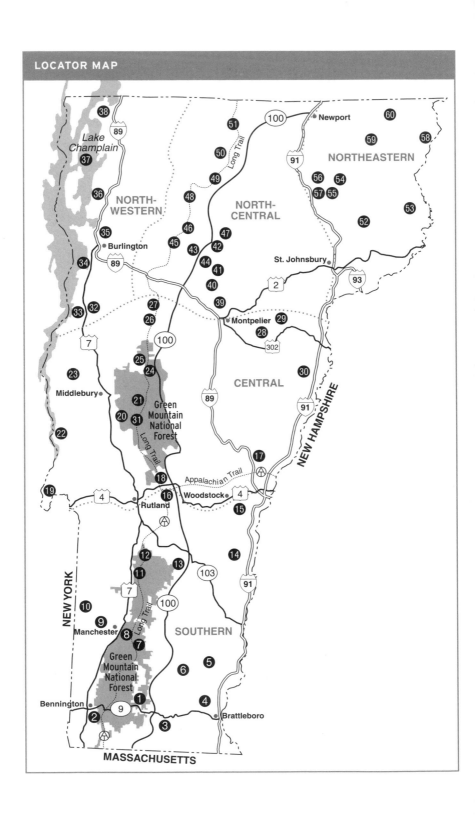

Lake Champlain

Newport

NORTHEASTERN

NORTH-WESTERN

NORTH-CENTRAL

Burlington

St. Johnsbury

Montpelier

CENTRAL

Middlebury

Green Mountain National Forest

Long Trail

NEW HAMPSHIRE

Appalachian Trail

Woodstock

Rutland

NEW YORK

Manchester

SOUTHERN

Green Mountain National Forest

Bennington

Brattleboro

MASSACHUSETTS

CONTENTS

Locator Map . . . . **iv**
At-a-Glance Trip Planner . . . . **viii**
Acknowledgments . . . . **xvi**
Introduction . . . . **xviii**
How to Use This Book . . . . **xx**
Trip Planning and Safety . . . . **xxii**

SECTION 1: SOUTHERN VERMONT

❶ Haystack Mountain 3
❷ Harmon Hill 7
❸ Mount Olga 10
❹ Black Mountain 13
❺ Putney Mountain 17
❻ Ledges Overlook 21
❼ Stratton Pond 25
❽ Lye Brook Falls 30
❾ Mount Equinox 35
❿ Merck Forest and Farmland 39
⓫ Little Rock Pond 43
⓬ White Rocks Ice Beds 47
⓭ Okemo Mountain 50
⓮ Mount Ascutney 54
⓯ Mount Tom 57
⓰ Pico Peak 61

SECTION 2: CENTRAL VERMONT

17 Gile Mountain 67

18 Deer Leap 72

19 Buckner Memorial Preserve. 75

20 Rattlesnake Cliffs and Falls of Lana 79

21 Robert Frost Trail 83

22 Mount Independence 87

23 Snake Mountain. 91

24 Sunset Ledge. 95

25 Mount Abraham 99

26 Burnt Rock 103

27 Camel's Hump 106

28 Spruce Mountain. 110

29 Owl's Head 113

30 Wright's Mountain. 118

31 Mount Horrid's Great Cliff. 122

SECTION 3: NORTHWESTERN VERMONT

32 Mount Philo State Park. 127

33 Williams Woods. 131

34 Allen Hill 135

35 Colchester Pond. 138

36 Eagle Mountain 142

37 Burton Island 145

38 Missisquoi National Wildlife Refuge 149

SECTION 4: NORTH-CENTRAL VERMONT

39 Hubbard Park. 154

40 White Rock Mountain 158

41 Mount Hunger. 163

42 Moss Glen Falls 167

43 Wiessner Woods 171

44 Stowe Pinnacle. 176

45 Mount Mansfield 180

46 Sterling Pond 185

47 Elmore Mountain 189

48 Prospect Rock 193
49 Devil's Gulch and Big Muddy Pond 197
50 Burnt Mountain. 201
51 Jay Peak. 205

SECTION 5: NORTHEASTERN VERMONT

52 Burke Mountain. 211
53 Maidstone State Park. 215
54 Mount Pisgah 220
55 Mount Hor 225
56 Wheeler Mountain 229
57 Wheeler Pond and Gnome Stairs 233
58 Monadnock Mountain 237
59 Bluff Mountain. 242
60 Brousseau Mountain 246

NATURE AND HISTORY ESSAYS

Thru-Hiking. . . . . - . . . 29
Tropical Storm Irene 34
Questing 71
Is It a Swamp or a Bog? 117
Vermont's Ancient, Illogical Rivers. 162
Where Are the Catamounts? 175
The Sparse Tundra of Vermont 184
Is the Water Clean? 219
Hiker Footsteps (or, the Psychology of Trail Maintenance) 224
From the CCC to the VYCC: Conservation Corps in Vermont 241

APPENDIX

Mountain Biking 251

Index 255
About the Author 259
Appalachian Mountain Club 260
AMC Book Updates 261

AT-A-GLANCE
TRIP PLANNER

#	Trip	Page	Location	Difficulty	Round-Trip Distance and Elevation Gain
	SOUTHERN VERMONT				
1	Haystack Mountain	3	Wilmington	Moderate	4.2 mi, 1,025 ft
2	Harmon Hill	7	Woodford	Moderate	3.7 mi, 975 ft
3	Mount Olga	10	Wilmington	Easy/Moderate	1.8 mi, 520 ft
4	Black Mountain	13	Dummerston	Moderate	2.8 mi, 975 ft
5	Putney Mountain	17	Putney	Easy	1.2 mi, 140 ft
6	Ledges Overlook	21	Townshend	Easy	1.5 mi, 400 ft
7	Stratton Pond	25	Stratton	Moderate	7.4 mi, 390 ft
8	Lye Brook Falls	30	Manchester	Moderate	4.4 mi, 740 ft
9	Mount Equinox	35	Manchester	Strenuous	6.0 mi, 2,805 ft
10	Merck Forest and Farmland	39	Rupert	Moderate	5.8 mi, 800 ft
11	Little Rock Pond	43	Mount Tabor	Easy	4.8 mi, 365 ft
12	White Rocks Ice Beds	47	Wallingford	Easy	1.8 mi, 336 ft

Estimated Time	Fee	Good for Kids	Dogs Allowed	X-C Skiing	Snow-Shoeing	Trip Highlights
3 hrs		🧍	🐕		📍📍	Views of Haystack Pond
2.5 hrs		🧍	🐕		📍📍	Wildlife and berries in ridgeline fields
1.5 hrs	$	🧍	🐕	🎿	📍📍	Loop hike, varied forests, fire tower
2.5 hrs					📍📍	Rare forest on ridge with blueberries
1 hr		🧍	🐕	🎿	📍📍	Ridgeline walk, grassy summit
1.5 hrs		🧍			📍📍	Views over lake, savanna on summit
4.5 hrs		🧍	🐕	🎿	📍📍	Flat walk to remote lake, swimming
3 hrs		🧍	🐕	🎿	📍📍	125-foot waterfall in steep valley
4.5 hrs			🐕		📍📍	Views and pretty ridge trail on highest Taconic Mountain
4 hrs		🧍	🐕	🎿	📍📍	Educational farm, parklike mature hardwood forests
3.5 hrs		🧍	🐕	🎿	📍📍	Loop around beautiful pond, swimming
1.5 hrs		🧍	🐕		📍📍	Open hemlock forest, microclimate at rock slide

#	Trip	Page	Location	Difficulty	Round-Trip Distance and Elevation Gain
13	Okemo Mountain	50	Mount Holly	Moderate/ Strenuous	6.0 mi, 1,950 ft
14	Mount Ascutney	54	Windsor	Strenuous	5.2 mi, 2,450 ft
15	Mount Tom	57	Woodstock	Easy/Moderate	3.0 mi, 550 ft
16	Pico Peak	61	Mendon/Killington	Strenuous	7.6 mi, 1,600 ft
	CENTRAL VERMONT				
17	Gile Mountain	67	Norwich	Easy	1.4 mi, 413 ft
18	Deer Leap	72	Killington	Easy/Moderate	2.0 mi, 430 ft
19	Buckner Memorial Preserve	75	West Haven	Moderate	2.6 mi, 315 ft
20	Rattlesnake Cliffs and Falls of Lana	79	Salisbury	Moderate	3.6 mi, 870 ft
21	Robert Frost Trail	83	Ripton	Easy	1.0 mi, 30 ft
22	Mount Independence	87	Orwell	Easy/Moderate	3.0 mi, 200 ft
23	Snake Mountain	91	Addison	Moderate	3.6 mi, 900 ft
24	Sunset Ledge	95	Lincoln	Easy	2.2 mi, 387 ft
25	Mount Abraham	99	Lincoln	Strenuous	5.2 mi, 1,582 ft
26	Burnt Rock	103	Fayston	Moderate/ Strenuous	5.2 mi, 2,090 ft
27	Camel's Hump	106	Duxbury	Strenuous	7.0 mi, 2,585 ft
28	Spruce Mountain	110	Plainfield	Moderate	4.4 mi, 1,300 ft
29	Owl's Head	113	Peacham	Easy/Moderate	3.8 mi, 210 ft
30	Wright's Mountain	118	Bradford	Easy/Moderate	2.7 mi, 326 ft

Estimated Time	Fee	Good for Kids	Dogs Allowed	X-C Skiing	Snow-Shoeing	Trip Highlights
4 hrs			✓		✓	Fire-tower views across southern Vermont
4 hrs			✓		✓	Waterfall, multiple view points, fire tower
2 hrs		✓	✓	✓	✓	Open, mature forest with historical significance
4 hrs			✓		✓	Open birch glade, views, historical camp
1 hr		✓	✓	✓	✓	Fire tower, views
1.5 hrs		✓	✓		✓	Rock outcrop, views
2.5 hrs		✓			✓	Rare wildlife, open hickory forest
3 hrs		✓	✓		✓	Waterfall, views, recreation hub
0.75 hr		✓	✓	✓	✓	Frost poems along fields, woods, and swamp
2 hrs	$	✓	✓	✓	✓	Historical site, Lake Champlain views
2 hrs		✓			✓	Mature hardwood forest, clifftop views
1.5 hrs		✓	✓		✓	Ridgeline walk, rock outcrop
3.5 hrs			✓		✓	Rare plants in above-treeline tundra, views
3.5 hrs			✓		✓	Boreal ridge, fun rock scrambles, views
5 hrs			✓		✓	Rare plants in alpine tundra, views
3.5 hrs		✓	✓		✓	Fire tower, views
2 hrs	$	✓	✓		✓	Open fern meadows, rocky outcrop, views
1.5 hrs		✓	✓	✓	✓	Rock outcrop, views, vernal pool

#	Trip	Page	Location	Difficulty	Round-Trip Distance and Elevation Gain
31	Mount Horrid's Great Cliff	122	Goshen	Moderate	1.6 mi, 630 ft

NORTHWESTERN VERMONT

#	Trip	Page	Location	Difficulty	Round-Trip Distance and Elevation Gain
32	Mount Philo State Park	127	Charlotte	Moderate	2.4 mi, 580 ft
33	Williams Woods	131	Charlotte	Easy	1.2 mi, minimal
34	Allen Hill	135	Shelburne	Easy	1.9 mi, 120 ft
35	Colchester Pond	138	Colchester	Easy/Moderate	3.2 mi, 150 ft
36	Eagle Mountain	142	Milton	Easy	2.1 mi, 200 ft
37	Burton Island	145	Saint Albans	Easy	2.8 mi, minimal
38	Missisquoi National Wildlife Refuge	149	Swanton	Easy	3.0 mi, minimal

NORTH-CENTRAL VERMONT

#	Trip	Page	Location	Difficulty	Round-Trip Distance and Elevation Gain
39	Hubbard Park	154	Montpelier	Easy/Moderate	3.5 mi, 250 ft
40	White Rock Mountain	158	Middlesex	Moderate/Strenuous	4.6 mi, 1,558 ft
41	Mount Hunger	163	Waterbury Center	Moderate/Strenuous	4.0 mi, 2,290 ft
42	Moss Glen Falls	167	Stowe	Easy	0.8 mi, 150 ft
43	Wiessner Woods	171	Stowe	Easy	1.5 mi, 100 ft
44	Stowe Pinnacle	176	Stowe	Moderate	2.8 mi, 1,520 ft
45	Mount Mansfield	180	Underhill	Strenuous	6.2 mi, 2,543 ft
46	Sterling Pond	185	Cambridge	Moderate	3.1 mi, 1,040 ft
47	Elmore Mountain	189	Elmore	Moderate	4.4 mi, 1,450 ft

Estimated Time	Fee	Good for Kids	Dogs Allowed	X-C Skiing	Snow-Shoeing	Trip Highlights
1.5 hrs			✓		✓	Rare plants, views
2 hrs	$	✓	✓	✓	✓	Scenic hike beneath cliff, views on top
1 hr		✓		✓	✓	Rare stand of mature, native forest; wildflowers
1.5 hrs		✓	✓	✓	✓	Lake Champlain views, swimming
2 hrs		✓	✓	✓	✓	Fields and woods, swimming and bird-watching
1 hr		✓	✓	✓	✓	Highest point on Vermont's shore of Lake Champlain
2 hrs	$	✓	✓	✓	✓	Loop hike, shoreline, swimming, views
1.5 hrs		✓	✓	✓	✓	Flat walk, unusual peatland, bird-watching
1.5 hrs		✓	✓	✓	✓	Stone lookout tower, varied forests
3.5 hrs			✓		✓	Fun rock scrambling, unusual summit terraces, views
3.5 hrs			✓		✓	Steep ledges, bald summit, views
0.75 hrs		✓	✓		✓	125-foot waterfall, scenic valley
1 hr		✓	✓	✓	✓	Loop hike, varied forests, view
2.5 hrs			✓		✓	Bald spot, views
4.5 hrs	$		✓		✓	Open ridgeline hike, alpine tundra, highest point in Vermont
3 hrs		✓	✓		✓	Steep, scenic notch, high-mountain pond
2.5 hrs	$	✓	✓		✓	Multiple rock outcrops, fire tower, views, balanced rock

#	Trip	Page	Location	Difficulty	Round-Trip Distance and Elevation Gain
48	Prospect Rock	193	Johnson	Easy/Moderate	2.0 mi, 540 ft
49	Devil's Gulch and Big Muddy Pond	197	Eden	Moderate	5.2 mi, 465 ft
50	Burnt Mountain	201	Montgomery	Moderate	4.8 mi, 1,600 ft
51	Jay Peak	205	Westfield	Moderate	3.4 mi, 1,638 ft

NORTHEASTERN VERMONT

52	Burke Mountain	211	Burke	Strenuous	6.2 mi, 2,080 ft
53	Maidstone State Park	215	Maidstone	Easy	1.5 mi, minimial
54	Mount Pisgah	220	Westmore	Moderate	4.8 mi, 1,395 ft
55	Mount Hor	225	Sutton	Easy/Moderate	2.9 mi, 601 ft
56	Wheeler Mountain	229	Sutton	Easy/Moderate	2.5 mi, 700 ft
57	Wheeler Pond and Gnome Stairs	233	Sutton/Barton	Easy	1.6 mi, 175 ft
58	Monadnock Mountain	237	Lemington	Moderate/Strenuous	5.0 mi, 2,108 ft
59	Bluff Mountain	242	Island Pond	Moderate	3.2 mi, 1,060 ft
60	Brousseau Mountain	246	Norton	Easy/Moderate	1.6 mi, 550 ft

Estimated Time	Fee	Good for Kids	Dogs Allowed	X-C Skiing	Snow-Shoeing	Trip Highlights
1.5 hrs		✓	✓		✓	Rocky outcrop, views
4 hrs		✓	✓		✓	Rock scrambling in narrow ravine, pond shore, views
3 hrs			✓		✓	Beaver ponds, fields, varied terrain
3 hrs			✓		✓	Open ridge and summit, views
4 hrs			✓		✓	Mature, open hardwoods, rocky outcrops
1 hr	$	✓	✓	✓	✓	Lakeshore, loons, swimming
3 hrs			✓		✓	High, rocky perches over lake
1.5 hrs		✓	✓		✓	Ridgewalk to varied views, including Lake Willoughby
2 hrs			✓		✓	Cliffs and rocky outcrops, views
1 hr		✓	✓	✓	✓	Loop hike, cascades, pond shore
3 hrs			✓		✓	Fire-tower view of valley and mountains
2.5 hrs			✓		✓	Loop hike, steep ledges, views
1 hr		✓	✓		✓	Rocky outcrop, views

ACKNOWLEDGMENTS

I HAD A TREMENDOUS AMOUNT OF HELP PUTTING THIS BOOK TOGETHER. First and most significantly, thanks to my husband, Kip Roberts, for taking care of our daughter, Indy, and me while I worked on this project. Thanks to Bob and Julie Roberts for generously sharing their time, talents, and love, not to mention many meals. My parents, Judy and Gary Lamphere, re-earned the title "Most Supportive Parents" (which they had first acquired in my ski-racing days) for going out of their way to help, for being reluctant models in photographs of the hikes, and, most important, for sending me into the mountains at a critical point in my life. Thanks to friends and family members who kept me company on the trail and shared photos for the book.

Vermont is fortunate to have a huge number of smart, dedicated professionals working for the benefit of the state's natural places. I am fortunate to have benefited from their time and expertise, which helped me improve the descriptions in this book. Thanks to the following people for reviewing trips and answering my many questions: Pete Antos-Ketcham, Matt Larson, and Megan Duni of the Green Mountain Club; Seth Coffey, David Lacy, Heather Thornton, Danna Strout, Joan McCloud, Holly Knox, and Ethan Ready of the U.S. Forest Service; Luke O'Brien of the NorthWoods Stewardship Center; Nate McKeen and the staff of the Vermont State Parks; Rick White, Diana Frederick, Susan Bulmer, and Sherry Winnie of the Vermont Department of Forests, Parks and Recreation; Emily Boedecker and Emily Seifert of The Nature Conservancy; Rick LaDue of the Equinox Preservation Trust; Tom Ward, Kathryn Lawrence, and Chris Wall of the Merck Forest and Farmland Center; Steve Giroux of the Ascutney Trails Association; Jennifer Waite of the National Park Service Rivers and Trails Program; Elsa Gilbertson of the Division of Historic Preservation; Nancy Jones of the Bradford Conservation Commission; Yumiko Jakobcic of the Winooski Valley Park District; Steve Anderson of the Putney Mountain Association; Jonathan Frishtick of the Norwich Trails Committee; Stephen Plume of the Westmore Association; Dave Frisque of the U.S. Fish and Wildlife Service; Lucie Fillion Daley of the Town of Lemington; Becca Washburn of the Stowe Land Trust; Betsy Cieplicki of Shelburne Parks and Recreation; Donna Vondle and Gary Pelton of the U.S. Army Corps of Engineers; Chris Boget of the Lake Champlain Land Trust; Kym Duchesneau and Meghan Grant of the Town of Milton; Rolf Anderson of Hazen's Notch Association; Alexis Nelson and Matt Tetreault of the Vermont Association of Snow Travelers; Marjorie Gale of the Vermont Geological Survey; Jerry Jenkins; Margaret Fowle of Audubon Vermont; Stephen Zeoli of the Mount Independence Coalition; Bill Shepard of the Connecticut River Birding Trail; Stephen Wright of the University of Vermont; David Sausville and Doug Blodgett of the Vermont Fish and Wildlife Department; Adam Piper of the Vermont Land Trust; Amy Diller Kelsey of Catamount Trail; Ed Metcalfe of the Southern Vermont Natural History Museum; Andrew Norkin of the Appalachian Mountain Club; Bob Proudman of the Appalachian Trail Conservancy; Laura Dintino of Vital Communities; and Kristian Omland.

And thanks, finally, to Kimberly Duncan-Mooncy, Heather Stephenson, and Athena Lakri at Appalachian Mountain Club Books, for the opportunity to work on this project, for sharing their professional knowledge, and especially for their good-natured support and flexibility along the way.

—Jennifer Lamphere Roberts, 2012

INTRODUCTION

VERMONT IS NAMED FOR ITS MOST DEFINING FEATURE: the Green Mountains. From border to border, the landscape is craggy, rumpled, and buckled. In some places, the stature and the sheer bulk of the mountains dominate the landscape; in other places, the hills roll more gently. Even the relatively level Champlain valley is flat only in comparison with the rest of the state, and is still hilly enough to have excellent hikes to peaks with long views.

The spine of the Green Mountains runs the length of the state, topped by the 270-mile Long Trail, the nation's oldest long-distance hiking trail. On either side of the high crest are lower parallel ridges called the First and Third ranges. The ancient Taconic Mountains roll across the southwestern corner of the state, while the northwest is dominated by the wide waters of Lake Champlain. Vermont's Northeast Kingdom is a highland of forests, cliffs, and lakes. The Connecticut River forms the state's eastern border, with the lower, rolling mountains of Vermont's Piedmont extending from there to the tall ridgelines in the center of the state. This widespread hilliness combined with Vermont's rural character encourages an outdoors culture—an appreciation for woods, undeveloped mountains, and the activities that happen in them: hiking, camping, paddling, fishing, and hunting.

All of these activities were practiced and perfected by Vermont's first settlers, the Abenaki. Part of the larger family called Wabanaki ("People of the Dawnland"), who moved into what is now the northeastern United States and southeastern Canada after the last ice age 12,000 years ago, the Abenaki settled from the shores of Lake Champlain eastward into the mountains. Today, the center of Abenaki culture in Vermont remains near the lake, in the northwestern corner of the state.

Though Vermonters have long appreciated the mountains and forests, hiking was not always as popular as it is today. The 1921 guide to the Long Trail began with a lament that more hikers were not visiting: "The Green Mountains of Vermont have been sadly neglected, which is strange, as the entire range is within plain sight of the much frequented White Mountain and Adirondack Mountain groups and their noble skyline might well have inspired excursions into a virgin mountain region. This neglect lies with the people of the State who failed to make the mountains accessible or to give them due publicity." Today the mountains are probably Vermont's most well-known feature, and hiking trails have made many of them accessible.

The hikes in this guidebook were chosen both for their remarkable features and for their representation of Vermont's different landscapes. They are spread across the state, including one on a Lake Champlain island that is accessible only by boat. They visit ponds, bogs, waterfalls, and interesting forests as well as cliffs and ridgelines. The hikes vary in difficulty, but the majority are easy or moderate, so that parents can keep up with their kids on the trail. Although I have seen children—even very young ones—on top of the highest Green Mountains, I have mostly been conservative and have designated only the easier hikes with the "good for kids" icon (see page xx).

Day-hiking is the perfect way to experience Vermont's special places. With a light pack containing a little food, some water, and a warm layer, hikers can explore woods, streams, waterfalls, and rocky summits for part of the day, then take a refreshing dip at a swimming hole or a state park beach, and finish with a hearty meal in a nearby village. I can't think of a happier way to spend a day.

HOW TO USE THIS BOOK

WITH 60 HIKES TO CHOOSE FROM, you may wonder how to decide where to go. The locator map at the front of this book will help you narrow down the trips by location, and the At-a-Glance Trip Planner that follows the table of contents will provide more information to guide you toward a decision.

Once you settle on a destination and turn to a trip in this guide, you will find a series of icons that indicate whether there are fees, whether the hike is good for kids, whether dogs are permitted, and whether cross-country skiing or snowshoeing is recommended. For those hikes with the "good for kids" icon, I suggest ages for children who would most likely enjoy the hike, but of course children vary tremendously. The suggestions are based on children who are not athletic prodigies but whose families hike together regularly. Some of the hikes designated for kids visit waterfalls or cliffy lookouts that are great rewards for children's efforts to get there, but that can be hazardous. Ultimately, to determine whether a hike is appropriate for their family, parents will have to gauge their own children's interest, motivation, and ability.

Information on the basics follows: location, rating, distance, elevation gain, estimated time, and maps. The ratings are based my perception and are estimates of what the average hiker will experience. You may find them to be easier or more difficult than stated. The distance and estimated hiking time shown are for the whole trip, whether it's an out-and-back hike (with distance noted as "round-trip") or a loop. The estimated time is also based on my perception. Consider your own pace when planning a trip. The elevation gain is calculated using measurements and information from U.S. Geological Survey (USGS) topographic maps, landowner maps, and Google Earth. Information is included about the relevant USGS maps, as well as about where you can find trail maps.

The boldface summary that follows the list of basics provides a basic overview of what you will see on your hike. The directions explain how to reach the trailhead by car and include Global Positioning System (GPS) coordinates for parking lots. Whether or not you own a GPS device, it is wise to bring an atlas such as the *DeLorme Atlas & Gazetteer for Vermont*, which shows small roads and forest roads in detail.

In the trail description, you will find instructions on where to hike, the trails on which to hike, and where to turn. You will also learn about the natural and human history along your hike, as well as about flora, fauna, and any landmarks or notable objects you will encounter.

The trail maps that accompany each trip will help guide you along your hike, but it would be wise to take an official trail map with you as well. Official maps are often—but not always—available online, at the trailhead, or at the visitor center.

Each trip ends with a More Information section that provides details about access times and fees, the property's rules and regulations, and contact information for the place where you will be hiking. There is also a Nearby section that offers suggestions for places to continue the experience when the hike is done—including swimming, paddling, or mountain-biking destinations—and where to find the closest restaurants.

TRIP PLANNING AND SAFETY

PLANNING YOUR TRIP WELL is the first step to having a safe hike. Some of the trips ascend to bare, high-elevation summits where winds and low temperatures necessitate extra clothing. Other hikes visit cliff tops or waterfalls where you'll need to use extra caution with children and dogs. Learn about the terrain you will travel through in order to pack the right gear and prepare for the experience. Allow extra time in case you get lost.

You will be more likely to have an enjoyable, safe hike if you plan ahead and take proper precautions. Before heading out for your hike, consider the following:

- Select a hike that everyone in your group is comfortable taking. Match the hike to the abilities of the least capable person in the group. If anyone is uncomfortable with the weather or is tired, turn around and complete the hike another day.
- Plan to be back at the trailhead before dark. Before beginning your hike, determine a turnaround time. Don't diverge from it, even if you have not reached your intended destination.
- Check the weather and assume it will be cooler and windier on the mountain than at the base. If you are planning a ridge or summit hike, start early so that you will be off the exposed area before the afternoon hours, when thunderstorms most often strike, especially in summer. Weather conditions can change quickly, and any changes are likely to be more severe the higher you are on the mountain.
- Bring a pack with the following items:
  ✓ Water: Two quarts per person is usually adequate, depending on the weather and the length of the trip.

✓ Food: Even if you are planning just a 1-hour hike, bring some high-energy snacks such as nuts, dried fruit, or snack bars. Pack a lunch for longer trips.

✓ Map and compass: Be sure you know how to use them. A handheld GPS device may also be helpful, but it is not always reliable.

✓ Headlamp or flashlight, with spare batteries.

✓ Extra clothing: rain gear, wool or fleece sweater, hat, and mittens.

✓ Sunscreen.

✓ First-aid kit, including adhesive bandages, gauze, nonprescription painkillers, moleskin, and any necessary prescription medication in case you are on the trail longer than expected.

✓ Pocketknife or multitool.

✓ Waterproof matches and a lighter.

✓ Trash bag.

✓ Toilet paper and two plastic bags to pack it out.

✓ Whistle.

✓ Insect repellent.

✓ Sunglasses.

✓ Cell phone: Be aware that cell phone service is unreliable in rural areas. If you are receiving a signal, use the phone only for emergencies to avoid disturbing the backcountry experience for other hikers.

✓ Binoculars (optional).

✓ Camera (optional).

• Wear appropriate footwear and clothing. Wool or synthetic hiking socks will keep your feet dry and help prevent blisters. Comfortable waterproof hiking boots will provide ankle support and good traction. Cotton clothing absorbs sweat and rain, making it effective at helping cool you down but problematic or even dangerous if the weather conditions change. If you choose to wear cotton while hiking, bring a synthetic, wool, or silk layer to change into. Polypropylene, fleece, silk, and wool all wick moisture away from your body and keep you warm in wet or cold conditions. To help avoid bug bites, you may want to wear pants and a long-sleeve shirt.

• When you are ahead of the rest of your hiking group, wait at all trail junctions until the others catch up. This avoids confusion and keeps people from getting separated or lost.

• If you see downed wood that appears to be purposely covering a trail, it probably means the trail is closed due to overuse or hazardous conditions.

- If a trail is muddy, walk through the mud or on rocks, never on tree roots or plants. Water-resistant boots will keep your feet comfortable. Staying in the center of the trail will keep it from eroding into a wide hiking highway.
- Leave your itinerary and the time you expect to return with someone you trust. If you see a logbook at a trailhead, be sure to sign in when you arrive and sign out when you finish your hike.
- After you complete your hike, check for deer ticks, which carry the dangerous bacteria that causes Lyme disease.
- Poison ivy is always a threat when hiking. To identify the plant, look for clusters of three leaves that shine in the sun but are dull in the shade. If you do come into contact with poison ivy, wash the affected area with soap as soon as possible.
- Wear blaze-orange items during hunting season. In Vermont, hunting begins in September; though most seasons end in December, some may extend later into winter. Yearly schedules are available at vtfishandwildlife. com and in fliers and brochures available at town halls, general stores, and other public areas.

Many trails are closed during mud season, and even if they are not, it's a good idea to avoid hiking during that time, when trails are especially susceptible to damage. Mud season is loosely defined as most of April and May—essentially, spring in Vermont—but in reality, mud season begins whenever the ground starts to thaw and lasts until the ground has dried out. The same conditions—saturated, partly frozen soils—can also occur in late fall and during winter thaws. If muddy conditions cause you to begin hiking on the side of the treadway, turn around. Mud season begins and ends earlier in the warmer valleys than on the cool mountain slopes; you may be able to stagger your hikes according to when the trails dry out, but sometimes the best choice is another activity altogether.

Winter hiking can be an enjoyable way to experience the Green Mountains in their snowy splendor, but it requires extra gear and planning. Once the snow piles up, many trailheads are not accessible by car, so plan to hike farther than the distance shown in this guidebook. The presence of alpine ski areas may alter your route and your experience, particularly on Pico and Jay peaks. Skis with traction (wax, skins, or a pattern etched in the base) or snowshoes keep you more or less on top of the snow, letting you travel more efficiently without creating "post holes" by sinking into the snowpack. Snowshoeing is an easy activity for beginners to pick up, as it is simply walking. Skiing on ungroomed, backcountry trails requires considerable skill. Cross-country skiers should be aware that the difficulty ratings given for hikes in this book do not apply to skiing, and that skiing is generally more challenging. All winter travelers need to bring more food and warm layers than they would in summer, and exercise more caution; fewer daylight hours, colder temperatures, and slower travel times magnify any problems that may occur, like getting lost or twisting an ankle. Prudent winter travelers do not go out alone, and make sure at least one person in the group has a sleeping bag and a small camp stove in case of emergency. When properly prepared, winter hikers can safely and comfortably experience the spectacular beauty of Vermont's frozen landscape.

When not frozen, Vermont's woods are home to biting insects. They can be a minor or significant nuisance, depending on seasonal and daily conditions. West Nile virus and eastern equine encephalitis (EEE) virus can be transmitted to humans by infected mosquitoes and cause rare but serious diseases. Reduce your risk of being bitten by using insect repellent, wearing long sleeves and pants, and avoiding hiking in the early morning and in the evening, when mosquitoes are most active.

THE GREEN MOUNTAIN CLUB

The Green Mountain Club (GMC) is a nonprofit organization founded in 1910. GMC built and maintains Vermont's Long Trail, and the organization's advocacy and education efforts also safeguard the state's many other hiking trails. At sensitive, high-use areas, GMC sponsors caretakers who perform trail and shelter maintenance, provide first aid, and talk with hikers about fragile summit ecosystems, local regulations, and Leave No Trace principles. For more information, visit GMC headquarters in Waterbury Center or go to greenmountainclub.org.

THE GREEN MOUNTAIN NATIONAL FOREST

The Green Mountain National Forest encompasses more than 400,000 acres in southwestern and central Vermont, forming the largest contiguous public land area in the state. The Forest includes eight designated wilderness areas and three nationally designated trails (the Appalachian Trail, the Long Trail, and the Robert Frost National Recreation Trail), as well as approximately 900 miles of multiple-use trails. For more information, visit fs.usda.gov/greenmountain.

LEAVE NO TRACE

The Appalachian Mountain Club (AMC) is a national educational partner of Leave No Trace, a nonprofit organization dedicated to promoting and inspiring responsible outdoor recreation through education, research, and

leave no trace
CENTER FOR OUTDOOR ETHICS

partnerships. The Leave No Trace program seeks to develop wildland ethics—ways in which people think and act in the outdoors to minimize their impact on the areas they visit and to protect our natural resources for future enjoyment. Leave No Trace unites four federal land management agencies—the U.S. Forest Service, National Park Service, Bureau of Land Management, and U.S. Fish and Wildlife Service—with manufacturers, outdoor retailers, user groups, educators, organizations such as AMC, and individuals.

The Leave No Trace ethic is guided by the following seven principles:

1. **Plan Ahead and Prepare.** Know the terrain and any regulations applicable to the area you're planning to visit, and be prepared for extreme weather or other emergencies. Small groups have less impact on resources and on the experiences of other backcountry visitors.

2. **Travel and Camp on Durable Surfaces.** Travel and camp on established trails and campsites, rock, gravel, dry grasses, or snow. Good campsites are found, not made. Camp at least 200 feet from lakes and streams, and focus activities on areas where vegetation is absent. In pristine areas, disperse use to prevent the creation of campsites and trails.

3. **Dispose of Waste Properly.** Pack it in, pack it out. Inspect your camp for trash or food scraps. Deposit solid human waste in catholes dug 6 to 8 inches deep, at least 200 feet from water, camps, and trails. Pack out toilet paper and hygiene products. To wash yourself or your dishes, carry water 200 feet from streams or lakes and use small amounts of biodegradable soap. Scatter strained dishwater.

4. **Leave What You Find.** Cultural or historical artifacts, as well as natural objects such as plants and rocks, should be left as found.

5. **Minimize Campfire Impacts.** Cook on a stove. Use established fire rings, fire pans, or mound fires. If you build a campfire, keep it small and use dead sticks found on the ground.

6. **Respect Wildlife.** Observe wildlife from a distance. Feeding animals alters their natural behavior. Store your rations and trash securely.

7. **Be Considerate of Other Visitors.** Be courteous, respect the quality of other visitors' backcountry experience, and let nature's sounds prevail.

AMC is a national provider of the Leave No Trace Master Educator course. AMC offers this five-day course, designed especially for outdoor professionals and land managers, as well as the shorter two-day Leave No Trace Trainer course, throughout the Northeast. For Leave No Trace information contact the Leave No Trace Center for Outdoor Ethics, 800-332-4100 or 302-442-8222; lnt.org. For a schedule of AMC Leave No Trace courses, see outdoors.org/education/lnt.

1

SOUTHERN VERMONT

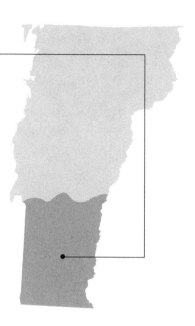

FROM ITS SOUTHERN BORDER TO RUTLAND, 60 miles north, Vermont is pretty consistently about 40 miles wide. Mountains and other large land features in the state tend to occur in swaths that trend north–south, and a lot of diverse landscape is packed into that 40-mile width of southern Vermont.

On the western side of southern Vermont, the Taconic Mountains spill north out of Massachusetts and reach their highest point at Mount Equinox (Trip 9) in Manchester. From there, the Taconics become progressively smaller and the peaks less frequent until they disappear altogether. The Taconics are part of the Appalachian Mountains, as the Green Mountains are, but their origins are different. In fact, the origin of the Taconic Mountains is somewhat mysterious. Their summits are made of older rock than their bases, which means that somehow older rock was pushed from someplace onto the younger mountains beneath them. How that happened continues to be a source of debate. The limestone so prevalent in the Taconic Mountains is easily eroded by trickling water, making caves inside the mountains and rich soils outside them. Rich soils create spectacular spring wildflower displays, and provide habitat for some rare plants. Extensive forests provide homes to animals large and small, including black bear, bobcat, white-tailed deer, and songbirds.

Tidily defining the border between the Taconic and Green mountains is the long, narrow Valley of Vermont. US 7 runs through this channel, as do the

Battenkill River and Otter Creek, Vermont's longest river. The valley is wide in some places, such as around Bennington, where it stretches over several miles, and constricted at others, such as at Emerald Lake, where the road and railroad squeeze past the water along the base of Mount Tabor.

The Green Mountains occupy the central part of southern Vermont (as well as the center of the state as a whole). Although their western edge at the Valley of Vermont is steep and sudden, for the most part the Greens consist of high, rolling land that is more a plateau than a sharply defined range of mountains. Some geologists speculate that this relatively flat, high place is what was left after its peaks were pushed west to become the new tops of the Taconics. Other geologists disagree, but either way this terrain was historically difficult for humans to settle and remained largely the domain of wildlife.

Today, the southern section of the Green Mountain National Forest boasts almost 60,000 acres of federally designated Wilderness. Wilderness areas are managed to preserve their wild character, and so are home to large animals like black bear, moose, and bobcat that prefer extensive tracts of undeveloped forests, such as the deep woods between Stratton Pond and Lye Brook Falls (Trips 7 and 8). Encircling the Peru Peak and Big Branch wildernesses, the White Rocks National Recreation Area conserves the surrounding scenic terrain—including the gem of Little Rock Pond and massive rock slides that created the White Rocks Ice Beds (Trips 11 and 12)—for hiking, camping, and snowmobiling. The Appalachian Trail and the Long Trail run together through the southern Green Mountains, paralleled by the Catamount Trail, a cross-country ski trail. Historical remnants of previous activity, such as fire towers, sawmills, and charcoal kilns, remain in many places.

East of the high plateau of the Green Mountains, the landscape generally consists of lower hills carved by a maze of rivers, streams, and, historically, glaciers. This region is called the Piedmont—literally "foothills"—and has some of the warmest temperatures in Vermont, leading to natural communities, such as on dry hilltops like Black Mountain (Trip 4), that don't exist in other parts of the state. Most of the mountains are small in the Piedmont; one notable exception is the massive monadnock of Mount Ascutney (Trip 14), which towers over the region and has high-elevation forests with their associated plants and wildlife.

On the far eastern edge of southern Vermont, the Connecticut River flows through floodplains and natural shoreline communities that are unusual in Vermont. Technically, only the beaches are in Vermont, since New Hampshire's border extends to the low-water mark on the Vermont side. But the valley and its plants, animals, history, and recreation are very much a part of southern Vermont life.

TRIP 1
HAYSTACK MOUNTAIN

Location: Wilmington, VT
Rating: Moderate
Distance: 4.2 miles round-trip
Elevation Gain: 1,025 feet
Estimated Time: 3 hours
Maps: USGS Mount Snow; fs.usda.gov/Internet/FSE_MEDIA/
stelprdb5315088.pdf

This pleasant cruise up a mellow ridge leads to a rocky top with views of nearby Haystack Pond and distant peaks.

DIRECTIONS

From the western junction of VT 100 and VT 9 in Wilmington, go west on VT 9 for 1.1 miles and turn right onto Haystack Road. (A large sign on the grass says Chimney Hill.) Drive 1.2 miles and turn left onto Chimney Hill Road. Proceed 0.2 mile and turn right onto Binney Brook Road, which weaves past many turnoffs and ends after 1.1 miles at Upper Dam Road. Turn right and follow Upper Dam Road for 0.3 mile (staying left at a junction as marked) to park on the right shoulder (space for about 6 cars), where a gravel road heads uphill into the woods. *GPS coordinates: 42° 53.99′ N, 72° 54.66′ W.*

TRAIL DESCRIPTION

Haystack Mountain (3,445 feet) is a recognizable pointed peak on the southern end of a ridge dominated by the ski trails of Mount Snow (3,586 feet) and its own, no-longer-operational alpine ski area. The hike to Haystack's small rocky summit traverses easy to moderate grades until the slightly steeper final 0.3 mile, making it a good hike for kids about ages 6 and older.

From the roadside parking, follow the gravel two-track uphill into the woods and around a metal gate. Occasional blue plastic diamonds mark the two-track, which leads to Wilmington's water supply at Haystack Pond. Hiking among yellow birch and beech trees, you begin to hear Binney Brook as it tumbles through a ravine on your left. At 0.5 mile, where the brook flows through a large culvert under the road, turn left onto a footpath. (The two-track continues into a watershed protection area that is marked No Trespassing.)

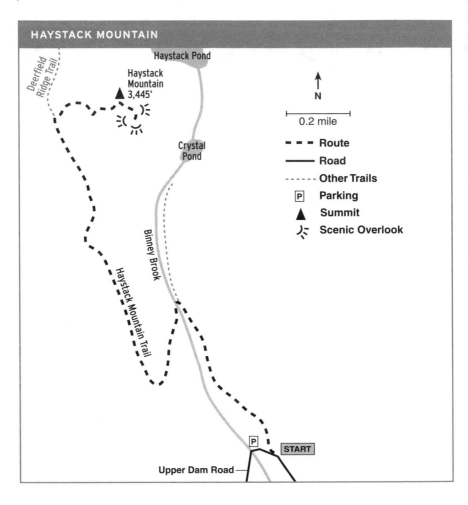

HAYSTACK MOUNTAIN

Haystack Pond

Deerfield Ridge Trail

Haystack
Mountain
▲ 3,445'

Crystal
Pond

Binney Brook

Haystack Mountain Trail

N

0.2 mile

- - - Route
——— Road
------ Other Trails
P   Parking
▲   Summit
)⁻ϟ   Scenic Overlook

P

START

Upper Dam Road

The narrow, rooty trail heads southwest to circle the end of the long
ridgeline leading to Haystack's summit. Wood nettle with its stinging hairs
spreads along the edges of the path as it rolls gently for 0.3 mile from the
two-track. The path then bends sharply back to the northwest and begins
a moderate, steady climb across a rocky hillside. The climbing is pleasantly
interrupted by level stretches and gradual pitches, and at 1.3 miles a sharp
S curve brings you to the ridgeline. Lilies and ferns fill in the forest floor
alongside rose twisted stalk, with its flowers and berries dangling, hidden
beneath its arched, leafy stem.

Passing through some wide muddy areas, the path rounds the western side
of Haystack's summit cone. At 1.8 miles, blue arrows direct you to turn right
off the ridge path, which continues straight. The trail immediately moves from
a northern hardwood forest on the ridgeline to a shady, tight boreal forest as

Haystack Pond spreads across 27 acres on the east side of Haystack Mountain's summit; West Dover and Rice Hill are in the distance.

you climb the summit knob. The path ascends switchbacks to a small rocky opening at the summit. The view east is dominated by Haystack Pond in the basin below. Beyond that, the north–south valley carrying VT 100 is backed by rows of gentle low hills. In the distant northeast, Mount Ascutney (3,144 feet) juts above the horizon, and far to the east the large hump of Mount Monadnock (3,165 feet) rises over southwestern New Hampshire. Mount Snow's summit chairlift is just visible over the treetops to the north.

For views to the south and west, climb down through a narrow cleft in the rocks to another outlook on the south face of the summit. This perch provides a great view of the 2,200-acre Harriman Reservoir (also called Lake Whitingham), the largest body of water within Vermont's borders. Built in 1923 to provide hydroelectric power, the lake is a dammed stretch of the Deerfield River. The Deerfield Valley village of Mountain Mills was abandoned to make way for the reservoir, and boaters today can occasionally spot the submerged foundation of the old mill. Another version of electrical production is visible to the west, where wind towers in Searsburg spin on top of a ridge. On a clear day, Massachusetts's highest point, Mount Greylock (3,491 feet), can be seen in the distant southwest.

DID YOU KNOW?

Haystack Mountain's alpine ski area ceased full-time operations in 2001 after almost 40 years. Since then, investors have made updates to its buildings and lifts with hopes of someday bringing the area out of retirement.

MORE INFORMATION

Haystack Mountain is part of the Green Mountain National Forest; Manchester Ranger District, 2538 Depot Street, Manchester Center, VT 05255; 802-362-2307; fs.usda.gov/greenmountain.

NEARBY

Swim and paddle on Harriman Reservoir, 3.5 miles south. Camp at Woodford State Park, which also has great swimming and paddling on a high-elevation lake 6.4 miles west, or at Molly Stark State Park, 6.1 miles east (see Trip 3). Food and shops are in Wilmington, 3.8 miles southeast.

TRIP 2
HARMON HILL

Location: Woodford, VT
Rating: Moderate
Distance: 3.7 miles round-trip
Elevation Gain: 975 feet
Estimated Time: 2.5 hours
Maps: USGS Woodford; USGS Bennington; USGS Pownal; fs.usda.
gov/Internet/FSE_MEDIA/stelprdb5317929.pdf

**Fields atop this long ridge attract wildlife and provide western
views across Bennington and the Taconic Mountains.**

DIRECTIONS

From the junction of US 7 and VT 9 in Bennington, head east on VT 9 for 5.0
miles. A large Appalachian Trail/Long Trail parking lot (space for about 20
cars) is on the left. *GPS coordinates:* 42° 53.12′ N, 73° 06.94′ W.

TRAIL DESCRIPTION

Harmon Hill (2,325 feet) is a steep-sided ridgeline running east of the large
town of Bennington. Its relatively flat top conveys the Long Trail south toward
its terminus at the state line. On the mountain's northern end, City Stream and
VT 9 carve a twisting path around its base and provide the starting place for
hikes up onto the long ridge. This hike is steep for the first 0.6 mile, but the
remainder is a rolling walk along the ridge, making it a reasonable challenge
for kids about ages 7 and older. Winter hikers need to take extra precautions
when the steep hillside is icy.

From the parking lot, cross VT 9 to the trailhead and immediately begin
ascending the eastern slope of Harmon Hill. The white-blazed Appalachian
Trail/Long Trail (AT/LT) heads northward at first, paralleling the highway as it
rises. Bending left, then right, then left again, the trail climbs steadily up rock
steps through a mixed hardwood forest that includes shaggy-barked hophornbeam and large old maples. Trillium, jewelweed, and ferns sprout between
rocks that poke out of the ground all across the hillside.

The pitch and the amount of rock in the trail both moderate toward the
top of the hillside, where a southern-trending leg of trail bends to the right
and suddenly reaches flat ground. Heading southwest through widely spaced

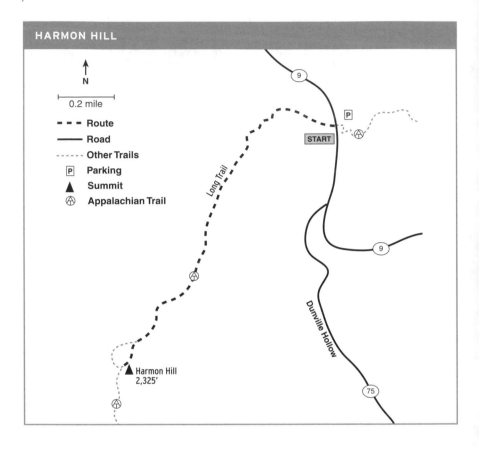

HARMON HILL

N

0.2 mile

- - - Route
——— Road
------ Other Trails
P Parking
▲ Summit
Ⓐ Appalachian Trail

Long Trail

9

P

START

Ⓐ

9

Dunville Hollow

Ⓐ

▲ Harmon Hill
2,325'

Ⓐ

75

hardwoods, the trail descends slightly. The height of the ridge is out of sight through the forest on your right as you make your way through the thick beds of ferns between the tree trunks.

At around 1.1 miles, pass through a low, wet area on bog bridges and begin climbing gradually toward the summit. The forest begins to open, with another fern meadow and trees that branch widely because they receive more sunlight in these clearings. The U.S. Forest Service uses fire to maintain this historical clearing and its views. Raspberries, quick to sprout after a burn, become thick as you reach the top. Winding through small stands of trees, unofficial paths are mowed or trampled through fields to the right. The best views from Harmon Hill are from these open areas west of the trail.

You can make a small loop by heading right to the cleared edge of the ridge, then winding your way back to rejoin the AT/LT farther down the trail. Looking west, you'll see the rooftops of Bennington spread out across the valley. The 306-foot stone spire of the Bennington Monument is visible just to the north of the forested hump of Mount Anthony (2,340 feet). Mount Anthony and Harmon Hill face each other across the geologically important divide of the Valley of Vermont. This narrow basin is a long finger of lowland stretching south from Lake Champlain through Rutland to Bennington—the perfect corridor for a north–south road like US 7.

The Valley of Vermont divides the Green Mountains—including Harmon Hill—from the Taconic Mountains to the west. The Taconic Range is geologically distinct from the Green, Adirondack, and Berkshire ranges that surround it, formed from a collision of continental plates millions of years before the rest of the Appalachian Mountains were pushed up. Other Taconic peaks in Vermont include Mount Equinox (Trip 9), Mount Antone (Trip 10), Snake Mountain (Trip 23), and Mount Philo (Trip 32).

The summit of Harmon Hill is marked by a register box and a list of distances to points north and south. Follow the AT/LT north to return to the trailhead the way you climbed up. As you walk through the fields on top of Harmon Hill, be on the lookout for animals that appreciate the berries as much as we do; these openings in the forest provide food and habitat for bears, deer, rabbits, and many kinds of birds.

DID YOU KNOW?

Ebenezer Emmons, who in 1844 discovered that the Taconic Mountains were distinct from surrounding ranges, was banned from practicing geology in New York because the state geologist disagreed with him about the mountain range's age. Emmons was later found to be correct.

MORE INFORMATION

Harmon Hill is in the Green Mountain National Forest; Manchester Ranger District, 2538 Depot Street, Manchester Center, VT 05255; 802-362-2307; fs.usda.gov/greenmountain. The Green Mountain Club maintains the Appalachian Trail/Long Trail. Green Mountain Club, 4711 Waterbury–Stowe Road, Waterbury Center, VT 05677; 802-244-7037; greenmountainclub.org.

NEARBY

Swim, paddle, and camp at Woodford State Park, Vermont's highest-elevation state park, 6 miles east. Harriman Reservoir (Lake Whitingham) has a rail trail as well as swimming and paddling, 14 miles east. Head to Bennington, 5 miles west, for food, shops, and the Battle Monument.

TRIP 3
MOUNT OLGA

Location: Wilmington, VT
Rating: Easy to Moderate
Distance: 1.8 miles
Elevation Gain: 520 feet
Estimated Time: 1.5 hours
Maps: USGS Wilmington; vtstateparks.com/pdfs/mollystark_trails.pdf

This loop trail to Mount Olga's lookout tower is a pleasant ramble through a rich forest.

DIRECTIONS
From the western junction of VT 9 and VT 100 in Wilmington, drive 3.3 miles east on VT 9 to Molly Stark State Park. Parking for 20 cars is near the office. (When the park is closed, park at the base of the entrance road and add 0.2 mile round-trip to the hike.) *GPS coordinates:* 42° 51.29′ N, 72° 48.88′ W.

TRAIL DESCRIPTION
Mount Olga (2,418 feet) has all the attractive features of a big mountain—including a variety of hiking terrains and terrific views—in a small package, making it a great destination for families or those with limited time. The trail on the north side of the loop is a little shorter (0.7 mile to the summit) and therefore a little steeper—a better choice for the ascent. Descend on the more gradual, 1.0-mile trail that ends at the top of the campground. The southern side of the loop is good cross-country ski terrain, while the northern leg is more suited to snowshoes. Children about ages 5 and older will enjoy the accomplishment of summiting this small mountain.

Begin across the park road from the office, where Mount Olga Trail descends wooden steps to cross a stream. Follow blue blazes up a moderate climb through a young forest of yellow birch, spruce, and fir. Where a rock wall ascends from the right, the trail turns sharply left and zigzags up a steep, rooty pitch. Mount Olga Trail climbs moderately for the first few tenths of a mile. Then, entering a spruce/fir stand, the trail levels and crosses more rolling terrain. Canada violets blossom during early spring in these damp woods, their white petals unfurling to reveal a yellow center and striking purple veins.

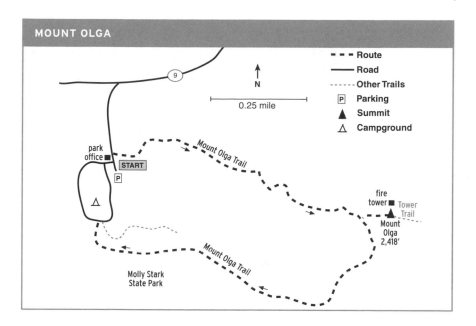

Climbing moderately again, the trail leaves the coniferous forest and emerges into mixed deciduous woods. You will ascend rock steps to a trail junction on the hillside with ledges rising around you. Go left, climbing the 0.1-mile spur trail to a grassy summit area surrounded by tall trees.

From the cab (lookout room) of Mount Olga's steel fire tower, Mount Greylock (3,491 feet), the highest point in Massachusetts, is visible in the southwest. To the northwest, Haystack Mountain's pointed peak (3,445 feet) juts from the prominent ridgeline leading north over Mount Snow (3,586 feet) and Stratton Mountain (3,936 feet). A small slice of Harriman Reservoir (Lake Whitingham) is visible, tucked into the hills directly west. Searsburg Wind Farm turbines sprout from the ridge just north of the reservoir. Far to the east, Mount Monadnock (3,165 feet) rises 2,000 feet higher than the New Hampshire hills surrounding it.

Go back down the summit spur trail (making sure not to descend a trail that heads east to Marlboro). Returning to the junction with Mount Olga Trail, head straight onto the southern leg of the loop, climbing over a little ridge before dropping downhill through a beech stand with remarkably twisted branches. After passing through a corridor between big rocks and crossing a stream on a low bridge, the trail curves to the right and begins a gentle downward grade, which it maintains for most of the remainder of the hike.

The deciduous woods here are rich with understory plants. In spring, look for tall, slender stalks of wild oats, as well as trout lilies and early yellow violets. Mats of evergreen partridgeberry and ferns spread across the forest floor.

Before the trees leaf out in spring, wildflowers carpet the woods along the southern leg of the Mount Olga loop.

Shelf fungus and big, rectangular pileated woodpecker holes appear on rotting trunks. About 0.8 mile from the summit, the trail meets a rock wall and follows it to the campground. Emerge next to site 10, turn right, and follow the campground road back to the trailhead.

DID YOU KNOW?

When completed in 1997, Searsburg Wind Farm became the largest wind-power facility in the eastern part of the country. The eleven 198-foot towers can generate up to 6 megawatts of electricity—enough to power 1,600 average Vermont households.

MORE INFORMATION

Molly Stark State Park operates Memorial Day to Columbus Day, from 10 A.M. to official sunset. A day-use fee applies in summer. Off-season use is allowed; contact Vermont State Parks for details. Molly Stark State Park, 705 Route 9 East, Wilmington, VT 05363; 802-464-5460 or 888-409-7579; vtstateparks.com.

NEARBY

Swim and boat at the Harriman Reservoir, 5 miles west, or at Adams Reservoir in Woodford State Park, 13 miles west. Food and shops are along VT 9/VT 100 in Wilmington, 3 miles west.

TRIP 4
BLACK MOUNTAIN

Location: Dummerston, VT
Rating: Moderate
Distance: 2.8 miles round-trip
Elevation Gain: 975 feet
Estimated Time: 2.5 hours
Map: USGS Newfane

Hike through a blueberry-covered forest to an unusual rocky woodland community on Black Mountain's summit, including a sprawling mountain laurel population.

DIRECTIONS
From the junction of VT 30, VT 9, and US 5 in Brattleboro, head north on VT 30 (Linden Street, then West River Road) for 4.3 miles. Turn right onto the Green Iron Bridge and cross the West River. At the end of the bridge, turn right onto Rice Farm Road and drive 1.0 mile to the trailhead parking area (space for about 5 cars) on the left, marked with a Nature Conservancy sign. *GPS coordinates: 42° 54.68′ N, 72° 36.38′ W.*

TRAIL DESCRIPTION
Black Mountain (1,280 feet) is a steep-sided, horseshoe-shaped mountain with a rolling, wooded summit ridgeline studded with granite outcrops. Its dry crest supports Vermont's only pitch-pine/scrub-oak woodland, a natural community that is more commonly found along New England's coasts. The hike features frequent steep climbs, but the footing is not difficult and the variety of landscapes is pleasantly distracting. White- and blue-painted blazes are left from earlier iterations of trails; follow the yellow diamond-shaped trail markers put in place by The Nature Conservancy (TNC).

Black Mountain Trail begins climbing northward from the parking lot, crossing the hillside on a grassy two-track speckled with wild strawberries and violets. At a metal gate, the trail enters the woods, rounds a switchback, and climbs onto a flat bench. Tall pines make a shady path leading to a hallway of dense pine saplings. At 0.3 mile, after passing a TNC registration box fixed high on a tree, the trail crosses a series of boardwalks that lead to a moderate climb across a rooty slope. Dwarf ginseng blooms in early summer

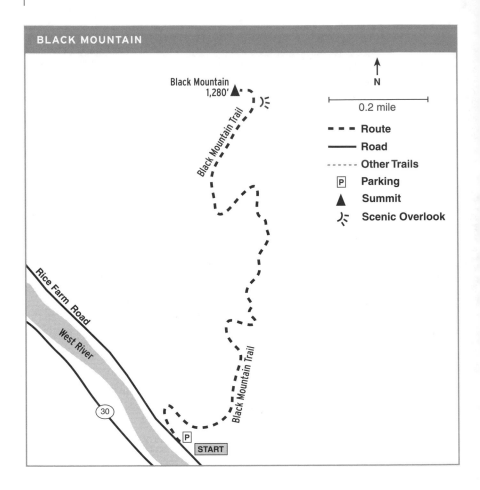

BLACK MOUNTAIN

Black Mountain
1,280'

Black Mountain Trail

N

0.2 mile

--- Route
—— Road
------ Other Trails
P Parking
▲ Summit
Scenic Overlook

Rice Farm Road

West River

30

Black Mountain Trail

P
START

here, with yellowish berries replacing the clusters of white flowers in mid- to late summer.

Now the trail begins a series of switchbacks up a steep hill. Black Mountain's steep sides are a result of its volcanic history. Unlike most Vermont mountains, which were pushed up by tectonic plate movement, Black is a granite pluton: the cooled, hardened magma from inside an ancient volcano that never erupted. Softer rocks surrounding it wore away over time, revealing the granite dome. As you climb, notice the change in the forest that occurs as the soils become thinner and more acidic on the upper mountain: Partway up this steep slope, red oaks and blueberries mix in with the beech, pine, and hemlock. As you hike higher, you'll see more blueberries and oaks, and fewer—and then no—beech and hemlock.

Climb several rock staircases onto a dry, ledgy plateau. Look for pileated woodpecker holes in the pines and spotted wintergreen, with its pale stripe

Granite outcrops and blueberry bushes spread beneath the open forest of pine and oak atop Black Mountain.

on dark, pointy leaves, growing low among the blueberries on the forest floor. Mounting this more moderate slope, you will zigzag through large beech trees and moss- and lichen-covered ledges to the base of another steep pitch, where switchbacks begin again.

You will ascend into a dry forest of scrub oak (endangered in Vermont), pitch pine, and the occasional red maple. The low canopy allows in a fair amount of sunlight, and blueberry bushes and granite ledges cover the ground between the small trunks. At about 1.1 miles, the trail begins its undulating course over the summit ridge. Continue northward, passing several stands of mountain laurel. In June, white and pink flowers blanket these evergreen shrubs in a stunning display.

Descending briefly, the trail arrives at a series of southeast-facing ledges. Obstructed views through the branches reveal the tall point of Mount Monadnock (3,165 feet) in the distance and rock slabs on the eastern half of Black Mountain in the foreground. The south-facing bowl within the horseshoe of Black Mountain captures solar heat, supporting plants that normally thrive 200 miles south of here. Follow the trail left, uphill to the highest ledge, surrounded by blueberries and wintergreen. Return downhill the way you came up.

DID YOU KNOW?

Pitch pines are adapted to wildfires. Their bark is heat-resistant, and some of their pinecones do not open to disseminate seeds until they've been exposed to the heat of a fire.

MORE INFORMATION

Black Mountain Natural Area is limited to passive recreational activities such as hiking, snowshoeing, bird-watching, photography, and nature study. Bicycles and motorized vehicles are not allowed. Dogs are not allowed. Remove no plants, animals, artifacts, or rocks; do not build fires. The Nature Conservancy, 27 State Street, Montpelier, VT 05602; 802-229-4425; nature.org/vermont.

NEARBY

The West River has excellent paddling opportunities and a number of swimming holes, including one under the 267-foot-long West Dummerston Covered Bridge (the longest covered bridge open to traffic in Vermont), 2 miles north. (Before swimming, double-check the safety of swimming holes where flooding caused by Tropical Storm Irene in 2011 may have altered the landscape.) Head to downtown Brattleboro, 6 miles south, for food and shopping. Camp at Fort Dummer State Park, 6.4 miles south, or Townshend State Park, 12.5 miles northwest.

TRIP 5
PUTNEY MOUNTAIN

Location: Putney, VT
Rating: Easy
Distance: 1.2 miles round-trip
Elevation Gain: 140 feet
Estimated Time: 1 hour
Maps: USGS Putney; USGS Westminster West; putneymountain.org/web/trails-maps

Walk through a variety of lovely forests on this loop hike to a grassy summit with views across southern Vermont and New Hampshire.

DIRECTIONS

From I-91, Exit 4, drive north 0.7 mile on VT 5 and turn left onto Westminster Road/Kimball Hill. After 1.1 miles, turn left onto West Hill Road and go 2.3 miles to Putney Mountain Road on the right. Drive 2.2 miles to the trailhead parking area (space for 15 cars) on the right. *GPS coordinates: 42° 59.78′ N, 72° 35.93′ W.*

TRAIL DESCRIPTION

Putney Mountain's open, fieldlike summit (1,660 feet) is the reward at the end of a pleasant ridgeline ramble. Interesting natural features, including an enormous, oddly shaped white ash called the Elephant Tree, are described in a nature-trail guide available at the trailhead kiosk. Just beyond the kiosk, a trail junction marks the beginning and end of the loop hike. Go left onto West Cliff Trail and follow the yellow trail markers into a shady hillside of mature hemlocks that effectively block so much sun that the understory is sparse. Rock cairns—piles of stones used to mark backcountry routes—have been artfully arranged along this stretch of trail, appearing frequently. Step across small streams and the remnants of an old stone wall—evidence that this steep slope was previously cleared. At 0.7 mile, leave West Cliff Trail as it turns left, and follow blue trail markers straight onto Summit Trail.

As soon as you start uphill on Summit Trail, the deep red-gold hues of the conifer forest recede, replaced by the light, airy white and green of a birch stand. Climb a steep slope onto the open summit of Putney Mountain. Small footpaths wander this grassy, shrubby area, looping and dead-ending, provid-

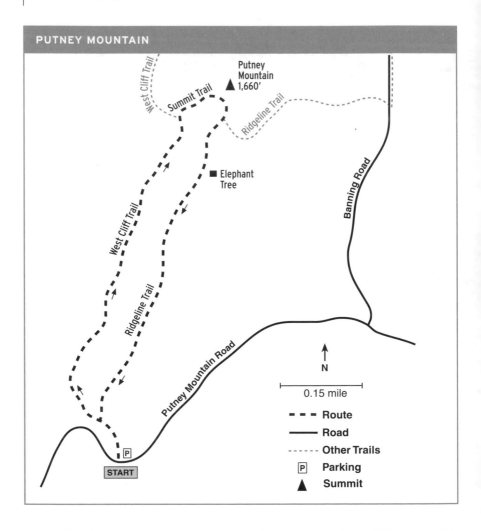

PUTNEY MOUNTAIN

ing paths through the variety of plants that colonize cleared forests at this latitude and elevation. Nubs and stripes of durable white quartzite jut out of the softer bedrock of gray phyllite.

Walk up to the height-of-land to see the rocky summit of New Hampshire's Mount Monadnock (3,165 feet), distantly visible to the southeast. Turn around to see the long ridgeline of the Green Mountains to the west. The pointed peak of Haystack Mountain (3,445 feet) anchors the southern end of this chain, and the ski trails on Stratton Mountain (3,936 feet) are visible at the more northern end.

The broad views and easy access make Putney Mountain a favorite observation site for autumnal hawk migrations.

Ferns, scrub oak, and raspberries spread across Putney Mountain's summit, which offers views across southern Vermont and New Hampshire.

From the height-of-land on the eastern side of the summit meadow, follow blue trail markers south, reentering the woods. After a short distance, you will meet Ridgeline Trail, which goes left (north) around Putney's summit and straight ahead (south) toward the parking area. Go straight on Ridgeline Trail, following white trail markers along the forested crest of the mountain. Shortly after crossing a stone wall, descend a ledge into a clearing; look left for the Elephant Tree, an enormous white ash with a "trunk" protruding from the main stem. The tree is thought to be more than 200 years old; its size marks it as one of the oldest trees in the vicinity.

Continue south along the rolling ridgeline, watching for the white trail markers to indicate the maintained trail amid what is sometimes a maze of unofficial trails that wander across the open areas. Hikers create these informal trails by trying to avoid muddy spots, but they tend to enlarge the wet areas, trample vegetation, and increase erosion. Walking through a puddle or rockhopping across it causes less impact and requires less repair work than going around wet spots.

Water accumulates in shallow basins along this ridge, and at least one vernal pool—a seasonal breeding pond for amphibians—appears each spring near the trail and dries up in summer. Vernal pools have an important place in forest ecosystems, allowing tadpoles and salamander larvae to hatch and complete their aquatic stage before maturing into terrestrial adults as the pool dries up.

**The Elephant Tree, a landmark along Ridgeline Trail, is an example of a "wolf tree"–
a tree left standing when the forest was cleared.**

Descending the final rock ledge, you will arrive back at the junction of West Cliff Trail and the parking lot.

DID YOU KNOW?

The Putney Mountain Association, a membership-supported group that owns Putney's summit and maintains the trails, sponsors the annual Fall Putney Mountain Hawk Watch to gather data about raptor migration patterns.

MORE INFORMATION

Camping and fires are not permitted on Putney Mountain. Mountain biking is permitted, but motorized vehicles are not, except as needed to make the trails accessible to people with disabilities. Snowmobiles are permitted in winter. Putney Mountain Association, P.O. Box 953, Putney, VT 05346; putneymountain.org.

NEARBY

West Dummerston's historical covered bridge spanning the West River on VT 30 is a popular spot to picnic and swim. A few restaurants and a food co-op can be found in Putney, near the junction of Westminster Road and VT 5, with more dining options 10 miles south in Brattleboro.

TRIP 6
LEDGES OVERLOOK

Location: Townshend, VT
Rating: Easy
Distance: 1.5 miles round-trip
Elevation Gain: 400 feet
Estimated Time: 1.5 hours
Map: USGS Saxtons River

Watch for bald eagles and osprey soaring over Townshend Lake, and walk through a pretty woodland savanna high above the valley.

DIRECTIONS

From the junction of VT 30 and VT 35 in Townshend, head north on VT 30 for 2.0 miles and turn left at Townshend Dam. Cross the dam and turn right into the Townshend Lake Recreation Area. Drive 0.6 mile, passing the swimming area parking lots and continuing on to park on the right by the picnic pavilion and playground. (Off-season hikers: Park in the lot at the gate—space for 5 cars—and walk the road to the trailhead, adding 1.2 miles round-trip to the hike.) *GPS coordinates:* 43° 03.06′ N, 72° 42.43′ W.

TRAIL DESCRIPTION

The loop hike to Ledges Overlook (1,140 feet) is an often steep, 0.6-mile ascent to views of the West River valley, followed by a more leisurely 0.9-mile return. Hikers about ages 6 and older will be able to scramble up to the lookout point. Dogs are not allowed when the recreation area is open but are welcome in the off-season.

Begin on the southern leg of the loop, which starts opposite the picnic pavilion, just uphill from the swimming area. Follow yellow blazes into the woods on an old two-track. The trail curves north for a short distance, then narrows to a footpath and proceeds northwest. Following alongside a stone wall, the grade steepens. Enormous white pines punctuate the mixed hardwood forest, and many downed trees lie scattered across the forest floor.

At 0.1 mile, a sharp curve southward brings the trail up a steep, rooty pitch into the shade of a hemlock stand. From here, the trail crosses a soggy saddle then climbs a steep hillside for 0.2 mile. Rock ledges appear in the woods above on the right—the base of the lookout. Where a stone wall descends

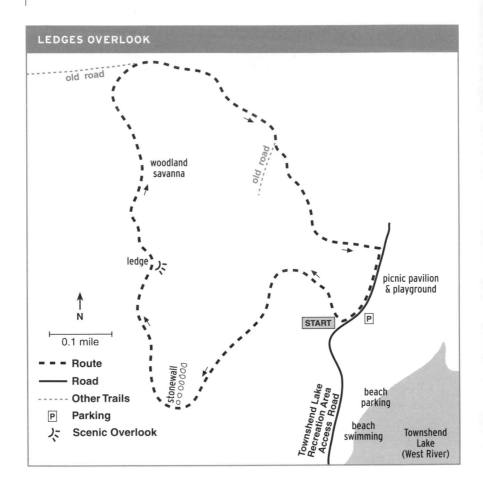

LEDGES OVERLOOK

old road

woodland
savanna

old road

ledge

picnic pavilion
& playground

N

0.1 mile

START

P

- - - Route
——— Road
------ Other Trails
P   Parking
Scenic Overlook

stonewall

beach
parking

beach
swimming

Townshend Lake Recreation Area Access Road

Townshend
Lake
(West River)

from the ridge above, the trail starts swinging in a long curve around a knoll, passing through red oak and beech and finishing on a northward heading. Edge along the top of the steep hill for 0.2 mile to arrive at the outlook. The impounded West River's Townshend Lake fills the valley below.

High-water marks from Tropical Storm Irene's flooding in August 2011 may still be visible along the banks. Also visible on the far shore is a former railroad bed, now the multiuse West River Trail. Beyond the massive earthen dam, the West River bends around the flank of Bald Mountain (1,680 feet). As you gaze eastward across the lake to the ridge of Rattlesnake Mountain (1,380 feet), keep an eye out for bald eagles and osprey, both of which nest in the area.

If you visit the ledges at dusk, you may see bats swooping and feeding. Little brown bats, big brown bats, red bats, and northern long-eared bats have all been spotted around Lake Townshend, though a devastating disease called white-nose syndrome has decimated populations in recent years. Two species

Townshend Lake fills the West River valley below Ledges Overlook, providing a recreation area as well as flood control.

that were once the most common—the little brown and the northern long-eared—are now endangered in Vermont, their numbers having declined by more than 90 percent over three years.

From the ledges, the trail continues north and west, climbing a short distance to enter a flat woodland savanna of hophornbeam trunks rising from a grassy lawn. Lacking the usual undergrowth of shrubs and young trees, the savanna is open, airy, and bright. Spring beauties sprout here early in the season, alongside violets.

Leaving the savanna, descend gradually northward through deciduous woods with a number of huge, old conifers. A sharp right turn brings the trail into the trough of an old road, which drops more directly down the hill. After 0.2 mile of a rocky and sometimes steep descent, watch for the yellow blazes to guide you left as the road curves right and drops into a gully. At this junction, look for dwarf ginseng, with its early-summer ball of miniature white flowers. Follow the footpath a final 0.2 mile to its end in a recently cleared field above the recreation area road. Turn right on the road for 0.1 mile to return to the trailhead.

DID YOU KNOW?

The 1,700-foot-long, 133-foot-high Townshend Dam was completed in June 1961 to control flooding. Its 11-billion-gallon capacity was tested in April 1987, when water filled to the spillway's 96-foot level and then rose 2.5 feet higher. The excess water was discharged over the spillway. During Tropical Storm Irene in 2011, the water level rose to 88 feet.

MORE INFORMATION

Townshend Lake Recreation Area is open 8 A.M. to 8 P.M. daily between the third Saturday in May and the Sunday after Labor Day, free of charge. Pets are not allowed, except in the off-season. The recreation area is operated by the U.S. Army Corps of Engineers, Townshend Lake, 3845 Route 30, Townshend, VT 05353; 802-365-7703; nae.usace.army.mil/recreati/tsl/tlhome.htm.

NEARBY

Swimming, boating, and picnicking are available at the trailhead. Groceries and restaurants are in Townshend, 3 miles south. The 16-mile West River Trail parallels VT 30, linking Townshend, Jamaica, and South Londonderry for biking, walking, or skiing. Camping is at Townshend State Park, 2 miles south.

TRIP 7
STRATTON POND

Location: Stratton, VT
Rating: Moderate
Distance: 7.4 miles round-trip
Elevation Gain: 390 feet
Estimated Time: 4.5 hours
Maps: USGS Stratton Mountain; fs.usda.gov/Internet/FSE_MEDIA/
stelprdb5315046.pdf

The wide, sparkling waters of this remote pond greet you after an easy walk through gently rolling woods.

DIRECTIONS
From the junction of VT 100 and Stratton–Arlington Road (Kelley Stand Road) in West Wardsboro, drive west on Stratton–Arlington Road for 7.9 miles to the Stratton Pond trailhead parking lot on the right (space for about 12 cars). (In winter, the road is closed 0.9 mile east; winter travelers park in the Appalachian Trail/Long Trail lot and add 1.8 miles round-trip to the hike.) *GPS coordinates:* 43° 03.70′ N, 72° 59.21′ W.

TRAIL DESCRIPTION
Stratton Pond (2,559 feet) spreads across 46 acres on a high plateau covered by ponds and streams between Stratton Mountain (3,936 feet) rising to the east and the Valley of Vermont descending to the west. On the edge of Lye Brook Wilderness, the pond's remote, pristine waters attract both day-hikers and campers, while thru-hikers skirt by the eastern shoreline, making this one of the most-visited spots on the Long Trail. The hike or ski to the pond is mostly flat—only the first 0.2 mile or so feels like it has any elevation gain—but the distance pushes this trip into moderate difficulty. Kids who can sustain a few hours of walking will accomplish this hike and probably never break a sweat.

Stratton Pond Trail follows blue blazes northeast into the woods from a signboard along the road (don't be misled by the two-track at the back of the parking lot). A couple of gentle inclines at the beginning are interspersed with flat stretches, and then the trail becomes mostly flat, with bog bridges and step stones traversing the many wet areas. Hobblebush, club moss, and trout lilies fill in the spaces between paper birch and beech trunks that get larger and

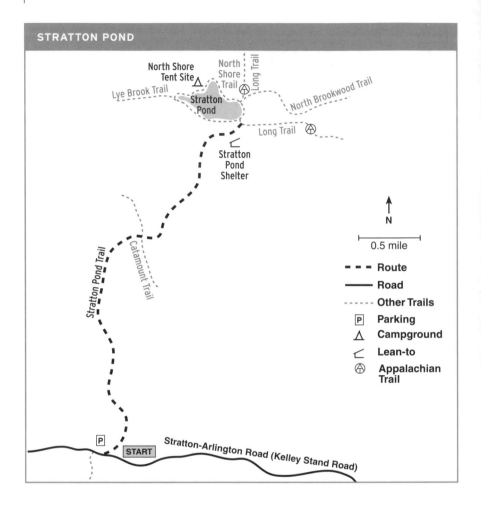

STRATTON POND

older the deeper you get into the woods. False hellebore's clusters of poisonous ribbed leaves sprout from the damp forest floor early in spring, with flowers emerging from a tall stalk (2 to 6 feet) in midsummer. By August, this plant has withered away.

A little over 1.0 mile into the hike, you will cross over the highest point of the trail, but since that point occurs on a long, flat-topped rise, it's almost imperceptible. At 2.0 miles, cross a grassy two-track, originally built as a logging road when International Paper owned this area. Now the Catamount Trail uses the path, coming from the south to join Stratton Pond Trail here.

Reentering the woods, the trail continues on bog bridges that curve past two chunks of recently (in geologic time) cleaved boulder, the taller piece wrapped with mossy roots of several trees growing from its top. The trail gradually ascends another small high point before descending over damp

Stratton Pond supports native populations of brook trout and bullheads, which attract herons, loons, mink, and river otters.

ground. The trail passes close to several ponds, though you won't see them; these ponds, along with the large tracts of unbroken forest in this area, support a diversity of animals. Aquatic vegetation in the ponds attracts moose, and you will likely see their large, two-toed tracks in the mud and piles of oval-shaped scat along the trail. Red efts—the juvenile, terrestrial stage of the eastern, or red-spotted, newt—also wander these damp woods between their aquatic larval and adult stages. Their bright-orange skin acts as a warning of toxicity to potential predators.

At 3.4 miles, you will arrive at a T junction. The trail to Stratton Pond Shelter departs to the right. Go left for 150 feet to meet the Long Trail/ Appalachian Trail, joining from the right. Continue downhill 0.1 mile on the now white-blazed trail to the shore of Stratton Pond. The water stretches west toward its outlet from this spot at the top of the pond. A grassy area next to one of several springs that feed the pond makes a nice picnic spot. Beavers are active here and have recently caused some flooding along North Shore Trail, one of several trails that together make a lovely 1.5-mile circuit around the pond.

Return to the trailhead the way you hiked in.

Red efts, the juvenile stage of the eastern, or red spotted, newt, move slowly through moist woods, eating small insects and snails.

DID YOU KNOW?

Nearby Stratton Mountain provided creative inspiration that led to the birth of long-distance hiking in the United States. James P. Taylor dreamed up the Long Trail in 1909 while sitting in a tent on the mountainside, waiting for rain to clear, and Benton MacKaye conceived the Appalachian Trail while perched in a tree on the summit.

MORE INFORMATION

Stratton Pond is in the Green Mountain National Forest; Manchester Ranger District, 2538 Depot Street, Manchester Center, VT 05255; 802-362-2307; fs.usda.gov/greenmountain. The Green Mountain Club maintains the shelter and the Long Trail (and this section of the Appalachian Trail). Green Mountain Club, 4711 Waterbury–Stowe Road, Waterbury Center, VT 05677; 802-244-7037; greenmountainclub.org.

NEARBY

The West River, renowned for paddling, offers good swimming holes and camping at Jamaica State Park, 15 miles northeast. Restaurants and shops are along VT 100 in West Dover, 15 miles southeast, or in Manchester, 21 miles northwest.

THRU-HIKING

"No person should attempt to tramp The Trail without a light axe, and a good compass." So advised the 1921 edition of the *Long Trail Guide*. Hiking was not novel in America at that time, but the idea of a long-distance hiking trail was. The Green Mountain Club formed in 1910 to create better access to the mountains, began cutting the Long Trail (LT) that same year. By 1920, the trail extended almost 200 miles, from Johnson, Vermont, to the Massachusetts border. Long-distance hiking in America had begun.

The LT now extends the length of Vermont—272 miles—and was the likely inspiration for the 2,180-mile Appalachian Trail (AT), which was born as a proposal in an architectural journal in 1921. Today, the AT and LT share their corridors for 105 miles in southern Vermont, and hiking either one end-to-end has become a badge of fortitude.

The two long-distance trails have developed similar subcultures of ambitious hikers striving to walk great distances over rugged terrain, and there are as many ways to hike as there are adventurous spirits to try it. Thru-hikers complete the trail in one long walk, while section-hikers cover the distance in smaller chunks over a longer time. Some hikers adopt ultralight practices, forgoing luxuries to shave weight (going without a sleeping bag in warmer months, for instance, or cutting the handle off a toothbrush if you're really counting ounces). Others travel old-school style, wearing wool and leather. Some people hike barefoot, and one man who is blind completed the AT with a Seeing Eye dog. Slack-packers carry just water and snacks along the trail, heading to town at day's end for dinner, a shower, and a bed. Some thru-hikers are purists, resisting the urge to blue-blaze—that is, to skip a section by hiking a blue-blazed side trail—and rejoin later on, perhaps after a pizza and a beer and a pint of ice cream. Others view the hike as a series of experiences linked by the general route of the trail, but not bound to it. (Bill Bryson's book *A Walk in the Woods* is a humorous example of this philosophy.) However it's tackled, the challenge of a thru-hike requires as much emotional stamina as it does physical, and for most who complete it, the hike is transformational.

TRIP 8
LYE BROOK FALLS

Location: Manchester, VT
Rating: Moderate
Distance: 4.4 miles round-trip
Elevation Gain: 740 feet
Estimated Time: 3 hours
Maps: USGS Manchester; fs.usda.gov/Internet/FSE_MEDIA/
stelprdb5321982.pdf

A magnificent 125-foot waterfall and an astounding recent land-slide hide deep in a narrow wilderness valley just outside one of Vermont's most-visited towns.

DIRECTIONS
From the junction of US 7 and VT 11/VT 30 in Manchester, head east on VT 11/VT 30 for 0.5 mile. Turn right onto East Manchester Road and go 1.2 miles. Turn left onto Glen Road, which quickly forks. Stay right on Lye Brook Access Road and drive 0.4 mile to the road's end at the Lye Brook Wilderness parking area (space for about 20 cars). *GPS coordinates:* 43° 09.55′ N, 73° 02.50′ W.

TRAIL DESCRIPTION
From bustling Manchester Village, Lye Brook Valley appears as an intriguing narrow slice in the steep wall of eastern mountains. The valley provides access to the 18,122-acre Lye Brook Wilderness, a high forested plateau laced with streams, ponds, and bogs. On the way to this upland Wilderness, Lye Brook Falls, one of the highest waterfalls in Vermont, plummets down the wall of the valley. Lye Brook Trail alternately climbs and then crosses level stretches; it is most likely to be enjoyed by kids about ages 8 and older. It is also fun terrain for a cross-country ski adventure.

Lye Brook Trailhead is marked with a small, unpainted wood sign charac-teristic of the minimal signs used in designated Wilderness areas (although the actual Wilderness boundary is 0.4 mile up the trail). Start across densely rocky ground into a tall, dim hardwood and hemlock forest. About 350 feet in, arrive at an unsigned junction of several trails—mostly informal exploratory paths around the river and parking area. A small brown arrow directs you left onto the most developed path, which ascends along the edge of Lye Brook's

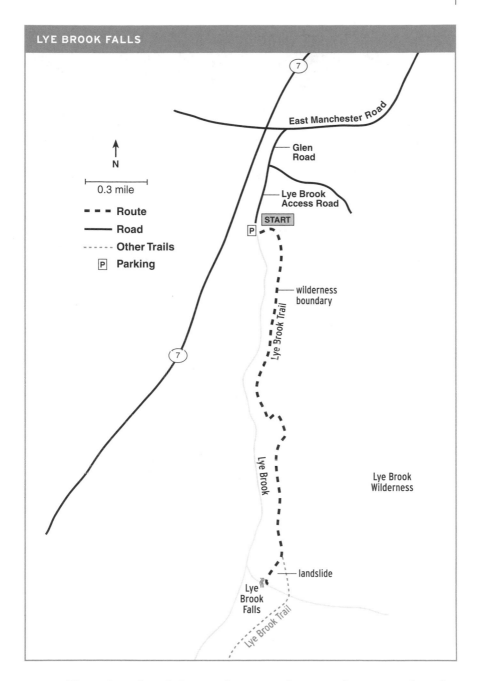

LYE BROOK FALLS

7

East Manchester Road

N

0.3 mile

- - - Route
— Road
----- Other Trails
P Parking

Glen
Road

Lye Brook
Access Road

START

P

wilderness
boundary

Lye Brook Trail

7

Lye Brook

Lye Brook
Wilderness

landslide

Lye
Brook
Falls

Lye Brook Trail

ravine. The wide path and the woods surrounding it are bursting with rocks, though shortly you cross onto smoother ground. Lye Brook Trail continues this pattern of alternating between very rocky and very smooth terrain the whole way to the Falls Trail junction.

Lye Brook Falls fans out as it tumbles over many small steps in the rock on its 125-foot drop.

Leveling out, the trail passes a hiker registration box and briefly follows the straight corridor of a former railroad bed before arriving at the Wilderness boundary. Continuing in a southwesterly direction across a gentle slope, Lye Brook Trail crosses a wide tannic stream on rocks. Climbing gradually, you will pass a small stand of brilliantly white smooth gray birches on the left.

You will step easily across several small streams before entering a steeper, narrower section of Lye Brook Valley at 1.0 mile. Curving left, the trail begins to climb a moderate pitch, entering a hemlock stand. Lye Brook drops away to the right, deep in its ravine. Curving north and then back to the south again, the trail climbs steadily for 0.6 mile over alternately rocky and then smooth gravelly ground before leveling across the steep hillside high above Lye Brook.

Evidence of Tropical Storm Irene's flooding can be seen in the jumbles of rocks spilling down the hillside in narrow columns. These once-tiny streambeds roared with tumbling water and rock for a couple of days in August 2011 before returning to rivulets.

At 1.8 miles, Lye Brook Falls Trail diverges to the right while Lye Brook Trail continues uphill to the left. Heading right, the narrow path to the falls crosses a rocky sidehill, gradually descending past dripping ledges and more rock-filled stream gullies. Then, at 2.1 miles, the destructive power of Irene's heavy rains is displayed on a massive scale. The woods end abruptly where the whole hillside—trees, rocks, the footpath, and all—slid into the valley far below. The next stretch of trail, approximately 60 feet, crosses the bare hillside about halfway down the steep, 500-foot slide. Then, just as abruptly, the woods begin again and seem untouched by the nearby devastation.

The approach to Lye Brook Falls, 0.1 mile past the landslide, is a little unclear, as multiple trails spiderweb off the main path. Staying high, head left for the best view of the cascade. The steep edges of the stream's ravine are unprotected—use caution here. Lye Brook Falls spills down a narrow rock chute for at least 125 feet—some estimates put it at 160 feet—before twisting and turning through boulders in the streambed below. The winter landscape here is a marvel of frozen sheets of ice draped over the rocks and hanging from the sides of the ravine.

Return to the trailhead the way you hiked in.

DID YOU KNOW?

Lye Brook Trail follows a former railroad line and woods road that facilitated removal of most of the trees here about a century ago. The remains of charcoal kilns and sawmills are still scattered across this once-again-wild landscape.

MORE INFORMATION

Lye Brook Wilderness is within the Green Mountain National Forest; Manchester Ranger District, 2538 Depot Street, Manchester Center, VT 05255; 802-362-2307; fs.usda.gov/greenmountain.

NEARBY

A swimming hole is just downstream from Glen Road's bridge over Bromley Brook, 0.4 mile away. Swim, paddle, and camp at Emerald Lake State Park, 8 miles north, off US 7. Food and shops are in Manchester, 2.5 miles west.

TROPICAL STORM IRENE

On the morning of August 28, 2011, Tropical Storm Irene roared north along the Atlantic coast and funneled into the mouth of the Connecticut River. As it headed inland, Irene's wind speeds dropped and it was downgraded to a tropical storm. That change in status did not result in low impacts for Vermont, though. The storm dumped heavy rains over the Green Mountains, which had already experienced a wet summer following heavy snowfall the winter before. Twelve inches of rain poured down on parts of Vermont that day, turning small streams into torrents and rivers into raging floods that tore out roads and bridges, washed away buildings and vehicles, and claimed four lives. The worst flooding since 1927 ravaged the state, closing 321 sections of road, 124 road bridges, and 6 railroad bridges, according to the Vermont Agency of Transportation. Thirteen towns were isolated as temporary islands and had to have food, water, and medical supplies airlifted in.

Southern and central Vermont were hit particularly hard by Irene, and hiking trails took a pounding along with the rest of the landscape. The Green Mountain National Forest was entirely closed for more than a week to assess the condition of its deluged footpaths and roads. While most of the forest reopened by mid-September, some trails and roads were so heavily damaged that they remained closed through the following summer to give crews a chance to make repairs. Five state parks were so pummeled that they turned away Labor Day visitors in order to clean up and rebuild. The Green Mountain Club, which maintains trails and shelters throughout the state, pulled all of its backcountry staff out of the woods the day before the storm and spent weeks afterward organizing and dispatching cleanup and assessment crews. Some trails were closed until they could be repaired, and some were relocated altogether.

The Vermont Agency of Natural Resources, which manages many of the state's public lands and hiking trails, was one of several state offices inundated by the swollen Winooski River in Waterbury. Staff members were displaced to a variety of temporary workspaces while the state undertook a massive reorganization plan that included building new offices on higher ground as well as figuring out if the historical Waterbury location, which had been damaged in the 1927 flood as well, could be salvaged and made floodproof. After the devastation of 1927 and 2011, no one in Vermont was willing to bet the waters wouldn't rise again.

TRIP 9
MOUNT EQUINOX

Location: Manchester, VT
Rating: Strenuous
Distance: 6.0 miles round-trip
Elevation Gain: 2,805 feet
Estimated Time: 4.5 hours
Maps: USGS Manchester; equinoxpreservationtrust.org/mapdown. php; equinoxmountain.com/mountain_trailmap.php

A long boreal ridgeline with incredible views awaits at the top of this challenging hike up the highest peak in the Taconic Mountains.

DIRECTIONS
From the junction of VT 7A and VT 11/VT 30 in downtown Manchester, head south on VT 7A for 1.2 miles. Turn right onto Seminary Avenue and follow it 0.2 mile to its end, where it bends left and becomes Prospect Street. Take the second right onto West Union Street and go 0.2 mile to the end of the public road. The parking lot (space for about 10 cars) is on the right. *GPS coordinates:* 43° 09.73' N, 73° 04.93' W.

TRAIL DESCRIPTION
Mount Equinox (3,840 feet) steals the show in the Battenkill Valley, towering impressively over the village of Manchester. Its very steep sides support diverse natural communities, including rich northern hardwood forests and rich fen on the lower mountain, an old-growth red spruce/yellow birch stand on the midmountain, and boreal forest and calcareous outcrops on the upper mountain. The range of habitats led to conservation of much of the eastern slope in the 1990s, with the Equinox Preservation Trust (EPT) organized to manage it. Blue Summit Trail, formerly called Burr and Burton Trail, is the only route on the mountain that EPT designates double black diamond (most difficult), due to its relentlessly steep climb to the ridgeline at 2.1 miles, at which point the pitch lessens for the final 0.5 mile to the summit. Another 0.5 mile of gently sloped trail leads along the crest to Lookout Rock.

Pass through the parking-area gate and begin your hike on Red Gate Trail. After a kiosk, Blue Summit Trail (still called Burr and Burton Trail on the signpost) joins from the right. Together, the two trails follow a gravel

MOUNT EQUINOX

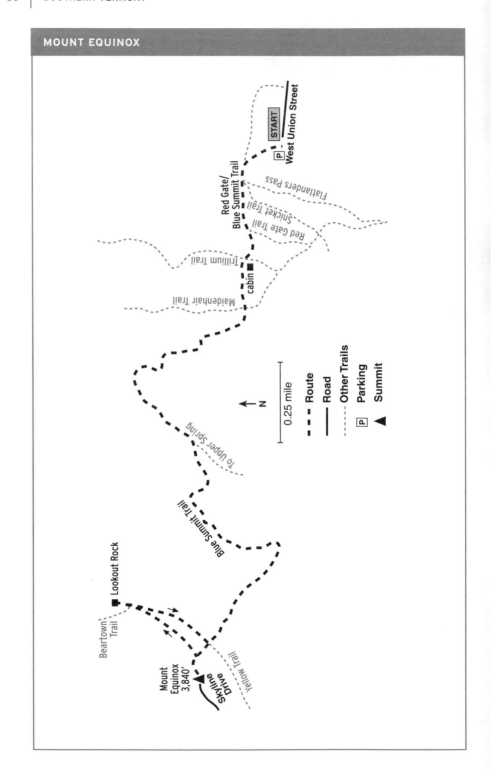

The crest of Mount Equinox supports a boreal forest and a beautiful, tree-lined path to Lookout Rock.

two-track past Flatlanders Pass and Snicket Trail. Following a moderate climb, the two trails separate at a fork at 0.3 mile. Go right on Blue Summit Trail and pass through private land where Trillium Trail crosses next to a small cabin.

The trail reenters EPT land at 0.7 mile, at the crossing of Maidenhair Trail, and the grade steepens. For the next 0.8 mile, the two-track jogs back and forth across the mountainside, maintaining a steep rise on every leg. The steady climb passes through beech, red oak, and bitternut hickory, with pale jewel-weed, hobblebush, and a variety of ferns and wildflowers spreading across the angled slopes. In spring, look for bloodroot, hepatica, lady's slipper, and trillium; in summer, you may see herb Robert as well as whorled aster.

At about 1.5 miles, you will cross a very steep rock band where thin yellow birch saplings line the trail like sentries and small spruces crowd along the narrow shelf; here you will arrive at a junction. The two-track continues to Upper Spring; go right, leaving the road for a rugged footpath, and continue up steeply for 0.6 mile more.

The grade eases and the forest becomes more boreal at 2.1 miles, where an enormous yellow birch growing next to a large fir marks your arrival on the ridge. Climbing directly up a moderate slope, you will arrive at Yellow Trail (your return path) at 2.4 miles. If you want to skip the developed summit with its cars, roads, and building, head right on Yellow Trail for 0.5 mile to reach Lookout Rock. To continue to the top, stay straight, pass around a cell tower station, and go left where a wide path leads right to Lookout Rock. Climb the last 0.1 mile to the summit, where a new visitor center was constructed in 2012 to replace the long-closed Equinox Inn. Carthusian Monks own 7,000 acres of the western side of Mount Equinox, including the road and summit, and manage the trails along the ridgeline. Views from the top are expansive, reaching across four states on a clear day.

To go to Lookout Rock, follow Blue Summit Trail the way you ascended and stay left at the cell tower junction, following a wide, rocky path. Yellow Trail becomes visible, paralleling your route before eventually merging with it. Beartown Trail drops off the ridgeline to the left just before you arrive at Lookout Rock's bench with its bird's-eye view of Manchester.

To descend, follow Yellow Trail back through the forest below the ridgeline and meet Blue Summit Trail in 0.5 mile. Turn left and go down the way you hiked up.

DID YOU KNOW?

The Taconic Mountains are so steep because the lower slopes are composed of soft rock that erodes more readily than the rock that forms the upper slopes, thus washing away what once were more-gradual hillsides.

MORE INFORMATION

Most of the trails and eastern side of the mountain are managed by the Equinox Preservation Trust; P.O. Box 986, Manchester, VT 05254; 802-366-1400; equinoxpreservationtrust.org. Summit trails are managed by Mount Equinox Skyline Drive; 1A Saint Bruno Drive, Arlington, VT 05250; 802-362-1114; equinoxmountain.com.

NEARBY

Camp, swim, and paddle at Emerald Lake State Park, 10 miles north. The Battenkill River has many scenic paddling stretches. Food and shops are abundant in Manchester.

TRIP 10
MERCK FOREST AND FARMLAND

Location: Rupert, VT
Rating: Moderate
Distance: 5.8 miles round-trip
Elevation Gain: 800 feet
Estimated Time: 4 hours
Maps: USGS Pawlet; merckforest.org/pdf/TrailMap.pdf

Wander through a working farm and beautiful hardwood forests on your way to a grand vista on Mount Antone.

DIRECTIONS
From the junction of VT 30 and VT 315 in East Rupert, follow VT 315 west for 2.6 miles to the height-of-land. Turn left and follow the 0.5-mile driveway to Merck's parking area (space for about 100 cars). *GPS coordinates:* 43° 16.46′ N, 73° 10.45′ W.

TRAIL DESCRIPTION
Climbing Mount Antone (2,600 feet) at Merck Forest and Farmland Center is a pleasantly different kind of hiking experience. The nonprofit center uses its 3,160 acres of farm and forest to demonstrate sustainable agriculture, and the public is invited to observe, participate, or simply explore the landscape on 30 miles of trails. Mount Antone is steep but not terribly high, with an amazing picnic spot on its wide grassy shoulder. Kids about ages 8 and older will enjoy the hike if you can get them past the farm animals. Dogs need to be leashed near the visitor center and farm.

Next to the parking area, the visitor center has maps and restrooms, among other offerings. Go around a gate and walk 0.3 mile on a dirt road to the field that is the hub of farm activities. Animals graze along the road, and a large sugarhouse and barn invite further exploration. Continue straight through a four-way junction of dirt roads, descending between open fields on Old Town Road. As you climb from the low spot, Wildlife Trail heads right through a pasture and, a little farther on, Gallop Road heads left. At 0.6 mile, turn right onto McCormick Trail.

Drop across the hillside through birches and maples. Leveling out through widely spaced hardwoods, the trail passes through ferns and jewelweed that

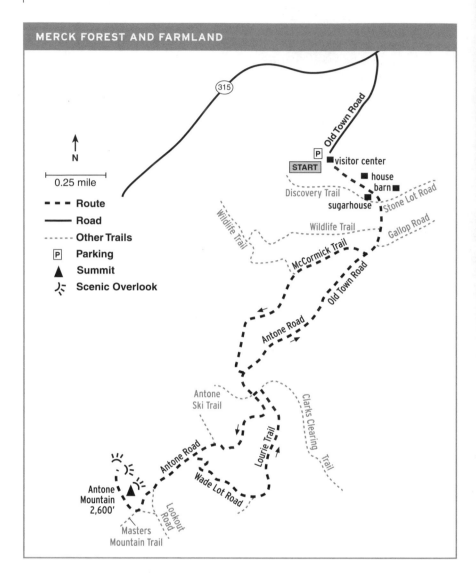

MERCK FOREST AND FARMLAND

315

N

0.25 mile

- - - Route
——— Road
------ Other Trails
P Parking
▲ Summit
⅄ᶻ Scenic Overlook

START ■ P ■ visitor center
■ house
barn ■
Discovery Trail sugarhouse ■ Stone Lot Road

Wildlife Trail Wildlife Trail Gallop Road

Old Town Road

McCormick Trail Old Town Road

Antone Road

Antone
Ski Trail Clarks Clearing Trail

Antone Road Lourie Trail

Antone
Mountain
2,600' Wade Lot Road

Lookout Road

Masters
Mountain Trail

make a meadow across the forest floor. At the lowest point, Wildlife Trail joins from the right, and McCormick Trail begins a moderate climb that becomes steep as it curves left and follows the edge of a ravine. Reaching the top of a ridge, the trail descends for a short distance to meet Antone Road in a clearing at 1.5 miles. Bear right across this small field and head south on Antone Road.

Antone Ski Trail diverges to the right next to a little cabin, and Clarks Clearing Trail heads left next to sap lines strung in sugar maples. Stay straight on Antone Road for a steep, 0.3-mile climb to the ridge of the mountain. The grassy two-track switches back and forth a few times, but some pitches are

The cleared shoulder of Mount Antone is a beautiful picnic spot with northern views of the Champlain Valley, the Taconic Mountains, and the Green Mountains.

simply straight up. Arriving on top, the trail rolls along the high land, passing the top of Antone Ski Trail on the right and then Wade Lot Road, your return route, on the left at 2.2 miles. Pass Lookout Road and climb a rocky, rooty pitch to a four-way junction at 2.5 miles. Turn right and ascend the last 0.2 mile to the summit.

A small clearing provides a window northeast, back to where you started. For the really spectacular view, go 350 feet down the far side of the summit to a grassy field with a bench under an oak tree. A northern panorama stretches across the horizon, from the Champlain Valley in the northwest over the diminishing Taconics and tall Green Mountains to the big, 160-year-old barn anchoring Merck's farm fields.

Return 0.6 mile along Antone Road, and turn right down Wade Lot Road. This curving, grassy two-track drops steeply through one of the most beautiful forests on the property, with ferns and grass spread beneath widely spaced hardwood trunks. Ned's Place, a camping cabin, is visible downhill to the right.

At 3.6 miles, turn left onto Lourie Trail and continue through the same lovely forest until, curving north around the mountain, the woods fill with shrubby saplings. Blackberries, raspberries, and purple-flowering raspberries (also called thimbleberries) line the path as it crosses the steep mountainside

Purple-flowering raspberry, with its edible, late-summer fruit, is a common sight along mountain trails in Vermont.

before arriving at Clarks Clearing Trail at 4.3 miles. Go left to the junction of Antone Road and follow it right, retracing your steps to the meadow at the top of McCormick Trail. From there, follow Antone Road's gradual descent for 0.4 mile to Old Town Road. Go left on Old Town, and return downhill 0.6 mile to the barn and sugarhouse. Retrace your steps to the parking lot.

DID YOU KNOW?

In 1850, most of the forest on this property was pasture cleared for sheep, with only the mountaintops remaining forested. See historical photos of the changing landscape at the visitor center.

MORE INFORMATION

Open dawn to dusk, seven days a week, year-round. Merck Forest and Farmland Center, P.O. Box 86, Rupert VT 05768; 802-394-7836; merckforest.org.

NEARBY

Camping is available here on the property, or at Emerald Lake State Park, which also has swimming and paddling, 14.5 miles east. The Battenkill River has scenic paddling 20 miles southeast. Dorset Quarry is a popular swimming hole 6.6 miles east. Some food is available in Dorset, 5 miles east, with more options in Manchester, 11 miles southeast.

TRIP 11
LITTLE ROCK POND

Location: Mount Tabor, VT
Rating: Easy
Distance: 4.8 miles round-trip
Elevation Gain: 365 feet
Estimated Time: 3.5 hours
Maps: USGS Danby; USGS Wallingford

A gentle valley hike leads to a fun loop trail around a beautiful pond with lots of swimming spots.

DIRECTIONS

About 17 miles south of Rutland, crossroads between Danby and Mount Tabor meet US 7. From US 7, turn east onto Brooklyn Road/Forest Road 10 at an industrial-looking lot next to the railroad. Go 3.1 miles up this winding mountain road to the Appalachian Trail/Long Trail parking lot (space for about 20 cars) on the right. (Winter hikers park at the USFS Mount Tabor Work Center on Forest Road 48, 0.4 mile along Brooklyn Road from US 7.) *GPS coordinates: 43° 22.36′ N, 72° 57.76′ W.*

TRAIL DESCRIPTION

The clear waters of Little Rock Pond (1,854 feet) gather in a pretty basin along the high crest of the Green Mountains. The hike follows gradual grades along a stream, then circles the berry-lined pond, passing some beautiful swimming spots. All of these factors make this a great hike for kids about ages 7 and older, but they also make Little Rock Pond a popular area. If solitude is your goal, head to the pond in the off-season (late fall to early spring), when the pond's beauty is perhaps even more luminous.

Cross Forest Road 10 from the parking area and follow the white-blazed Appalachian Trail/Long Trail (AT/LT) north. For 0.2 mile, the trail rises moderately along the wide, rocky Big Branch. Then, curving west, the path leaves the river and settles into the gentle, almost level pitch it maintains the rest of the way to the pond. The waters of Little Black Brook become audible in the ravine on your left before they become visible at 0.6 mile, when you cross the stream on a narrow metal I beam. Small cascades tumble downhill as you follow the left bank for 0.2 mile, then cross again on large rocks. Hobblebush,

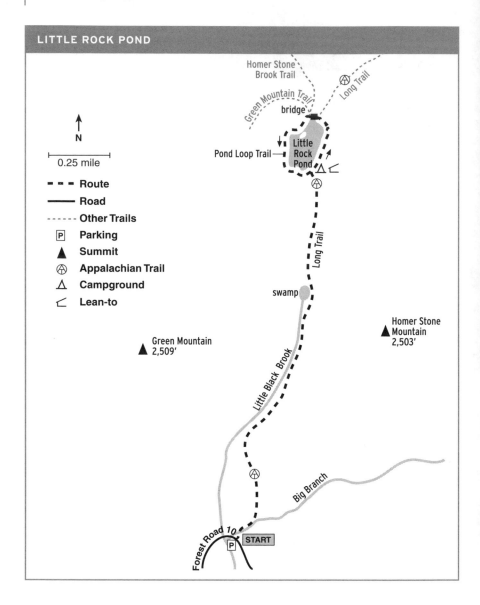

LITTLE ROCK POND

Homer Stone
Brook Trail

Green Mountain Trail

Long Trail

bridge

Little
Rock
Pond

Pond Loop Trail

N

0.25 mile

- - - Route
——— Road
----- Other Trails
P   Parking
▲   Summit
Ⓐ   Appalachian Trail
△   Campground
⊏   Lean-to

Long Trail

swamp

Homer Stone
▲ Mountain
2,503'

Green Mountain
▲ 2,509'

Little Black Brook

Big Branch

Forest Road 10

P START

Indian cucumber, blue cohosh, and blue-bead lilies sprout from the mossy ground alongside the trail.

Bog bridges and chunky rock underfoot characterize the second half of the 2-mile hike to the pond. At 1.5 miles, skirt the right side of a small swamp and climb a little higher on the hillside. A final long string of bog bridges leads to the T intersection at the shore of the pond at 2.0 miles. Go right, past the camping area with its large shelter, built in 2010 to replace the Lula Tye Shelter and the old Little Rock Pond Shelter, both of which were removed.

The approximately 30-foot-high Little Rock provides a lovely rest spot along the western shore of the pond that shares its name.

Continue on the AT/LT along the rocky eastern shore of the pond. As you round the north end, openings in the trees provide access to the water and views of Homer Stone Mountain (2,503 feet) to the east and Green Mountain (2,509 feet) above the western pond edge. Around the swampy area at the pond's outlet, where Pond Loop Trail breaks off from the AT/LT, lady's slippers bloom in early summer. After the pouchlike flower has shriveled, a single nodding leaf remains atop the tall stalk, with two large ribbed leaves at ground level. Go left on the blue-blazed Pond Loop/Green Mountain Trail and cross a bridge over the outlet, passing Homer Stone Brook Trail. Follow the shoreline into shady hemlocks, and climb to the junction where Pond Loop Trail diverges from Green Mountain Trail. Staying left on Pond Loop Trail, descend along the narrow channel separating the mainland from a small island. A great place to picnic and swim is on your left here, across from the southern tip of the island. A wide ledge eases into the water, and blueberry bushes grow abundantly beneath white pines.

Continuing south, cross an inlet stream and clamber over rocks before climbing to the top of the Little Rock of the pond's name. Watch kids and dogs here, because the trail edges close to the drop before descending back to water level. Cross the swampy pond inlet in the final 0.2 mile to the AT/LT trail junction. Return to the trailhead the way you walked in.

Mature Indian cucumber has two layers of whorled leaves and drooping flowers in spring. In summer, green berries replace the pollinated flowers. By fall, the berries darken to a bluish-purple color while the center of the top whorl of leaves turns red.

DID YOU KNOW?

The camping area at Little Rock Pond has attracted people since the ancestors of the Wabanaki and Mohican moved into the Green Mountains shortly after the last ice age. An archaeological excavation at the campsite between 2009 and 2012 found evidence that this area may have been used as far back as 11,000 years ago, "when they could have still heard the glaciers calving," the lead archaeologist noted.

MORE INFORMATION

Green Mountain National Forest, Manchester Ranger District, 2538 Depot Street Manchester Center, VT 05255; 802-362-2307; fs.usda.gov/greenmountain. The Appalachian Trail/Long Trail and Little Rock Pond Campsite are maintained by the Green Mountain Club; 4711 Waterbury–Stowe Road, Waterbury Center, VT 05677; 802-244-7037; greenmountainclub.org. Camping fees are $5 per person between Memorial Day and Columbus Day weekends.

NEARBY

If backcountry camping isn't on your agenda, Emerald Lake State Park has car camping as well as swimming and paddling 7.5 miles south. General stores have limited food along US 7 in either direction; restaurants and shops are in Manchester, 17 miles south, and Rutland, 20 miles north.

TRIP 12
WHITE ROCKS ICE BEDS

Location: Wallingford, VT
Rating: Easy
Distance: 1.8 miles round-trip
Elevation Gain: 336 feet
Estimated Time: 1.5 hours
Maps: USGS Wallingford; fs.usda.gov/Internet/FSE_MEDIA/
stelprdb5315073.pdf

Hike to a rock slide, where pockets of ice last through summer and release a cold stream and cool breezes on even the hottest days.

DIRECTIONS
From the junction of US 7 and VT 140 (School Street) in Wallingford, follow VT 140 east for 2.1 miles. Bear right on Sugar Hill Road and take the next right onto Forest Road 52 (White Rocks Picnic Road). Follow it 0.5 mile to its end in the trailhead parking lot (space for about 25 cars). (Winter hikers park alongside the road at the gate and add 0.4 mile round-trip to the hike.) *GPS coordinates: 43° 27.05' N, 72° 56.61' W.*

TRAIL DESCRIPTION
The steep northwestern side of White Rocks Mountain (2,682 feet) is eroding in a series of dramatic rock slides easily viewed from a nearby ridge. After a short climb to the lookout, descend to the foot of one of the slides to experience the microclimate created by sheltered ice beds slowly melting deep within the rocks. This hike ascends and descends in both directions and would be fun for kids about ages 5 and older. The rocky outcrops atop the lookout ridge are particularly amusing places for kids to explore—with supervision, because there are some cliffs—and are far more appealing picnic spots than the tables next to the parking lot.

From the parking area, Keewaydin Trail departs east and White Rocks Trail goes southwest to climb a low ridge, where it meets Ice Beds Trail. Follow the blue blazes of White Rocks Trail into a hemlock forest. A ridge of chunky rocks descends toward you through the trees, with many unofficial trails that were beaten up it by explorers looking for views. The actual trail crosses the base of the rocks to rise gradually along the right slope. A series of switchbacks

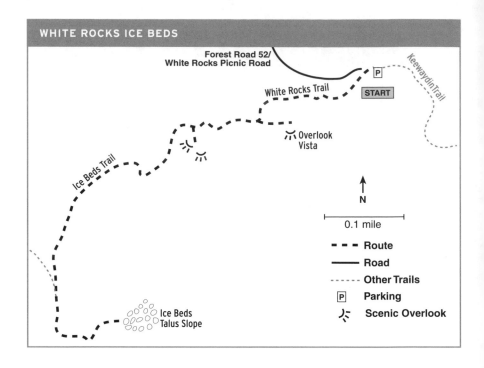

then climbs the steep pitch to arrive at a T junction on top of the rocky crest at 0.2 mile. Go left to the Overlook Vista, where a low rock wall and blueberry bushes line the edge of a cliff. A narrow valley separates the outlook from steep talus slopes on White Rocks Mountain. A sharp escarpment descends from its pointy peak to the valley, and conifers rim the rock slides.

Follow the path back to the junction and go straight onto Ice Beds Trail, which immediately scrambles up a ridge bristling with rock. After 0.1 mile, the trail encounters a wall of ledge and turns sharply right to descend off the ridge. Before going down, climb onto the wide, smooth ledge and take in the view south and west. The western slope of White Rocks Mountain is now visible, dominated by an enormous rock slide that tumbles about 1,000 feet from the summit cliffs. The Valley of Vermont stretches south, with Otter Creek—the longest river within Vermont, at 112 miles—snaking northward along the bottom. A limestone quarry is visible along the valley floor, and the Taconic Mountains stack up along the southern and western horizons.

Return to the trail and descend into the wooded valley. The route can be challenging to follow through the hemlocks, because there is almost no undergrowth to define the path; keep an eye out for blue blazes. As you drop over the left side of the ridge, a dirt road intersects the trail. Go left on the road, continuing downhill into a thicker, more diverse forest. Cross the wide stream

Rock slides on White Rocks Mountain create pockets where ice remains into summer.

and the flat valley floor, trending left as a rocky hillside rises steeply on the right. Bog bridges extend over damp ground before the trail begins gradually to rise. The open white slope of talus becomes visible through the trees, and the air turns noticeably cooler. Feel the stream running out of the base of the slide—the ice beds hidden in the rocks produce an achingly cold rivulet of 35 to 40 degrees Fahrenheit. Ice Beds Trail ends at the bottom of the slide. The jumble of boulders calls to be climbed, but use caution here and don't assume the rocks are stable.

Return to the trailhead the way you hiked in.

DID YOU KNOW?

In a rock slide, the size of the rocks differs from the top to the bottom. The momentum of large rocks carries them farther, and they end up lower on the slope, while smaller rocks stopped by obstacles remain higher on the slide.

MORE INFORMATION

Robert T. Stafford White Rocks National Recreation Area is within the Green Mountain National Forest, 231 North Main Street, Rutland, VT 05701; 802-747-6700; fs.usda.gov/greenmountain. Dogs must be leashed.

NEARBY

Swim, paddle, and camp at Emerald Lake State Park, 16 miles south.

TRIP 13
OKEMO MOUNTAIN

Location: Mount Holly, VT
Rating: Moderate to Strenuous
Distance: 6.0 miles round-trip
Elevation Gain: 1,950 feet
Estimated Time: 4 hours
Maps: USGS Mount Holly; vtstateparks.com/pdfs/okemo_sf_trails.pdf

A historical fire tower on this big peak gives 360-degree views across all of southern Vermont.

DIRECTIONS
From the junction of VT 100 and VT 103, go west on VT 103 for 2.8 miles and turn left onto Station Road. Go 0.7 mile and cross active railroad tracks. Turn left and proceed about 500 feet to the end of the road at the Healdville Trail parking area (space for about 6 cars). *GPS coordinates:* 43° 25.95′ N, 72° 45.70′ W.

TRAIL DESCRIPTION
Okemo Mountain (3,343 feet) is the name often used for Ludlow Mountain, due to the ski area on its eastern side and the 7,323-acre state forest encompassing most of the peak. The hiking trail on its western side, built by youth crews in the early 1990s, is a steady climb for the first half and a cross-mountain trek for most of the second.

Leaving the parking area, walk parallel to the train tracks for a short distance, then curve right, following blue-blazed Healdville Trail uphill. Catamount Trail shares the path for a little ways, then breaks off at a wide wooden bridge. The path starts out wide and mostly smooth as it climbs alongside a stream, then becomes narrower and rockier. Pretty cascades tumble down on your right, while rose twisted stalk, blue and white cohosh, trillium, and Indian cucumber line the sides of the trail.

At 0.8 mile, cross a plank bridge and continue up the valley for 0.2 mile more. Then a hard left bend begins a series of switchbacks that lead you up through a northern hardwood forest and among glacial erratics for almost 0.5 mile. A final push straight up the moderate pitch brings you to the cross-mountain section of trail at 1.6 miles.

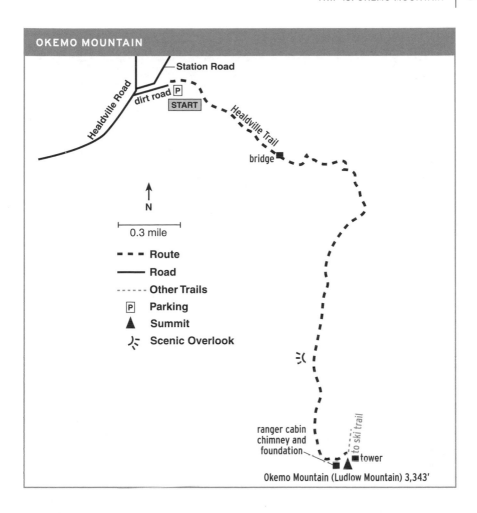

OKEMO MOUNTAIN

Station Road

Healdville Road

dirt road

P

START

Healdville Trail

bridge

N

0.3 mile

- - - Route

——— Road

----- Other Trails

P Parking

▲ Summit

Scenic Overlook

ranger cabin chimney and foundation

to ski trail

tower

Okemo Mountain (Ludlow Mountain) 3,343'

Walk south, high on the mountainside, rising and falling gradually and crossing muddy areas on wide, flat step stones. At 2.4 miles, a small outlook opens to the north and west. The Coolidge Range, including Killington Peak (4,235 feet), Vermont's second highest, extends north. To the west, a gap allows VT 103 and the railroad to pass out of the Green Mountains and into the Valley of Vermont, beyond which the Taconic Mountains rise. The Taconics were pushed up millions of years before the Greens and have weathered into steep-sided, round-topped humps that extend from the Champlain lowlands south along the Vermont–New York border and through western Massachusetts and Connecticut (where they are generally lumped in with the neighboring Berkshire Mountains).

Continue across the mountain, climbing moderately as the forest becomes more boreal, with bunchberry and Canada mayflower growing beneath paper birch, spruce, and fir. About 0.25 mile below the summit, Healdville Trail

Boreal forests like this one on Okemo Mountain thrive above about 2,900 feet in southern Vermont (or 2,500 feet farther north), where thin, rocky soils and cold temperatures favor red spruce, balsam fir, paper birch, and mountain ash.

curves left and climbs steeply, skirting a tall rock ledge and winding through a damp boreal forest. Look for ghostly Indian pipe sprouting from the shady forest floor here. Arriving on the summit ridge, descend gradually to a stone chimney in a clearing, backed by the moss-covered foundation of the former forest ranger's cabin. Continue 25 feet farther to the summit spur trail on the right. Go up a short, rocky pitch to the fire tower.

The roofed cab of the tower provides an immense view over southern Vermont. Beyond the chairlifts and slopes of Okemo Ski Area, Ludlow Village extends east along the valley. The massive ridge of Mount Ascutney (3,144 feet) dominates the northeastern horizon. Lake Ninevah rests in a high basin to the north, with Salt Ash Mountain (3,286 feet) and the Coolidge Range beyond it. Due west, the White Rocks National Recreation Area covers the high ground, with its scenic hikes to White Rocks Ice Beds (Trip 12) and lovely Little Rock Pond (Trip 11). South Mountain (3,200 feet) is the appropriately named bump close by to the south, with Bromley (3,260 feet) and Stratton (3,936 feet) mountains in the southwest beyond it.

Return downhill the way you hiked up.

DID YOU KNOW?

The 4.5-mile auto road up Okemo Mountain and the fire tower and ranger cabin were built in the 1930s by Civilian Conservation Corps crews. The auto road can be biked or driven in summer, but it's the mountain's longest ski trail in winter.

MORE INFORMATION

Healdville Trail is open to foot travel only. It is closed during mud season, from snowmelt to around the third week in May. Okemo State Forest, Vermont Department of Forests, Parks and Recreation, 100 Mineral Street, Suite 304, Springfield, VT 05156; 802-885-8845; vtstateparks.com.

NEARBY

Swim, picnic, hike, and rent a camping cabin at Camp Plymouth on Echo Lake, 8 miles north, where group camping is available. Individual campsites are available at Gifford Woods State Park, 25 miles north; Ascutney State Park, 27 miles east; or Emerald Lake State Park, 27 miles southwest. Food and shops are in Ludlow, 5 miles east.

TRIP 14
MOUNT ASCUTNEY

Location: Windsor, VT
Rating: Strenuous
Distance: 5.2 miles round-trip
Elevation Gain: 2,450 feet
Estimated Time: 4 hours
Map: USGS Windsor

Cascades and ledges provide scenic rest spots along this hike to the top of southeastern Vermont's most recognizable landmark.

DIRECTIONS
From the junction of US 5 and VT 44 in Windsor, follow VT 44 west for 3.3 miles. Make a left hairpin turn onto VT 44A (Back Mountain Road) and travel 0.2 mile to an Ascutney State Park parking lot (space for about 10 cars) on the right, marked by a small sign on the opposite side of the road reading "Windsor Trail Parking." *GPS coordinates: 43° 27.42′ N, 72° 25.33′ W.*

TRAIL DESCRIPTION
Mount Ascutney (3,144 feet) towers over the hills of the Connecticut River valley, its granite and syenite dome—once the magma inside a volcano—more durable than the landscape around it and therefore slower to be worn down. The steep sides of the mountain have long drawn adventurers whose marks remain: an auto road (still in use), ski area (closed), and stone hut (now just a foundation). Five hiking trails ascend from points around the dome and converge along the summit ridgeline. Windsor Trail ascends the northeast side, climbing steadily and often steeply past numerous points of interest on its way to an observation tower for spectacular views over the treetops.

From the parking area, follow a mowed path uphill through a field and enter the woods on a white-blazed trail. Pass through hardwoods and sumac to enter a dim hemlock stand, where the trail comes alongside a steep ravine. Windsor Trail follows the right side of this stream valley for about a mile, climbing steadily. Hemlocks give way to hardwoods as you ascend, and views of Mountain Brook become more common as the ravine becomes less deep. At 0.8 mile, a side trail leads left to a view of the long, cascading tumble of Gerry Falls. Use caution on the slick ledges if you explore along the stream.

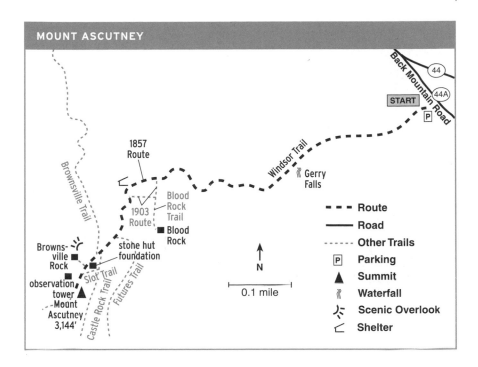

MOUNT ASCUTNEY

1857
Route

Brownsville Trail

Windsor Trail

Gerry
Falls

Blood
Rock
Trail

1903
Route

Blood
Rock

Browns-
ville
Rock

stone hut
foundation

observation
tower

Mount
Ascutney
3,144'

Slot Trail

Castle Rock Trail

Futures Trail

START

44

44A

P

N

0.1 mile

- - - **Route**

——— **Road**

----- **Other Trails**

P   **Parking**

▲   **Summit**

≀   **Waterfall**

⅄   **Scenic Overlook**

⊏   **Shelter**

After ascending a short, steep distance above the falls, cross the stream with the help of ropes strung at hand height between trees, and continue ascending over slippery slab. Windsor Trail zigzags across Mountain Brook several more times and then heads right to cross a hillside littered with large chunks of rock. A steep, rocky climb leads to the junction of two sections of Windsor Trail at 1.6 miles—the 1857 route leads right, and the 1903 route goes left. (The two legs rejoin in 0.2 mile.) Go right on the 1857 route. After 0.1 mile, the open front of a log shelter appears, jutting from the steep hillside. The trail veers left, climbing close to the impressive stone chimney as it ascends the slope above. Switchbacks bring you to the upper junction with the 1903 route. Stay right.

Climb over roots and mossy rocks for 0.2 mile to reach the junction of Futures Trail on your left. Go right for 0.2 mile more, ascending switchbacks to a boreal forest ridge and a little rock-walled bowl in the mountainside. Castle Rock Trail departs left, and Windsor Trail climbs to the right, meeting Brownsville Trail. Stay left and climb another 0.1 mile to arrive at the stone hut foundation. From the right side of the clearing, walk 200 feet down a spur trail to find western views from Brownsville Rock.

Continuing along the ridge on Windsor Trail, pass Slot Trail on the left and climb a small slope to the observation tower at 2.5 miles. From its open platform, you can see across New Hampshire and Vermont, and north into

Mount Ascutney give hikers a broad view of the ridge of the Green Mountains to the west.

Quebec and south into Massachusetts. The Connecticut River slips in and out of view between the hills. The southern view is dominated by a cell tower rising from Ascutney's true summit, 0.1 mile farther along the trail.

Return downhill the way you ascended. For variety, go right onto the 1903 route, which has the same mileage as the 1857 route. Blood Rock Trail extends 0.3 mile from the 1903 route to a nice view east and north from an uncomfortably angled slope above a cliff. If you check out the view from Blood Rock, add 0.6 mile to your total trip distance.

DID YOU KNOW?

The origin of the ominous name of the Blood Rock is less dramatic than you might guess: According to the Dartmouth Outing Club, a climber cut his hand trying to carve his initials into the rock.

MORE INFORMATION

Windsor Trail is maintained by Ascutney Trails Association, P.O. Box 147, Windsor, VT 05089; ascutneytrails.org.

NEARBY

Take a dip in the Black River's Twenty Foot Hole, 10 miles west, off Tyson Road in Reading. Camp at Mount Ascutney State Park, 2.5 miles south. For food, head into Windsor, 4 miles northeast.

TRIP 15
MOUNT TOM

Location: Woodstock, VT
Rating: Easy to Moderate
Distance: 3.0 miles round-trip
Elevation Gain: 550 feet
Estimated Time: 2 hours
Maps: USGS Woodstock North; NPS map available at Billings Farm and Museum

Gentle switchbacks up the southeast side of Mount Tom make a leisurely outing for the whole family.

DIRECTIONS

Follow US 4 into downtown Woodstock. In the center of the village, from the westbound lane of US 4/North Park Street, turn right onto Mountain Avenue and cross the Ottauquechee River on the covered Middle Bridge. Continue to follow Mountain Avenue as it turns sharply left at the end of the block. The trailhead is in Faulkner Park, which is on your right; parking is along the street. *GPS coordinates:* 43° 37.44' N, 72° 31.48' W.

TRAIL DESCRIPTION

With its gradual grade and many resting benches, Faulkner Trail replicates the gentle rehabilitation trails of the famous spas in Baden-Baden, Germany, though numerous informal shortcuts indicate energetic hikers' desires for a more direct route. Only the final hundred or so yards (never part of the original trail), from a viewpoint to the summit, are rugged and steep. The trail-head's walking proximity to the shops and restaurants of Woodstock make this a good postbrunch hike or simply an excuse to earn ice cream cones.

Find the trailhead at woods' edge at the back of Faulkner Park. The paved path turns to dirt as the trail sets out through large oaks and hemlocks. Rustic benches appear at intervals as the wide path heads north, then south, then north again, switching back and forth approximately 15 times in its ascent. Large stones stabilize the hairpin turns, and a small stone bridge arches over a stream. The mature forest is airy and tall, with big, mossy boulders and little undergrowth.

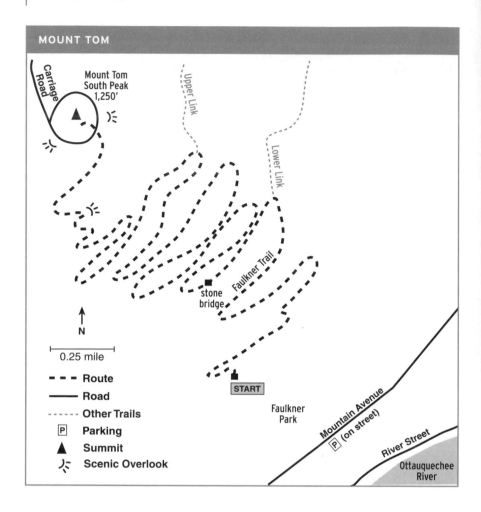

MOUNT TOM

Carriage Road

Mount Tom
South Peak
1,250'

▲

Upper Link

Lower Link

Faulkner Trail

stone
bridge

↑
N

0.25 mile

- - - Route
——— Road
------ Other Trails
P Parking
▲ Summit
⅄ Scenic Overlook

START

Faulkner
Park

Mountain Avenue
P (on street)

River Street

Ottauquechee
River

At about the fifth turn, stay left as Lower Link Trail departs to the right. This is one of several junctions connecting Faulkner Trail to an extensive network of footpaths and carriage roads in Billings Park and the abutting Marsh-Billings-Rockefeller National Historical Park. Vermont's only national park opened in 1992 as a new kind of park, committed to telling "the story of conservation history and the evolving nature of land stewardship in America." Today, Mount Tom's forest is the oldest professionally managed woodland in Vermont and one of the oldest in the nation.

The national park partners with the Faulkner Trust, the Vermont Land Trust, and the Billings Park Commission (Town of Woodstock) to manage 30 miles of continuous trails, making this jaunt on Mount Tom just the beginning of explorations of these hills and forests. Questing, a kind of game in which

A stone bridge and intermittent resting benches offer a touch of civility in the mature forests on Mount Tom.

clues lead hikers through a landscape, is popular in this part of Vermont (see page 71).

After several more turns up Mount Tom, Upper Link Trail appears on the right. Stay left and follow the final long leg across the hillside to the beginning of the shortened switchbacks that lead to the overlook. This rocky knoll below Mount Tom's South Peak was the original destination of Faulkner Trail. Wooden benches and a clearing in the trees provide a view of the town below. From here, the character of the hike changes dramatically as Faulkner Trail now ascends a steep, rugged pitch. Railings mark the edge of sharp dropoffs as the path scrambles up rocky ledges before arriving on the wide, flat, grassy summit. A carriage road ascends through the national park and ends in a loop here, lined with benches. The views extend northeast and southwest along the Ottauquechee River valley. Mount Peg, with its own network of trails, is on the other side of the village. Near the summit benches, a large wooden framework with lightbulbs provides an electric star to shine over Woodstock in winter.

Winter recreation is popular in this area. Many of the trails were first cut as carriage roads and now make good cross-country ski and snowshoe routes.

Return to the trailhead the way you hiked up.

DID YOU KNOW?

Frederick Billings, for whom Billings Park is named, owned large tracts of land in this area in the late 1800s. He reforested the denuded Mount Tom using progressive forestry methods, and he built a network of carriage roads and trails. Billings's goal was to create a template for farming, timber harvest, and recreation without ruining the land. By the time Billings died in 1890, his work was well known across the country.

MORE INFORMATION

Camping, mountain biking, and unleashed dogs are not allowed on Faulkner Trail, which is managed by the Faulkner Trust and the Town of Woodstock's Billings Park Commission. For more information, contact Woodstock Area Chamber of Commerce, P.O. Box 486, Woodstock, VT 05091; 802-457-3555; woodstockvt.com. Connecting trails are managed by Marsh-Billings-Rockefeller National Historical Park, 54 Elm Street, Woodstock, VT 05091; 802-457-3368; nps.gov/mabi.

NEARBY

Restaurants, groceries, and shops are just a couple of blocks away in downtown Woodstock. The Marsh-Billings-Rockefeller National Historical Park operates out of the visitor center of Billings Farm and Museum, an educational working farm carrying on the conservation practices of Frederick Billings (0.8 mile northeast). Head to Silver Lake State Park (8 miles north) for swimming and paddling.

TRIP 16
PICO PEAK

Location: Mendon and Killington, VT
Rating: Strenuous
Distance: 7.6 miles round-trip
Elevation Gain: 1,600 feet
Estimated Time: 4 hours
Map: USGS Pico Peak

Traverse rich hardwoods full of wildflowers, open birch glades, and a boreal ridgeline on this loop hike around the peak.

DIRECTIONS
From the junction of US 4 and VT 100 in Killington, head west on US 4 for 2.3 miles to the parking lot at the Appalachian Trail/Long Trail crossing (space for about 25 cars) on the left. *GPS coordinates:* 43° 39.97′ N, 72° 50.96′ W.

TRAIL DESCRIPTION
Sometimes you hike for big views, and sometimes you hike just because the trail is lovely. This loop falls in the latter category. The western slope of Pico Peak (3,957 feet) hosts one of the sweetest stretches of the Long Trail. Its open, airy forests; diverse wildflowers; and pleasant, undulating terrain almost mask the fact that you're ascending one of Vermont's tallest peaks (seventh highest, precisely). Pico's summit is less lovely, is heavily developed, and has limited views. This loop hike combines the Appalachian Trail/Long Trail (AT/LT) and its former route—Sherburne Pass Trail—to circle Pico's summit, taking in the outstanding beauty on the shoulders of this big mountain and bypassing the top. (Peak-baggers can climb a 0.4-mile spur trail to the true summit.) The hike can be done in either direction. I prefer the longer climb up the LT/AT because it's an enjoyable ascent through distractingly beautiful terrain. Near the end of the loop, food and drink await at the Inn at Long Trail before the final 0.8-mile road walk downhill.

From the parking lot, the LT/AT and Catamount Trail follow a path alongside US 4 for a short distance before turning left to enter the woods. After crossing a bridge, Catamount Trail departs to the right; stay left and begin a gentle climb. Flat stretches roll out between moderate rising pitches as you head south along the mountainside. Blue-bead lily, trillium, and false Solo-

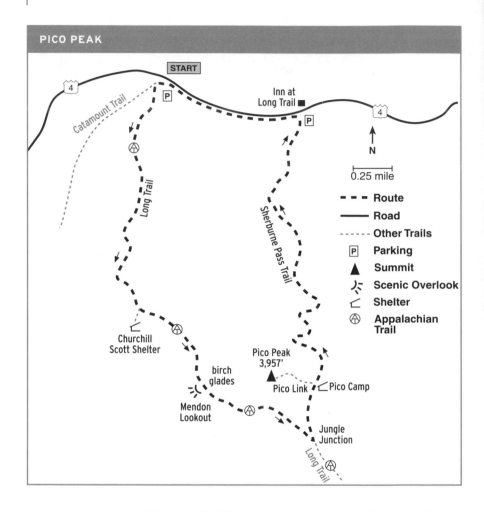

mon's seal grow amid ferns and hobblebush. The trail descends gradually into a damp area covered with thick clumps of jewelweed, blue cohosh, and Canada violets. From the moist slope, the trail climbs into a drier hardwood forest where the trees are widely spaced and the undergrowth is low. Watch for stinging wood nettle here, but also the delicate Virginia waterleaf and sweet cicely.

Saplings again thicken the understory as you crest the hillside, and the trail curves sharply left to mount the ridge. Indian cucumber's double-decker leaves rise on tall stems from club moss as you wind uphill through erratic boulders. Bending right again, the trail flattens across a bench, then drops steeply into a gully to cross a stream before climbing switchbacks out the other side.

At 1.9 miles, a short spur trail leads right to Churchill Scott Shelter and marks the beginning of one of the more interesting sections of this hike. Paper birch now starts to dominate the forest, and as the trail ascends onto a high

Pico Peak's loveliest sights—both short- and long-distance—are from its hillsides rather than from its summit.

shoulder of the mountain, the entire forest becomes white trunks. Ferns wave in the breeze between the widely spaced trees, and Mendon Lookout, on the right, provides an obstructed view west to the Taconics.

Rather suddenly, the trail leaves the paper birches and enters a spruce/fir forest. It rolls gently uphill to its highest point, 3,550 feet, and follows the contour of the hillside briefly before descending to Jungle Junction at 3.8 miles. The LT/AT southbound goes right here; turn left onto Sherburne Pass Trail. A flat, 0.4-mile walk through boreal woods and across a ski trail leads to the historical Pico Camp, which perches on the hill, its windows affording views of Killington (4,235 feet) and Ascutney (3,144 feet) peaks. (Behind the cabin, Pico Link leads steeply up an eroded trail to the summit.)

For 0.5 mile from Pico Camp, Sherburne Pass Trail slabs the hillside; it then descends briefly on a ski trail and reenters the woods. From here, the descent is rocky, rooty, and mostly moderate with some steep eroded pitches. At 5.5 miles, a small stream magnified by Tropical Storm Irene (see page 34) gouged a massive gully. Continue downhill, passing a bootleg trail on the left at 6.0 miles and skittering down bedrock to a flat, straight exit from the woods into the parking lot across from the Inn at Long Trail. Turn left on US 4 and descend 0.8 mile to the trailhead.

DID YOU KNOW?

The rich woods on the west side of Pico support many plants with edible and medicinal properties, such as sarsaparilla, blue-bead lily, Indian cucumber, jewelweed, bunchberry, and nettle. To learn more, consult a reputable field guide to edible and medicinal plants.

MORE INFORMATION

The Long Trail, Sherburne Pass Trail, and their shelters are maintained by the Green Mountain Club, 4711 Waterbury–Stowe Road, Waterbury Center, VT 05677; 802-244-7037; greenmountainclub.org.

NEARBY

Camp in an old-growth forest at Gifford Woods State Park on VT 100, 3 miles northeast. Chittenden Reservoir has paddling and swimming with spectacular mountain views, 11 miles northwest. Trails around the reservoir are good for cross-country skiing, as is the Catamount Trail. In addition to the restaurant at the Inn at Long Trail, more food options are found along Killington Road, 2.5 miles east, and on US 4 and in downtown Rutland, 8 miles west.

2

CENTRAL VERMONT

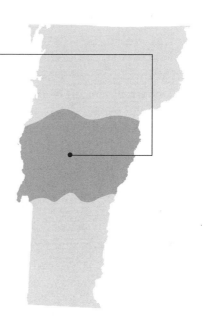

VERMONT METEOROLOGISTS OFTEN REFER TO CHANGES IN THE WEATHER happening north or south of Routes 2 or 4, because these corridors approximately define the geography of central Vermont. From Lake Champlain to the Connecticut River, the broad middle of the state is about 60 miles wide, and stretches about 55 miles north to south. The Green Mountains dominate this section, with their highest spine running just west of the center and parallel ranges descending on either side toward the eastern and western lowlands.

Lake Champlain forms the western border of the state here, but it is not the broad, dark expanse that usually comes to mind when the lake is mentioned. Instead, it looks more like a wide river along the shore of central Vermont, stretching about 2 miles across near Vergennes and narrowing to a snaky channel at its southern tail where it slips by the cliffs of Buckner Preserve (Trip 19). Champlain's waters, which support a variety of native and introduced plants and animals, are an important migratory stopover for many birds. The rolling expanse of the Champlain lowlands is the "banana belt" of Vermont—warmer and more fertile than most of the rest of the state—and consequently has ecological and human histories that are intertwined as far back as the departure of the last glacier, 11,000 years ago. The Taconic Mountains so prominent in southern Vermont extend northward into the Champlain Valley with occasional cliffy prominences like Snake Mountain (Trip 23), but for the most part they are overshadowed by the dominance of the surrounding farmland and the much more eye-catching Green Mountains to the east and Adirondacks across the lake. The state's longest river, Otter Creek, and the wide, turbid Dead Creek flow north side by side through the southern Champlain lowlands, draining the valley into the lake and providing miles of shoreline and wetland habitat as well as paddle-craft recreation.

East of the Champlain lowlands, the front range of the Green Mountains rises steeply, making a dramatic departure from the relatively flat valley floor. From there, mostly parallel ranges stack up to the east, covering the middle of the state with a wide swath of high land. The northern half of the Green Mountain National Forest encompasses a large chunk of this landscape, accompanied by numerous state forests. The Breadloaf, Bristol Cliffs, and Joseph Battell Wilderness Areas protect more than 41,000 acres of forest and crag, including the rare plants of Mount Horrid's Great Cliff (Trip 31). Moosalamoo National Recreation Area supports a wide variety of activities on almost 16,000 acres near Lake Dunsmore, such as watching hawk migrations from Rattlesnake Cliffs (Trip 20). The Appalachian Trail and the Long Trail part ways below Deer Leap (Trip 18), and the latter continues north parallel to the ski-specific Catamount Trail. In the northern part of central Vermont, two peaks—Mount Abraham (Trip 25) and Camel's Hump (Trip 27)—are high enough to support small above-treeline areas where rare arctic plants grow.

The smaller Braintree and Northfield mountain ranges—the third range of the Green Mountains—run parallel east of the big peaks, giving way to the unorganized hills of the Piedmont in eastern central Vermont. Although the Piedmont summits are smaller and less popular with hikers than the main range of the Green Mountains, there are some lovely small peaks, such as Wright's Mountain (Trip 30), and a few notable large ones, such as Spruce Mountain (Trip 28) in the Granite Hills. Appropriately named, as their provenance is closer to the granitic White Mountains of New Hampshire than the Green Mountains, some Granite Hills reach more than 3,000 feet and provide a large area of prime recreation in Groton State Forest.

The big, placid Connecticut River forms the eastern border of Vermont. The water mostly snakes through floodplain fields in central Vermont and then slowly backs up behind Wilder Dam in White River Junction. Hikers on the fire tower at Gile Mountain (Trip 17) get a good overview of the region known as the Upper Valley, a place defined by the geography of the river more than by the state line dividing it.

TRIP 17
GILE MOUNTAIN

Location: Norwich, VT
Rating: Easy
Distance: 1.4 miles round-trip
Elevation Gain: 413 feet
Estimated Time: 1 hour
Maps: USGS South Strafford; trailfinder.info/trail.php?id=222

A short climb leads to a fire tower with expansive views of the Upper Valley, a region around the Connecticut River that includes parts of Vermont and New Hampshire.

DIRECTIONS
From I 91, Exit 13, follow US 5 (South Main Street) north 0.5 mile into Norwich. When US 5 turns east, stay straight on Main Street for 0.6 mile. Turn left onto Turnpike Road and follow it 5.2 miles to the signed parking area on the left (space for about 10 cars). *GPS coordinates:* 43° 47.36′ N, 72° 20.57′ W.

TRAIL DESCRIPTION
It's no surprise that this short hike up Gile Mountain (1,860 feet) is a popular excursion in the Upper Valley, since its summit fire tower provides the best views in the region. Alongside the hiking trail, the switchbacks of a mountain-bike trail make good cross-country ski terrain during the colder parts of the year. The grade is never steep, but kids younger than 5 will probably need help with the many rock and log steps.

Gile Mountain Tower Trail begins at an information kiosk at the edge of the parking area. For the first 0.3 mile, the wide, blue-blazed trail is multiuse; keep an ear out for mountain bikers and give them room to pass. The rise is gradual, following the contour of the hillside and then turning to cross a wide wooden bridge.

Approaching the power-line swath, the mountain-bike trail splits off from the footpath. (The two trails cross several times on the way up.) After you pass beneath the power lines, the climb becomes more noticeable. Along the trail, rock steps and log cribbing provide erosion control, and step stones give dry footing across muddy patches. The trail makes gradual, sweeping curves as it rises through a mixed deciduous forest of paper and yellow birch, beech, and oak.

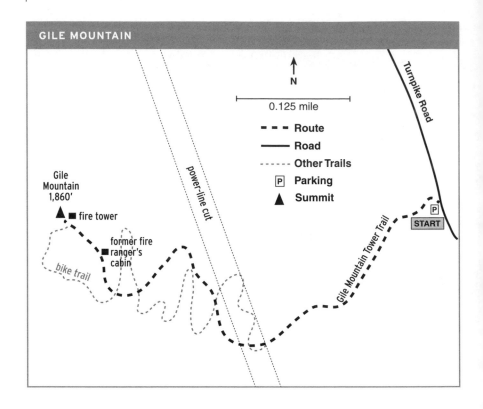

At 0.6 mile, a spur trail leads right a short distance to a shelter, formerly the fire ranger's cabin. From the shelter, the base of the fire tower is visible through the trees. One last rocky, rooty pitch brings you to the top of a gentle bulge that is the summit of Gile Mountain. The outcrop of ancient rocks on which the tower stands provides a picnic spot. Known as the Gile Mountain Formation, these rocks were once part of the ocean floor and rose to become mountains about 400 million years ago, when the continents that are now Africa and North America collided. Following that collision, pressure and heat created garnets in the rock; look for the small red or brown crystals in outcrops on the upper half of the mountain.

Tall trees surround the tower, so you have to climb up for the view. The forested hills that roll away in all directions from this summit are typical of Vermont's Piedmont landscape. Noticeably higher peaks rise beyond the foot-hills in all directions. Burke Mountain (3,267 feet) is to the north-northeast. East, across the Connecticut River, are the most dramatic peaks: New Hampshire's White Mountains. Moose Mountain (2,306 feet) forms the dominant low ridgeline to the east; running north from it, Smarts Mountain (3,238 feet) and Mount Cube (2,904 feet) lead your eye to the more distant bulk of Mount

A sturdy fire tower on top of Gile Mountain provides aerial views of the Connecticut River's Upper Valley, with its wall of tall White Mountains to the east and rolling Vermont piedmont to the west.

Moosilauke (4,802 feet). On a clear day, you may be able to see Mount Lafayette (5,249 feet) peeking over the top of Moosilauke.

The Appalachian Trail runs over the top of all five of these mountains on its 2,000-plus-mile path between Georgia and Maine. Beyond Moose Mountain, you may be able to make out the double tip of Mount Cardigan (3,127 feet). On the Vermont side of the Connecticut River, the pyramid of Mount Ascutney (3,144 feet) rises grandly in the south-southwest, and the high ridgeline of the Green Mountains marches across the western horizon. Vermont's second-highest peak, Killington (4,235 feet), is the distinctly large hump in the southwest, and the high crest of Mount Ellen (4,083 feet) points north to the solo peak of Camel's Hump (also 4,083 feet). Far to the north-northwest you may be able to make out Vermont's tallest peak, Mount Mansfield (4,393 feet at the Chin, on its northern end).

Return to the trailhead the way you came up.

DID YOU KNOW?

Norwich was the original home of a military academy, with the goals of educating cadets in the humanities and sciences in addition to military topics. Norwich University's campus was devastated by fire in 1866, and the school was relocated to Northfield, 54 miles northwest, where it still operates today.

MORE INFORMATION

Gile Mountain trails are maintained by the Town of Norwich Trails Committee, P.O. Box 376, Norwich, VT 05055; 802-649-1419; norwich.vt.us.

NEARBY

Paddling and bird-watching are popular activities on the lower Ompompanoosuc River and the Connecticut River. The Montshire Museum of Science has hands-on indoor and outdoor exhibits just south of downtown Norwich. Dining and groceries can be found along Main Street in Norwich and across the Connecticut River in Hanover, New Hampshire, 2.5 miles east.

QUESTING

Are you the kind of person who wonders as you wander? Do you like to play games or solve riddles? Do you have kids who prefer a little more mental stimulation than a quiet walk in the woods generally provides? If so, maybe your next outing should be a quest.

Questing is a kind of treasure hunt in which riddles or clues lead from a designated starting point to the goal: a hidden box. The point of the quest is not merely to find the treasure. (The box contains only a notebook for you to sign, a rubber stamp to mark your own logbook, and maybe a little more information about the clues you've been following.) Rather, the main point is to explore your surroundings and see them with new eyes.

This sounds familiar, you're thinking. Isn't this geocaching or letterboxing? It's true that questing is like both of those popular games; it is, in fact, an American version of the 150-year-old English game called letterboxing. Geocaching is similar but relies on a Global Positioning System device rather than riddles and clues to navigate to hidden boxes.

Questing has become a hot new trend in eastern Vermont, where hundreds of quests have been created by residents, with clues disseminated online and in books. Each clue starts with a difficulty rating, the distance the player will travel to find the box, and directions to the starting point. From there, clues lead the player through areas of natural or cultural significance—a wooded park, a historical graveyard, an overgrown orchard—pointing out interesting features and giving some context to the surroundings.

Here's the beginning of a quest for Gile Mountain (Trip 17):

Wood sign names this place
And the trail meanders right:
Proceed, eyes open.

Tiny turkey tails
Like little fuzzy brown ears
Mark stump on the left.

Sound like your kind of game? To find the rest of this quest—and many more—visit vitalcommunities.org/Valleyquest!

TRIP 18
DEER LEAP

Location: Killington, VT
Rating: Easy to Moderate
Distance: 2.0 miles round-trip
Elevation Gain: 430 feet
Estimated Time: 1.5 hours
Maps: USGS Pico Peak; www.fs.usda.gov/Internet/FSE_MEDIA/
stelprdb5315846.pdf

This short hike to a rocky promontory gives close-up views of the Coolidge Range towering over Sherburne Pass.

DIRECTIONS
From the junction of VT 100 and US 4 in Killington, follow US 4 west 1.5 miles to a parking area (space for 30 cars) on the left, across from the Inn at Long Trail. *GPS coordinates:* 43° 39.84′ N, 72° 49.94′ W.

TRAIL DESCRIPTION
Where US 4 crosses the height-of-land at Sherburne Pass, Deer Leap's cliffs seem to rise straight out of the Inn at Long Trail. Getting to the cliffs involves circling around behind the outcrop and approaching from the more gradual northern side. Although earlier generations of hikers scaled the steeps more directly, that route is no longer available due to its erosion and danger, as well as to protect areas special to the Abenaki. The Sherburne Pass and Deer Leap Mountain trails to the outlook have rocky, uneven footing, but the short distance and gradual rise make the hike suitable for children about ages 5 and older. The 100-foot drop from the edge of the cliff appears suddenly; bring a leash for your dog.

From the parking area, Sherburne Pass Trail extends on both sides of US 4; it is the renamed former route of the Appalachian Trail (AT) and Long Trail (LT). Cross US 4 to the northern trailhead on the far right side of the Inn at Long Trail. At first, the blue-blazed trail parallels the road below, gaining elevation gradually as it crosses jumbles of rocks along the hillside. At 0.3 mile, a gentle left curve steers the route deeper into the woods. Climbing easily through an open hardwood forest, Sherburne Trail arrives at a junction at 0.5 mile. The AT north to Maine heads right; stay straight, following the white-

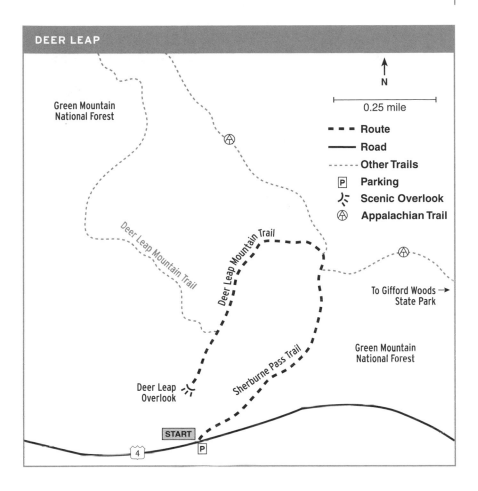

DEER LEAP

Green Mountain
National Forest

N

0.25 mile

- - - Route
——— Road
----- Other Trails
P Parking
)̷ Scenic Overlook
Ⓐ Appalachian Trail

Deer Leap Mountain Trail

Deer Leap Mountain Trail

To Gifford Woods →
State Park

Green Mountain
National Forest

Sherburne Pass Trail

Deer Leap
Overlook

START

P

4

blazed southbound AT for 200 feet across a flat bench, then turn left onto Deer Leap Mountain Trail, once again following blue blazes.

The route now curves south toward the cliffs, climbing a hardwood hillside. As the trail levels out on top of this knoll, it enters an enchanting forest of widely spaced spruce and paper birch trunks. Weaving between them, cross the flat top of the hill and descend over rooty, rocky ground. Look for birch roots arching out of the dirt here—their bark is surprisingly black, with striking red stripes. Paper birch is distinguishable from its yellow and gray relatives by its sheets of peeling bark. Paper birch is often called white birch—a name also used sometimes for gray birch—or canoe birch, since its bark is used to construct traditional Abenaki boats.

The woods become thick with spruce and fir as you descend from the knoll to a trail junction. Deer Leap Mountain Trail curves sharply downhill on your right. Stay straight on Deer Leap Overlook Spur, continuing over rocky terrain. A boardwalk and wood steps facilitate the last, steep descent to the overlook. Keep children and dogs close as you leave the woods; the edges of Deer Leap are steep.

Dominating the view across Sherburne Pass are the ski trails and wooded slopes of Pico Peak (3,957 feet). Over Pico's eastern shoulder, the top of the ski trails at Killington can be seen farther south. Killington Peak (4,235 feet) is the second tallest in Vermont and supports the largest ski resort in eastern North America. These are the two highest peaks of the Coolidge Range, a section of the Green Mountains stretching south from US 4, connecting the southern and northern tracts of the Green Mountain National Forest. The Catamount Trail, a winter-travel version of the Long Trail, parallels the combined route of the AT and LT through the Coolidge Range, though it stays at lower elevations.

Nearby in the west, Blue Ridge Mountain (3,278 feet) rises in a solitary hump. US 4 curves between Blue Ridge and East Mountain (2,390 feet) as it descends toward Rutland in the Valley of Vermont, a long, narrow lowland running north–south between the Green and Taconic mountains.

Return downhill the way you hiked up.

DID YOU KNOW?

"One could do worse than be a swinger of birches." In his poem "Birches," Robert Frost described the remarkable flexibility of birch trunks and a couple of reasons—factual and fanciful—why you may see them arched, their branches sweeping the forest floor.

MORE INFORMATION

Deer Leap is within the Green Mountain National Forest, 231 North Main Street, Rutland, VT 05701; 802-747-6700; fs.usda.gov/greenmountain.

NEARBY

Camp in an old-growth forest at Gifford Woods State Park on VT 100, 2 miles northeast (or hike there on the Appalachian Trail from Sherburne Pass Trail). Chittenden Reservoir has paddling and swimming with spectacular mountain views, 12 miles northwest. Trails around the reservoir are good for cross-country skiing, as is the Catamount Trail. In addition to the Irish pub at the trailhead inn, there are restaurants, grocery stores, and shops along Killington Road, 1.5 miles east, and on US 4 and in downtown Rutland, 9 miles west.

TRIP 19
BUCKNER MEMORIAL PRESERVE

Location: West Haven, VT
Rating: Moderate
Distance: 2.6 miles round-trip
Elevation Gain: 315 feet
Estimated Time: 2.5 hours
Map: USGS Whitehall, NY

This loop hike follows cliffs through a parklike forest with rare species and overlooks the southern reach of Lake Champlain.

DIRECTIONS
Although the trailhead is in Vermont, you must drive through New York to reach it. Traveling west on US 4, 5.1 miles after crossing from Vermont into New York, cross railroad tracks. Take the second right after the tracks (0.2 mile west of them) onto NY 9A, which is not well marked. Go 0.9 mile, to the end of the road, and turn left onto NY 9. Drive 0.2 mile and take the first right onto NY 10/Doig Street. After 0.5 mile, where NY 10 curves right, bear left onto an unmarked dirt road and follow it 0.1 mile over the Poultney River, reentering Vermont. After crossing the bridge, go left on Galick Road and follow it 0.7 mile to a small pullout (space for about 3 cars) at Tim's Trail on the right. *GPS coordinates:* 43° 34.41' N, 73° 24.26' W.

TRAIL DESCRIPTION
The Helen W. Buckner Memorial Preserve at Bald Mountain sits on an ecologically rich peninsula of Vermont that dips into New York, defined by the Poultney River and a long, narrow arm of Lake Champlain. The 3,959-acre preserve provides habitat for a wide array of rare and uncommon species: 11 animals, 18 plants, and 15 natural community types. Some species are notable because of their general rarity, such as peregrine falcons and bald eagles; others are rare or unusual in Vermont because this landscape supports the very northern extent of species that generally live farther south, such as chestnut and bur oaks, timber rattlesnakes, and the five-lined skink, Vermont's only lizard.

On the southern tip of the peninsula, a band of low cliffs supports a beautiful, dry oak/hickory/hophornbeam forest that is unusual in Vermont. Tim's Trail explores the talus slope beneath the cliff before climbing through a va-

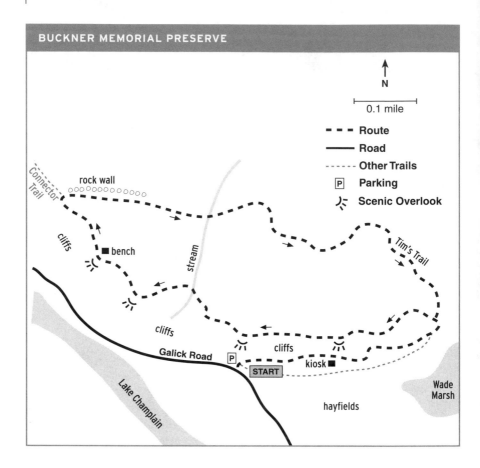

BUCKNER MEMORIAL PRESERVE

N

0.1 mile

- - - Route
——— Road
------ Other Trails
P Parking
⅄ Scenic Overlook

Connector Trail

rock wall
○○○○○○○○○○○○

cliffs

■ bench

stream

cliffs

Tim's Trail

cliffs

Galick Road

P

cliffs

START

kiosk ■

Lake Champlain

hayfields

Wade Marsh

riety of forest types on top. South-facing outcrops are the preferred basking spots for reptiles that need to absorb solar heat; watch for snakes as you walk. Rattlesnakes are reserved unless they are directly stepped on or intentionally harassed, and will not strike unless they feel threatened. The land's owner, The Nature Conservancy (TNC), recommends wearing long pants and ankle-high boots; inspecting the ground before you sit; and, if you encounter a rattlesnake, backing away slowly and giving the snake a 20-foot berth. Dogs are not allowed on the Buckner Preserve.

Begin the hike following green-and-yellow TNC markers along talus slopes at the base of the cliffs. A kiosk with brochure maps is 0.2 mile along the trail.

At 0.4 mile, the trail curves right and appears to go both directions on a two-track. To the right, the mowed path goes back to the parking lot along the edge of the field. Go left over bog bridges to the intersection of the two ends of Tim's Trail loop. Go left on the southern leg and climb for a short distance to arrive on top of the cliffs, where grasslike sedges spread across the forest floor

Unusual in Vermont, the dry oak/hickory/hophornbeam forest atop the cliffs in Buckner Preserve provides a parklike setting for a hike with dramatic views and rare species.

beneath widely spaced shaggy trunks of hickory, hophornbeam, cedar, and oak. Climbing along the edge of the cliffs, you will pass viewpoints over Wade Marsh in the field below, and the Champlain Canal and Whitehall, New York, in the distance. Use caution moving around the edge of the cliff.

After passing directly over the trailhead at 0.8 mile, the trail turns sharply right, crosses an open area, and descends into a dim hemlock forest. Cross a small stream and resume climbing through a wide hickory meadow, entering an area where the ground and tree trunks are scorched from a 2012 fire. A bench at 1.2 miles looks out over steep mountainsides dropping dramatically to Lake Champlain's South Bay.

From here, the trail rises for 0.1 mile to the junction with Connector Trail on the left. Turn right and follow an impressive stone wall downhill, passing eventually into a thicker mixed forest with beech and hemlock. For 0.9 mile, Tim's Trail descends through a varied forest and crosses two small streams. Joining a two-track, it curves around the edge of a deep ravine and drops back to the loop junction.

Return across bog bridges and follow either the trail along the base of the cliffs or the parallel path along the field edge to the trailhead.

Northern leopard frogs may leap out of your path atop the cliffs of Tim's Trail, and can also be seen in the grassy meadow below. These adaptable amphibians eat insects, worms, other frogs, and even birds and garter snakes.

DID YOU KNOW?

Recently, many northern leopard frogs have had missing or deformed legs. Biologists have been studying them, using short aluminum fences you may notice along the field wetlands.

MORE INFORMATION

The Nature Conservancy owns the preserve; 27 State Street, Montpelier, VT 05602; 802-229-4425; nature.org/vermont.

NEARBY

Paddle on the Poultney River, 0.7 mile east. Camp, swim, and paddle at Lake Bomoseen State Park, 15 miles northeast. A limited selection of food is in Whitehall, New York, 2.5 miles south. More options are along VT 4A in Castleton, 14 miles east.

TRIP 20
RATTLESNAKE CLIFFS
AND FALLS OF LANA

Location: Salisbury, VT
Rating: Moderate
Distance: 3.6 miles round-trip
Elevation Gain: 870 feet
Estimated Time: 3 hours
Maps: USGS East Middlebury; www.fs.fed.us/r9/forests/
greenmountain/htm/greenmountain/links/recreation/hiking/docs/
north_pdf/rattlesnake_cliffs_auntjenny.pdf

**Tall waterfalls, exceptional views from a rocky promontory, and
a wide array of activities within the 20,000-acre Moosalamoo
National Recreation Area make this a hike not to miss.**

DIRECTIONS
From the junction of US 7 and VT 125 south of Middlebury, follow US 7 south
for 3.1 miles. Turn left onto VT 53 (Lake Dunmore Road) and go 4.0 miles to
Silver Lake Parking Area on the left (space for about 25 cars). *GPS coordinates:*
43° 54.01′ N, 73° 03.85′ W.

TRAIL DESCRIPTION
Rattlesnake Cliffs hovers high above Lake Dunmore, giving views across the
water to the Taconic and Adirondack mountain ranges. On the way up, a short
side trail leads to an overlook of the spectacular Falls of Lana. The Moosalamoo National Recreation Area is a hub of recreation activities, providing
places to mountain-bike, camp, cross-country ski, and even pick wild berries. The particular habitat needs of peregrine falcons and bluebirds, along
with those of many other wildlife species, are supported within Moosalamoo.
Rattlesnake Cliffs may be closed March 15 to August 1 if peregrine falcons are
nesting in the area; check with Audubon Vermont (vt.audubon.org) or Green
Mountain National Forest (fs.usda.gov/greenmountain) for details. Kids about
ages 8 and older will enjoy the hike to Rattlesnake Cliffs, but keep in mind that
both the outlook and the Falls of Lana have unprotected ledges.

From the parking area, start up the wide Silver Lake Trail. You may share
this path with mountain bikers or the occasional utility truck. At 0.3 mile,

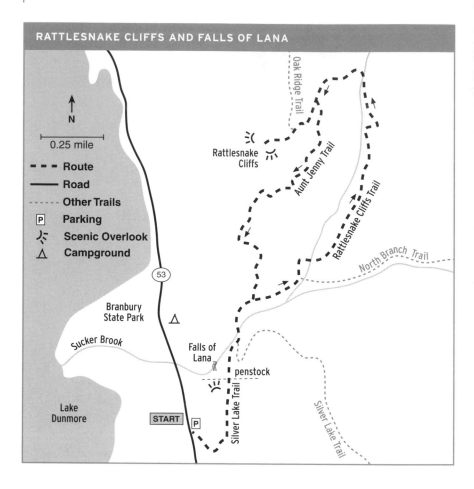

RATTLESNAKE CLIFFS AND FALLS OF LANA

the penstock (water pipe) from the power-generating impoundment of Silver Lake passes overhead in a clearing. For a view across the gorge to the Falls of Lana, head 300 feet down the penstock's corridor to a fenced opening on the right. To continue uphill, pass under the penstock and follow Silver Lake Trail along the upper section of Sucker Brook as it tumbles toward the falls. The side of the brook is well worn by explorers looking for views of the falls; use caution if you venture downhill here.

With pretty cascades on the left and a tall, mossy ledge on the right, Silver Lake Trail proceeds upstream to a trail junction at 0.5 mile. Turn left onto North Branch Trail. Cross Sucker Brook on a wide bridge and continue upstream on its left bank.

At 0.7 mile, Aunt Jenny Trail forks to the left; this will be the way you descend. Stay right, climbing moderately for 0.2 mile through a young stand

The remarkable Falls of Lana is a multi-tiered waterfall (of which only one section is shown here) near the trail on the way to Rattlesnake Cliffs in Moosalamoo National Recreation Area.

of birch speckled with hemlock saplings. At the next junction, turn left onto Rattlesnake Cliffs Trail.

Climb away from the river for a short distance, then return to cross it on a short bridge. The trail rises steeply out of the gorge, curving left at the top of the hill and paralleling the stream high above it. Hemlocks give way to a mixed hardwood forest on the steady ascent. Watch for trail blazes at a sharp right curve away from the stream valley, where a bootleg trail continues straight uphill. Rattlesnake Cliffs Trail wends its way back to cross two branches of the stream and then crosses the hillside, passing the top of Aunt Jenny Trail. The trail narrows and scoots around rocks and logs before climbing a series of wood steps through scrubby beech trees.

Views appear intermittently through the branches on your left as you arrive at the junction of Oak Ridge Trail on your right. Stay left, descending slightly as you edge around the height-of-land to a junction. Both trails lead to cliff lookouts: left, downhill to southerly views; straight ahead, to westerly views. The western view sweeps across the bulging north end of Lake Dunmore and the fields and forests of the southern Champlain lowlands. From the south-facing cliffs, Silver Lake shines in its high bowl, held back from tumbling into the valley by the thin ridge of Oak Hill (1,563 feet). The Green Mountains rise above Silver Lake to the east, and Lake Dunmore stretches south to Fern Lake.

Returning downhill, turn right onto Aunt Jenny Trail and follow blue blazes down the ridgeline. Turning right on a flat bench, follow a short section of old road, then descend on a foot trail again through red oak and beech. A few white oaks mix with red where a discontinued trail heads uphill to the right. Aunt Jenny Trail edges around the top of a steep hemlock-filled ravine dropping to Lake Dunmore, then rejoins the North Branch Trail. From here, hike out the way you came in.

DID YOU KNOW?

The "bluebird trail" at Moosalamoo is a group of 40-plus birdhouses in open fields around the region where you may spot birds. See moosalamoo.org/birdingandnature.asp for locations.

MORE INFORMATION

The Moosalamoo National Recreation Area is within the Green Mountain National Forest and is managed by the nonprofit Moosalamoo Association, P.O. Box 148, Brandon, VT 05733; 802-779-1731; moosalamoo.org.

NEARBY

The best recreation options are right here in the Moosalamoo National Recreation Area and Branbury State Park. Restaurants, grocery stores, shops, and cultural attractions are in downtown Middlebury, 8 miles northwest, and to a lesser degree in Brandon, 8 miles south.

TRIP 21
ROBERT FROST TRAIL

Location: Ripton, VT
Rating: Easy
Distance: 1.0 mile round-trip
Elevation Gain: 30 feet
Estimated Time: 45 minutes
Maps: USGS East Middlebury; fs.usda.gov/Internet/FSE_MEDIA/
stelprdb5315866.pdf

This winding path through woods and berry fields is adorned with poems inspired by these landscapes.

DIRECTIONS

From the junction of US 7 and VT 125 south of Middlebury, head east on VT 125 for 6.2 miles. The trailhead parking area (space for about 10 cars) is on the right. *GPS coordinates:* 43° 57.48′ N, 73° 00.67′ W.

TRAIL DESCRIPTION

Two connected trail loops wander through varied landscapes that inspired the poet they honor and that are in turn augmented by his poems, mounted on posts throughout. Interpretive signs identify plants, while occasional benches offer the opportunity to linger along this short hike. The first loop, 0.2 mile, is wheelchair accessible, and the entire route is friendly to all ages of hikers. The Robert Frost Trail is a great place to explore on skis, with rolling terrain and a connector trail leading to Water Tower Trails, a series of cross-country ski loops. Dogs must be leashed.

From the cluster of signs near the bathroom at the trailhead, go right into the trees along a wide gravel path. After a short distance, past a bench and the first poem, the path becomes an elevated boardwalk traversing a wetland thick with alders. "A winter garden in an alder swamp" begins the poem posted here. Robert Frost (1874–1963), who won four Pulitzer Prizes for poetry and recited his work at John F. Kennedy's presidential inauguration, spent time almost every year from 1921 to 1963 here in Ripton, and many of his poems include references to the local landscapes. Curving left, the walkway returns to gravel and meets the junction of the trail to the second loop. The wheelchair-

ROBERT FROST TRAIL

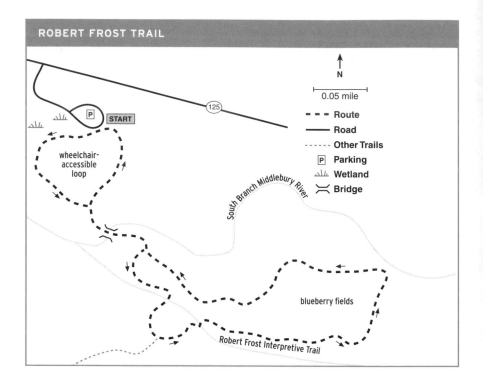

accessible path curves left here; go right, climbing onto a wood bridge over the South Branch of the Middlebury River.

At the end of the bridge, enter a dim hemlock grove on a more natural footpath. The trail curves left, rising gently into a pine forest where it meets the second loop in a small clearing with one of Frost's most famous works, "The Road Not Taken." Go right, away from the river. Trout lilies and ferns cover the forest floor between birches and spruce, and hobblebush spreads its large leaves alongside the path. Cross a small stream on a low bridge to come alongside a large, wooden interpretive sign, where the poem "Nothing Gold Can Stay" accompanies a description of the fleeting woodland wildflowers found here: trillium, wood anemone, bunchberry, and spring beauty. From this panel, the trail climbs gradually to a junction with a trail leading to Water Tower Trails. This junction has the highest elevation of the hike, and the trail now bends left and returns downhill, crossing the small stream a little farther upstream.

The path curves right to follow the stream through varied woods, with a beaked hazelnut tree identified alongside a gray birch and a muscly-looking blue beech (also called ironwood, this tree is actually a member of the birch family). Of the birch, Robert Frost observed: "The only native tree that dares

"In Hardwood Groves" is one of many Robert Frost poems posted along this gentle path, illuminating the landscape that inspired the poet's work.

to lean, / Relying on its beauty, to the air. / (Less brave perhaps than trusting are the fair.)"

The trees give way to shrubs as you enter fields at the far eastern end of the trail loop. Blueberries and huckleberries attract many animals—including humans—to this open area, which the U.S. Forest Service maintains through prescribed burns. A bench and rumination from the poem "The Black Cottage" are situated with a view north across fields and river to the steep slope of Breadloaf Mountain (3,835 feet). With almost 25,000 acres, the Breadloaf Wilderness surrounding its namesake peak has large tracts of wooded and formerly logged areas that support black bear and moose in considerable numbers.

Head downhill through the fields and curve left along the bank of the Middlebury River. An interpretive sign and the poem "The Last Mowing" address the succession of fields and forests before you arrive back at the beginning of this loop. Go right, retracing your steps to the shorter hiking loop on the other side of the river. There, go right to finish the hike on a gravel path leading to the parking area.

DID YOU KNOW?

Robert Frost taught on the nearby campus of Middlebury College at the Bread Loaf School of English for 42 years, and the college maintains his Ripton farm as a National Historic Landmark.

MORE INFORMATION

The trail is in the Green Mountain National Forest. Middlebury Ranger District, 1007 Route 7 South, Middlebury, VT 05753; 802-388-4362; fs.usda.gov/ greenmountain.

NEARBY

Swim, hike, mountain-bike, and camp at Branbury State Park and the adjacent Moosalamoo National Recreation Area, 10 miles southwest. Food and shops are in Middlebury, 10 miles northwest.

TRIP 22
MOUNT INDEPENDENCE

Location: Orwell, VT
Rating: Easy to Moderate
Distance: 3.0 miles round-trip
Elevation Gain: 200 feet
Estimated Time: 2 hours
Maps: USGS Ticonderoga; handout maps at museum

Interpretive panels help you imagine the fort that once stood on this hill as you wander through regrown forest and fields to views across Lake Champlain.

DIRECTIONS

Go west on VT 73 from its junction with VT 22A in Orwell. After 0.3 mile, when VT 73 curves right, stay straight to go onto Mount Independence Road. After 4.7 miles, stay on Mount Independence Road around a sharp left turn uphill to the parking area (space for 100 vehicles) for Mount Independence State Historic Site. *GPS coordinates:* 43° 49.07′ N, 73° 23.08′ W.

TRAIL DESCRIPTION

In 1776, Mount Independence (302 feet) was cleared of trees, topped with a star-shaped fort, and covered with buildings to support 12,000 American soldiers. Today, the only building on the reforested hill next to Lake Champlain is the boat-shaped Visitors Center Museum with swooping roofline and curved walls. The terrain is mild with gentle elevation changes, appropriate for hikers of varying ages and abilities.

To start, enter the museum to purchase an entry ticket ($5 per adult; no fee for children ages 14 and younger) and pick up an interpretive map. Checklists of the mountain's birds and wildflowers are also available. Find the Baldwin trailhead to the left of the building. Named for the fort of Mount Independence's chief engineer, whose diary provided important clues about the former fort, this wide, compacted path is suitable for outdoor wheelchairs. You will ascend gradually through open grass and enter the forest, where loose strips of bark on hophornbeam and shagbark hickory make it seem like the trees are shedding.

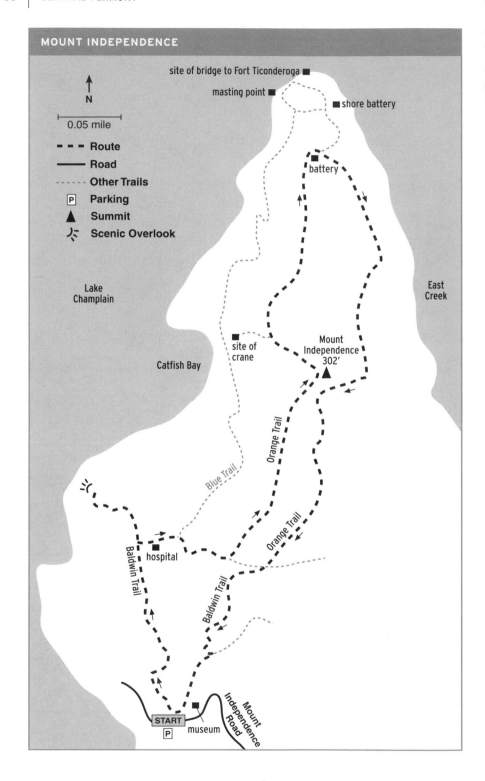

MOUNT INDEPENDENCE

N

0.05 mile

- - - Route
—— Road
----- Other Trails
P Parking
▲ Summit
⅄ Scenic Overlook

site of bridge to Fort Ticonderoga ■

masting point ■

■ shore battery

■ battery

Lake
Champlain

East
Creek

site of
crane ■

Catfish Bay

Mount
Independence
302'
▲

Orange Trail

Blue Trail

Orange Trail

hospital ■

Baldwin Trail

Baldwin Trail

START
P
museum

Mount Independence Road

Across Lake Champlain, Fort Ticonderoga remains, while its partner fortress on Mount Independence is long gone, leaving the natural beauty of woods, fields, and shoreline for hikers to explore.

Baldwin Trail flattens as it heads north along the ridge and, after a short distance, comes to a fork. Go left to a viewing area on a promontory. Look for bald eagles soaring over the lake here. While still endangered in Vermont, bald eagles are slowly returning to nest.

The walls of Fort Ticonderoga are visible across the narrow stretch of Lake Champlain. When the British came to attack in autumn 1776, the sight of the combined fortresses caused them to retreat. They returned the next summer, overwhelming the Americans and taking over Mount Independence, but when they learned of British general John Burgoyne's surrender in Saratoga that autumn, they burned all the buildings to the ground and abandoned the fort.

Return to the fork and go left, heading east to the middle of the peninsula. Pass Blue Trail on the left; a short distance farther, turn left onto the wide, grassy Orange Trail. The tree-lined swath leads along the height-of-land to a grassy clearing at the summit of Mount Independence, the center of the former star fort. The path continues northwest into a deciduous forest dotted with historical sites and to a clearing at the tip of the peninsula. Cannons were aimed at the lake from this high point. Return to the head of the clearing, where the trail continues left, back into the forest. Immediately, you arrive at a fork. Go right to return south toward the museum, gradually climbing the side of Mount Independence, surrounded by red oak, white pine, and eastern red cedar.

Orange Trail ends at a T junction with Baldwin Trail. Go right and immediately left, downhill on the return leg of Baldwin Trail. Descending through the woods, you will pass the former locations of a storehouse and a blockhouse. A spur trail leads left; stay straight to return to the grassy field next to the museum.

DID YOU KNOW?

More than 300 shipwrecks are scattered along the bottom of Lake Champlain, including at least two near the bridge that once connected Mount Independence and Fort Ticonderoga. The Lake Champlain Underwater Historic Preserve provides public access for divers who want to explore the wrecks, and it protects the artifacts from anchor damage and looting.

MORE INFORMATION

Camping and overnight parking are not allowed. Pets must be leashed. Digging, collecting any materials (including plants), and using metal detectors are all forbidden. The grounds of Mount Independence State Historic Site are open year-round; in winter the parking lot is not plowed and parking on the edge of Mount Independence Road is prohibited by the town. The museum is open from Memorial Day to Columbus Day, 9:30 A.M. to 5 P.M. daily; trail fees are charged during operating hours. Mount Independence State Historic Site Administrator, 8149 VT Route 17W, Addison, VT 05491; 802-759-2412 or 802-948-2000 in season; historicsites.vermont.gov/mountindependence.

NEARBY

Half Moon State Park has paddling and swimming 23 miles southeast in Hubbardton. Just north of Mount Independence, where VT 74 would cross the lake if there were a bridge, you can hop on a cruise boat to view Mount Independence (and sunken wrecks, detectable using sonar) in summer and during foliage season. Some food can be found in Orwell village, 7 miles east, or Benson, 12 miles south, with more options in Brandon, 18.8 miles east.

TRIP 23
SNAKE MOUNTAIN

Location: Addison, VT
Rating: Moderate
Distance: 3.6 miles round-trip
Elevation Gain: 900 feet
Estimated Time: 2 hours
Map: USGS Snake Mountain

Hike through a mature forest—rare in the Champlain lowlands—to panoramic views of Lake Champlain and the Adirondacks from summit cliffs.

DIRECTIONS
Follow VT 22A south 2.9 miles from its junction with VT 17 and turn left onto Wilmarth Road. Go 0.5 mile to a T intersection at Mountain Road. Go left to a parking lot (space for 10 cars) on the left. *GPS coordinates:* 44° 02.57′ N, 73° 17.31′ W.

TRAIL DESCRIPTION
Snake Mountain's serpentine ridge slithers north–south through farmlands along Lake Champlain. The 1,287-foot mountain's sudden rise from the surrounding lowlands creates an island of mature hardwood forest in the midst of open fields and gives hikers an extraordinary view of the broad Champlain Valley. The Nature Conservancy's 81-acre Willmarth Woods (spelled per the previous landowners' name, which differs from the spelling of the nearby road) protects the forest on the mountain's west side, and the 1,215-acre Snake Mountain Wildlife Management Area conserves wildlife habitat along its crest. Some of the summit area may be closed to hikers if nesting peregrine falcons are present; check with Audubon Vermont (vt.audubon.org) for current information. Dogs are not allowed in Willmarth Woods. Snowshoers share some sections of trail with snowmobiles.

A metal gate across from the end of Wilmarth Road marks the Snake Mountain trailhead; cross a clearing beyond it and enter the woods on a wide trail heading east. From the late 1700s to 1992, this land was part of the 200-acre Willmarth family farm. This area was a woodlot and a shady cow pasture; today it is one of the largest stands of mature mesic red oak/northern hard-

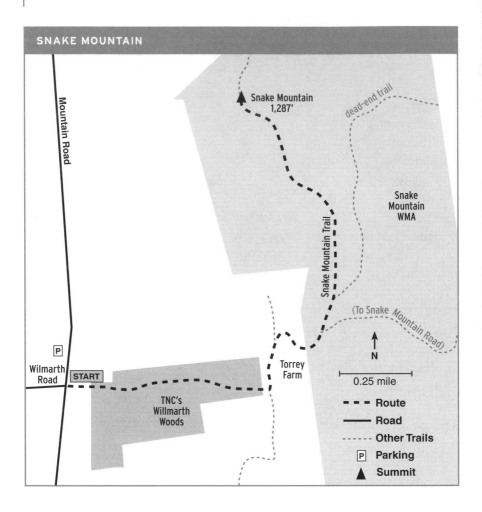

SNAKE MOUNTAIN

Mountain Road

Snake Mountain
1,287'

dead-end trail

Snake
Mountain
WMA

Snake Mountain Trail

(To Snake Mountain Road)

N

0.25 mile

Wilmarth
Road

START

TNC's
Willmarth
Woods

Torrey
Farm

- - - Route
——— Road
------ Other Trails
P Parking
▲ Summit

wood forest in the Champlain lowlands. The trail passes through large beech and maple trees, some of which are 150 years old and host breeding cerulean warblers. Look for the bright sky-blue back of the male and the more muted turquoise back of the female as they flit through the upper canopy, foraging for insects from spring through midsummer.

Snake Mountain Trail rises gradually on a rutted, sometimes muddy track. At 0.7 mile, the trail turns abruptly left at a T junction (no signs or blazes). You will encounter few directional signs on Snake Mountain, and logging activities may change the appearance of trail junctions; when in doubt, search for the most worn-looking footpaths and for a pile of brush or row of rocks across one trail that provides a vague suggestion to choose the other path.

Heading north, the trail climbs more steeply. After a very short distance, stay right at an unmarked fork, following red and blue blazes uphill. The trail

Take in the farmlands of Addison County, Lake Champlain, and the Adirondacks from Snake Mountain's west-facing cliffs.

now climbs eastward, entering the Snake Mountain Wildlife Management Area. Since the mountain is a small, rocky refuge of upland forest in an otherwise heavily farmed part of Vermont, it provides important wildlife habitat, including a white-tailed deer wintering area and a wetland near the summit known as Cranberry Bog. The trail turns north again and follows Snake Mountain's central ridgeline to the summit.

The climbing becomes rolling and pleasant, passing several unmarked trail junctions. At a final junction, stay left, heading toward open sky along the western edge of the ridge. The trail exits the woods and arrives on a concrete pad that once supported the Grand View Hotel.

The views south, west, and north are jaw-dropping. Immediately beneath you, a patchwork of farmland spreads in all directions, cut by the muddy, tree-lined bends of Dead Creek as it makes its way north to join Otter Creek before emptying into Lake Champlain. Across the lake, the foothills of the Adirondacks rise from the water, while the high peaks cut a jagged line across the sky. If you visit in autumn, Snake Mountain's quartzite cliffs provide an excellent seat from which to watch hawk migrations.

Return to the trailhead the way you climbed up.

Spotted knapweed grows in dry, disturbed areas such as the old hotel site on Snake Mountain. Native to Europe, spotted knapweed was accidentally introduced into the United States in the late nineteenth century. Because it crowds out native species, it is widely considered a pest.

DID YOU KNOW?

About 10,000 years ago, Snake Mountain was an island in the Champlain Sea, a temporary arm of the Atlantic Ocean. Marine life such as seals and beluga whales swam here, leaving behind skeletons that gave nineteenth-century settlers their first clues to the valley's oceanic past.

MORE INFORMATION

The first 0.5 mile of Snake Mountain's trail is managed by The Nature Conservancy's Vermont Chapter, 27 State Street, Montpelier, VT 05602; 802-229-4425; nature.org/vermont. Dogs, bicycles, motorized vehicles, camping, and fires are not allowed in Willmarth Woods. The Snake Mountain Wildlife Management Area is administered by the Vermont Fish and Wildlife Department (vtfishandwildlife.com) and is open to regulated hunting, trapping, hiking, and wildlife viewing. Snowmobile trails on Snake Mountain are maintained by the Vermont Association of Snow Travelers, 26 Vast Lane, Barre, VT 05641; 802-229-0005; vtvast.org.

NEARBY

Swimming areas and the magnificent Falls of Lana are 25 miles southeast at Branbury State Park in Salisbury. Middlebury, 11.4 miles southeast, has restaurants, groceries, and a variety of shops.

TRIP 24
SUNSET LEDGE

Location: Lincoln, VT
Rating: Easy
Distance: 2.2 miles round-trip
Elevation Gain: 387 feet
Estimated Time: 1.5 hours
Map: USGS Lincoln

Follow the Long Trail along a rolling ridge to west-facing ledges with views of Lake Champlain and the Adirondacks.

DIRECTIONS

From the intersection of VT 100 and Main Street in Warren, travel 0.7 mile south on VT 100. Turn right onto Lincoln Gap Road (labeled Lincoln Mountain Road in places) and follow it 4.0 miles to the Long Trail crossing at Lincoln Gap, where parking is along either side of the road. The height-of-land accommodates about 20 vehicles; a lower parking lot holds an additional 15. (Lincoln Gap Road is not maintained in winter; snowshoers park at the gate and add 1.2 miles round-trip to the hike.) *GPS coordinates:* 44° 05.70′ N, 72° 55.70′ W.

TRAIL DESCRIPTION

Sunset Ledge (2,811 feet) juts from the side of a gradually sloping ridge between Mount Grant (3,623 feet) and Lincoln Gap (2,424 feet). This section of the Long Trail undulates over rock slabs and through small hollows, making the walk almost as scenic and interesting as the broad views at the destination. Kids of most ages will enjoy scrambling along the ridgeline, after an initial steep pitch.

From Lincoln Gap, follow the Long Trail south into the Breadloaf Wilderness. The largest of Vermont's eight designated Wilderness areas, Breadloaf encompasses almost 25,000 acres of the main ridge of the Green Mountains between Lincoln Gap Road and VT 125. As in other designated Wildernesses, trail work and signage are not always evident. Once heavily logged, the mountains of Breadloaf Wilderness have mostly reforested and are now well populated by moose. A fair number of black bears roam here as well.

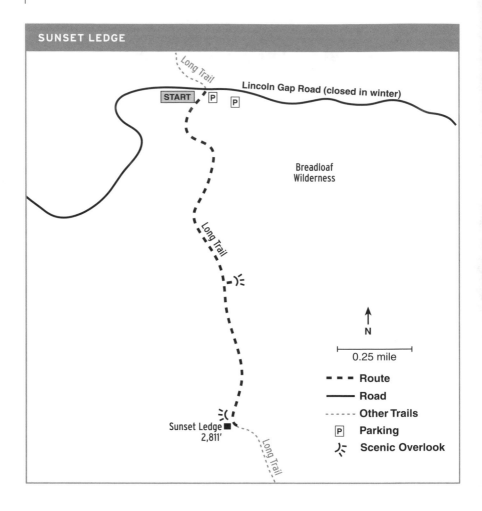

SUNSET LEDGE

Long Trail

Lincoln Gap Road (closed in winter)

START P P

Breadloaf
Wilderness

Long Trail

N

0.25 mile

- - - Route
——— Road
------- Other Trails
P Parking
⅄ Scenic Overlook

Long Trail

Sunset Ledge ■
2,811'

Long Trail

The Long Trail climbs steadily for a few tenths of a mile after entering the Wilderness Area. After a switchback at the top of a sidehill climb, the trail eases to a gradual pitch through beech and sugar maple, with hobblebush and ferns filling in the understory. A right turn leads to a ledgy, rooty scramble up an S curve. Halfway up, an informal trail leads left to a rock with a view north and east over the spruce trees to the Northfield Range, paralleling the high ridge of the Green Mountains on the opposite side of the Mad River valley.

Continuing uphill around another couple of curves, the trail tops the ridge; sky appears through the branches on both sides of the path. The trail rolls along over low ledges. In spring, look for the deep-maroon blooms of purple trillium and showy white-and-pink petals of painted trillium in these low spots. In late summer, look for a bright-red berry that replaces the flower, perched at the top of its stalk and surrounded by three broad leaves.

On the way to the western panorama at Sunset Ledge, an outlook high on the ridge gives a view east across the Mad River Valley to the Northfield Mountains.

At 1.1 miles, the forest opens on the right to reveal Sunset Ledge and wide views to the west. Leash dogs and keep children close in this cliffy area. The mountainside falls away beneath the ledge, swooping down into the forested and pastoral valley of the town of Lincoln and up into the Bristol Cliffs Wilderness.

A sharp notch in the ridgeline allows views of Lake Champlain spreading across broad lowlands. The Adirondacks rise above everything, the tallest of the distant peaks reaching elevations of more than 5,000 feet. If you're on Sunset Ledge in colder months, one of the most noticeable features of the Adirondacks is snow-covered landslide scars. Tropical Storm Irene expanded some slides and created a handful of new ones in 2011 (see page 34).

The cliffs you're resting on continue raggedly northward, with dark-green conifer spires on top and smooth deciduous canopy below. High above, the pointy peak of Mount Abraham pokes into the sky at just over 4,000 feet. Below it, the rounded peaks of the Hogback Mountains march northward. Farther south, Robert Frost Mountain (2,411 feet) rises between the towns of Middlebury and Ripton.

Return to the trailhead the way you hiked up.

Painted (shown) and red (also called purple) trillium bloom in Vermont woods in spring. They are easily recognizable by their three petals and three large leaves.

DID YOU KNOW?

Lincoln Gap and its namesake town were not named for our country's 16th president, as nearby Mount Abraham was. Instead, they honor Major General Benjamin Lincoln, a farmer from Massachusetts whose militia repelled the British in the Battle of Bennington during the Revolutionary War.

MORE INFORMATION

Breadloaf Wilderness is a place where human impact is kept to a minimum: Do not leave any personal property or use any wheeled device, such as a mountain bike or wagon. Breadloaf Wilderness is managed by the U.S. Forest Service, Rochester Ranger District, 99 Ranger Road, Rochester, VT 05767; 802-767-4261; fs.usda.gov/greenmountain. The Long Trail is maintained by the Green Mountain Club, 4711 Waterbury–Stowe Road, Waterbury Center, VT 05677; 802-244-7037; greenmountainclub.org.

NEARBY

Swim in the Mad River at various holes in Warren, 4 miles east, and along VT 100 north through Waitsfield, 10 miles northeast. The multiuse Mad River Path parallels the river, and whitewater paddling is popular downstream of Warren Village. Sugarbush, 8.2 miles northeast, has mountain biking, disc golf, and other outdoor activities. Dining and grocery stores are on VT 100 in Waitsfield and along VT 17 in Bristol, 9.5 miles west.

TRIP 25
MOUNT ABRAHAM

Location: Lincoln, VT
Rating: Strenuous
Distance: 5.2 miles round-trip
Elevation Gain: 1,582 feet
Estimated Time: 3.5 hours
Map: USGS Lincoln

Hike a section of the celebrated Monroe Skyline to find rare arctic plants and 360-degree views on this rocky summit.

DIRECTIONS

From the intersection of VT 100 and Main Street in Warren, travel 0.7 mile south on VT 100. Turn right onto Lincoln Gap Road (labeled Lincoln Mountain Road in places) and follow it 4.0 miles to the Long Trail crossing at Lincoln Gap, where parking is along either side of the road (space for 20 cars). A lower parking lot holds an additional 15 vehicles. (Note: Lincoln Gap Road is not maintained in winter; snowshoers park at the gate and add 1.2 miles round-trip to the hike.) *GPS coordinates:* 44° 05.70′ N, 72° 55.70′ W.

TRAIL DESCRIPTION

Mount Abraham (4,006 feet) is Vermont's fifth-highest peak, barely stretching above the 4,000-foot line that marks the approximate edge of alpine tundra in the Green Mountains (see page 184). The hike from Lincoln Gap is relatively short, but difficult footing in places makes this hike more challenging than the distance alone would imply.

The 272-mile Long Trail (see page 29) crosses the highest point of Lincoln Gap Road. Head north, following white blazes up a steep pitch from the road into the woods. The path traverses the hill above the road for a short distance, then turns away and climbs moderately through beech, maple, and fir. The trail is rocky and narrow, lined with club moss, trillium, and blue-bead lily.

After a short descent and a left curve over a sloping ledge, you will have a view of the ridgeline ahead through the trees. Mount Abraham marks the southern end of the spectacular ridge walk known as the Monroe Skyline. Extending north to the Winooski River valley, the 30-mile route follows high ridges with numerous vistas and bald summits.

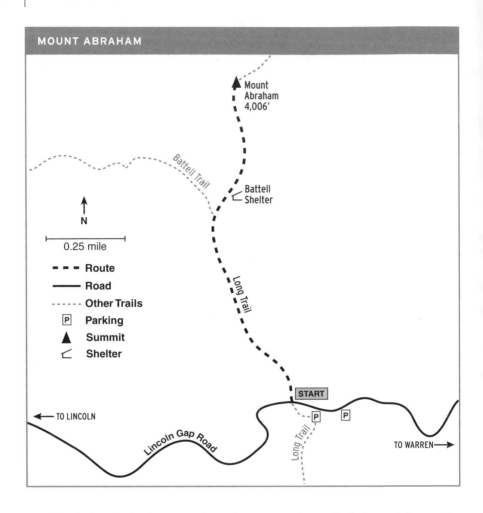

MOUNT ABRAHAM

Mount
Abraham
4,006'

Battell Trail

Battell
Shelter

N

0.25 mile

- - - Route
— Road
----- Other Trails
P Parking
▲ Summit
⊏ Shelter

Long Trail

START

TO LINCOLN

Lincoln Gap Road

Long Trail

P   P

TO WARREN→

The shift to high-elevation forest happens early on the hike up Mount Abe (as it is locally nicknamed). This forest transition generally happens around 2,700 feet, and your nose may alert you before your eyes do—balsam firs are exceptionally fragrant. As you enter the spruce/fir forest the climb steepens, but as you round the steep-sided mountain the pitches are interrupted by brief level respites. Where the path is not on sloping ledges, it's across uneven slopes of half-buried rocks crisscrossed with tannic streams.

At 1.7 miles, the blue-blazed Battell Trail joins from the left. One-tenth of a mile farther, the Battell Shelter provides a resting place before you make the final 0.8-mile push to the summit. (A Green Mountain Club caretaker collects a $5 fee from hikers who spend the night in the shelter.)

From there, the Long Trail climbs up ledges and over bog bridges. The trees grow shorter until, just over 0.5 mile above the shelter, you climb out of the

Just before reaching treeline and Mount Abraham's open summit, hikers are treated to a view south across the Breadloaf Wilderness.

branches. The views along the final ascent to the summit are magnificent. An enormous egg of quartz rests beside the trail, providing a good perch for viewing the ridge stretching south into the Breadloaf Wilderness. You can follow the route of the Long Trail with your eyes, scanning the high ground to cross the side-by-side peaks of Grant (3,623 feet) and Cleveland (3,482 feet), and beyond to the prow of Breadloaf Mountain (3,835 feet), which seems to plow westward.

At the summit, the ridgeline path of the Long Trail is evident as it continues northeast, first to Lincoln Peak (3,975 feet), 0.8 mile away, where a viewing platform perches over the ski trails of Sugarbush, and then over the high crest of Mount Ellen (4,083 feet). To the west, Lake Champlain sprawls 125 miles long beneath the Adirondack Plateau and its high peaks.

Mount Abraham's 1-acre summit is a patchwork of carpets of Bigelow's sedge; schist studded with quartz and covered with map lichen; and stunted, gnarled spruce and fir trees called krummholz ("crooked wood"). While hikers and their dogs should avoid trampling all summit vegetation, areas of particular concern may be designated by low rock walls or string perimeters.

Descend the way you came up.

DID YOU KNOW?

As you hike uphill, the temperature drops between 3.5 and 5.5 degrees Fahrenheit for every 1,000 feet you climb—and that's before accounting for windchill. Humidity traps heat, so on dry days the temperature drop is greater than when it's raining or snowing.

MORE INFORMATION

Mount Abraham is in the Green Mountain National Forest; Rochester Ranger District, 99 Ranger Road, Rochester, VT 05767; 802-767-4261; fs.usda.gov/greenmountain. The Long Trail and the Battell Shelter are maintained by the Green Mountain Club, 4711 Waterbury–Stowe Road, Waterbury Center, VT 05677; 802-244-7037; greenmountainclub.org.

NEARBY

Swim in the Mad River at various holes in Warren, 4.0 miles east, and along VT 100 north through Waitsfield, 10.0 miles northeast. The multiuse Mad River Path parallels the river, and whitewater paddling is popular downstream of Warren Village. Sugarbush has mountain biking, disc golf, and other outdoor activities 8.2 miles northeast. Dining and grocery stores are on VT 100 in Waitsfield and along VT 17 in Bristol, 9.5 miles west.

TRIP 26
BURNT ROCK

Location: Fayston, VT
Rating: Moderate to Strenuous
Distance: 5.2 miles round-trip
Elevation Gain: 2,090 feet
Estimated Time: 3.5 hours
Maps: USGS Waterbury; USGS Huntington

This bare summit provides a fun rock scramble and panoramic views along one of the most scenic sections of the Long Trail.

DIRECTIONS

From Waitsfield Village, follow VT 100 north 3.0 miles and turn left onto North Fayston Road. After 4.0 miles, at the forked junction with Center Fayston Road and unmarked Sharpshooter Road, go right onto Sharpshooter. Take an immediate left onto Big Basin Road and follow it 0.9 mile. Park on either side of the road (space for 8 cars). *GPS coordinates:* 44° 14.98′ N, 72° 52.43′ W.

TRAIL DESCRIPTION

This hike up Hedgehog Brook and along the Long Trail starts gently and gradually gets steeper and more challenging—and more fun! The payoff matches your efforts, because the ridgeline leads through a beautiful stretch of boreal forest and interesting rock formations before culminating in long views.

Hedgehog Brook Trail starts by descending to a rock hop across its namesake stream. Ascending rock steps on the far side, the narrow, blue-blazed trail leads you into a deciduous forest, paralleling the brook as it climbs gradually uphill. The trail undulates over hummocks and across small streams and then descends to cross the wide brook you are following. A short distance after this crossing, Hedgehog Brook Trail turns sharply left and begins up a wider, sandier path—the remnant of an old road. Look for the teeth marks and dangling strips of bark that indicate moose have visited the striped maple saplings along this section of trail. As you walk up the right side of the brook, an enormous mossy boulder with birch and spruce trunks sprouting from its scalp pushes the trail briefly off its straight track, which is lined with purple-flowering raspberry. Gradually, the trail becomes narrower and a little rockier, and begins to zigzag steeply uphill, leaving the stream far below. A double blaze marks a left

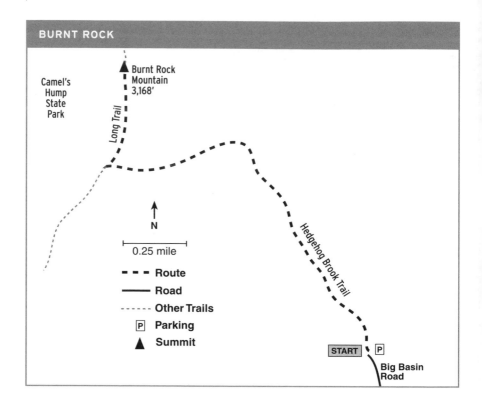

turn, and the trail crosses the slope, rising moderately and occasionally following smooth rock spines.

After a rocky stream crossing, the trail again heads steeply uphill. When you enter the Long Trail Easement Lands, the trees are noticeably shorter. A steep scramble over rocks and up three log ladders brings you into a spruce/fir forest with the occasional mountain ash. The trail jogs back and forth and climbs several ledges before arriving on the ridgeline, the end of Hedgehog Brook Trail. Turn right onto the white-blazed Long Trail and head north through a dim, mossy conifer forest. After scrambling through a narrow, rocky canyon and up a steep pitch, you break out of the trees and onto the open face of Burnt Rock Mountain. The white blazes are now painted on the rocks, though if you hike early in the season, some may have been scoured off by winter's ice. To the east, ridgelines stack up one behind the other into the distance. To the south, the dramatic bulk and crests of the high Green Mountains rise, the ski trails of Sugarbush and Mad River Glen tracing lighter paths through the dark-green forests from late spring to summer and fall.

The section of the Long Trail from Mount Abraham at the southern end, through where you stand on Burnt Rock Mountain, and north over Camel's

From the rugged crest of Burnt Rock, the section of Long Trail known as the Monroe Skyline extends south over General Stark Mountain, Mount Ellen, and Mount Abraham.

Hump is called the Monroe Skyline. Its long stretches of high elevation and magnificent views make it one of the most scenic and interesting parts of the 272-mile Long Trail. To the north, the humps of Mount Ira Allen and Mount Ethan Allen lead to the striking summit of Camel's Hump. To the west, the rounded bulges of foothills descend to the blue expanse of Lake Champlain.

Return downhill the way you climbed up.

DID YOU KNOW?

From the summit of Burnt Rock, the nation's last surviving single chairlift is visible on General Stark Mountain. Its continued use is one of many ways Mad River Glen ski area resists trends of modern alpine ski culture.

MORE INFORMATION

Hedgehog Brook Trail and this section of the Long Trail are located on private land. Hikers are allowed to use the trail thanks to the generosity of the landowners. Please stay on the trail and away from buildings. Inconsiderate hiker behavior could lead to trail closure. Both trails are maintained by the Green Mountain Club, 4711 Waterbury–Stowe Road, Waterbury Center, VT 05677; 802-244-7037; greenmountainclub.org.

NEARBY

Swim or paddle sections of the Mad River, flowing through Waitsfield, 7.0 miles southeast. Stores are along VT 100 in Waitsfield.

TRIP 27
CAMEL'S HUMP

Location: Duxbury, VT
Rating: Strenuous
Distance: 7.0 miles round-trip
Elevation Gain: 2,585 feet
Estimated Time: 5 hours
Maps: USGS Waterbury; USGS Huntington

Visit the craggy, windswept summit of Vermont's most famous peak on this challenging, rewarding day-hike loop.

DIRECTIONS

From I-89, Exit 10, go south on VT 100. Turn left at the stop sign and drive 0.2 mile. Turn right onto Winooski Street and follow it 0.4 mile to its end. Turn right onto River Road and drive 3.9 miles to turn left onto Camel's Hump Road. (Note that oncoming traffic on River Road stops at this junction, but downhill traffic on Camel's Hump Road does not.) Drive 3.5 miles up Camel's Hump Road to a parking lot on the right (space for 12 cars) or straight ahead to the upper lots (space for 25 cars). The upper lots are gated at dusk and re-opened at dawn. (The final 0.4 mile of Camel's Hump Road is not maintained in winter; winter hikers park in a lot at the end of the maintained road and add 0.8 mile round-trip to the hike.) *GPS coordinates:* 44° 18.99′ N, 72° 50.87′ W.

TRAIL DESCRIPTION

Camel's Hump (4,083 feet) cuts a large profile, literally and figuratively, in Vermont. The peak's isolated height and distinct shape are a National Natural Landmark, recognizable from great distances and featured as a symbol of the state in many places, including on the 2001 Vermont state quarter. One of the first stretches of the Long Trail (LT) was built here, and the mountain remains the only undeveloped 4,000-footer in the state. The summit is busy with hikers on most fair-weather days, so go for immense views, rare plants, and fun rock scrambles, but not necessarily for solitude and quiet.

This eastern-slope lollipop loop uses the Monroe, Dean, and Long trails and can be hiked in either direction, depending on preferences and abilities. The more scenic but more challenging route ascends Dean Trail and scales a steep, rocky ridge on the LT, treating hikers to views early and frequently. (This

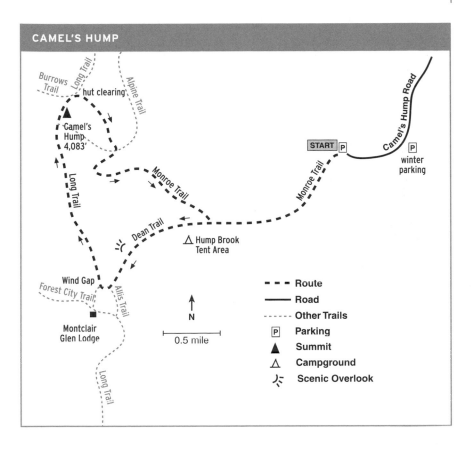

CAMEL'S HUMP

Burrows Trail
Long Trail
hut clearing
Alpine Trail
Camel's Hump 4,083'
Long Trail
Monroe Trail
Camel's Hump Road
START P
P winter parking
Monroe Trail
Dean Trail
△ Hump Brook Tent Area
Wind Gap
Forest City Trail
Allis Trail
Montclair Glen Lodge
Long Trail
N
0.5 mile

- - - Route
——— Road
------ Other Trails
P Parking
▲ Summit
△ Campground
⅄ Scenic Overlook

way may be safer as well, since descending those rock pitches can be tricky.) Monroe Trail is a steady green tunnel that is a slightly shorter route between the summit and the trailhead (3.3 miles versus 3.7), but not as fun or interesting, and better left for the descent.

From the upper parking area, the blue-blazed Monroe Trail rises gradually at first, heading south over rocky, gravelly terrain. Passing remnants of a stone wall, Monroe Trail bends west and climbs steadily and moderately alongside a ravine from which Hump Brook can be heard far below. After 1.3 miles, Dean Trail splits off to the left while Monroe Trail continues straight. Go left onto Dean Trail (also blue-blazed, as are all trails connecting to the LT). Initially, the cross-hill route gives respite from the climb, but after descending across a brook and past Hump Brook Tent Area at 0.2 mile, Dean Trail climbs steadily. After about 0.5 mile, the trail flattens and enters a spruce/fir forest, where a spur trail leads right to a big rock on the edge of a wetland and a view of Camel's Hump's sheer southern face above the trees. A closer cliff rises dramatically over the wetland and gives you a preview of the next leg of your hike.

When the trees become too small for trail markers on the upper elevations of Camel's Hump, blazes painted on rock lead hikers the final distance to the summit.

Dean Trail zigzags a final 0.2 mile to Wind Gap, where the Allis Trail and LT southbound head left. (Montclair Glen Lodge is 0.2 mile south on the LT.) Turn right onto the white-blazed northbound LT. A sign says the summit is 1.7 miles ahead, but you'll be heartened to know it's only 1.5 miles. A steep rock scramble brings you to a cliff top with a view northeast to the Worcester Range and south to Mount Ethan Allen (3,688 feet).

Following a rock path atop the ridge, clamber up another steep pitch, and another, and then squeeze through a jumble of giant boulders with dark, cave-like spaces between them. After a few more scrambles and open views, the trail descends into the trees. Occasional glimpses of the towering summit lead you through the forest and then up switchbacks to the base of the cliff. Alpine Trail heads right here, a bad-weather bypass to Monroe Trail if you need it. (Some remains of a 1944 B-24 bomber crash are flung across the mountainside along Alpine Trail, though most of the plane has been removed.) Stay left on the LT, cutting beneath the rock face and climbing its western side. Be careful of delicate mountain sandwort, Bigelow's sedge, and bilberry; leash your dog and step only on rock.

A clear day on the summit of Camel's Hump is a visual feast, with New Hampshire's White Mountains and New York's Adirondacks backing rows of

Green Mountains and the shining expanse of Lake Champlain. But whether or not it is sunny, be prepared for wind and cool temperatures.

Follow white blazes north, descending 0.2 mile to the Hut Clearing—now just a clearing. A mid-nineteenth-century hotel hosted adventurous guests at this location for about 15 years until it burned down, and a local hiking club maintained a series of shelters here in the first half of the twentieth century. Burrows Trail goes left, the LT continues straight, and Monroe Trail descends to the right. Go right, descending about 0.3 mile of moderately steep, rocky trail before the pitch eases. After 0.6 mile, Alpine Trail crosses, and 0.3 mile below that, Monroe Trail swings left, leaving the boreal forest and entering mixed hardwoods at the base of a cliff band. Walk beneath the cliffs for about 0.3 mile, where a sharp right turn steers your path downhill again. Two miles below the summit, you will arrive at the Dean Trail junction; continue straight down Monroe Trail the way you hiked up.

DID YOU KNOW?

Camel's Hump has had many names; its current appellation derives from Camel's Rump, the name given to it by Ira Allen, one of the founders of Vermont.

MORE INFORMATION

Trails are closed from snowmelt until Memorial Day weekend. Camel's Hump State Park is managed for multiple uses by the Vermont Department of Forests, Parks and Recreation, 111 West Street, Essex Junction, VT 05452; 802-879-5682; vtstateparks.com/htm/camelshump.htm. Trails and hiker facilities are maintained by the Green Mountain Club, 4711 Waterbury–Stowe Road, Waterbury Center, VT 05677; 802-244-7037; greenmountainclub.org.

NEARBY

Backcountry camping is available at Montclair Glen Lodge and Hump Brook Tent Area; fees may be charged. Frontcountry camping is at Little River State Park in Waterbury, 13 miles north. Paddle and swim at Waterbury Reservoir, 13 miles north, or the Winooski River, 4 miles north. Mountain biking is plentiful in the Waterbury–Stowe area (see Appendix). Food is in Waterbury, 8.5 miles northeast.

TRIP 28
SPRUCE MOUNTAIN

Location: Plainfield, VT
Rating: Moderate
Distance: 4.4 miles round-trip
Elevation Gain: 1,300 feet
Estimated Time: 3.5 hours
Maps: USGS Barre East; USGS Knox Mountain

A historical fire tower offers intimate views of Granite Hill peaks and long views to the highest Green and White mountains.

DIRECTIONS

From the blinking light at the junction of US 2 and Main Street in Plainfield, turn downhill onto Main Street. Follow it 0.5 mile and turn right onto East Hill Road. After 3.8 miles, turn left onto Spruce Mountain Road and drive 1.0 mile to the parking lot (space for 12 cars) at the road's end. *GPS coordinates: 44° 14.10′ N, 72° 22.68′ W.*

TRAIL DESCRIPTION

Spruce Mountain (3,020 feet) is on the western edge of a cluster of peaks in the 26,183-acre Groton State Forest. Access to the summit, though, is through the abutting 642-acre L. R. Jones State Forest. Spruce Mountain Trail passes through a variety of landscapes before topping out on a treed summit with a sturdy fire tower. The pitches are generally not steep, though the last part of the hike is a sustained climb. The footing is uneven on the upper half of the mountain, making this trail best suited to hikers about ages 10 and older.

Spruce Mountain Trail begins by heading downhill from the parking lot on the multiuse Tower Road, which accommodates forestry vehicles as well as hikers. For the first few tenths of a mile, heading south, the terrain is flat.

At about 0.5 mile, the wide track passes near a spring and enters a small log landing. When this land was bought for Vermont's first state forest in 1909, it was mostly open fields. Between 1910 and 1916, 300,000 trees were planted, many of which have since matured and been harvested. You may see evidence of forestry practices on your hike. Proceed straight through the clearing, reenter the forest, and begin a moderate climb. Where the road turns east, a cellar hole (the remains of a farmhouse that predated the state forest) sits a little way off the

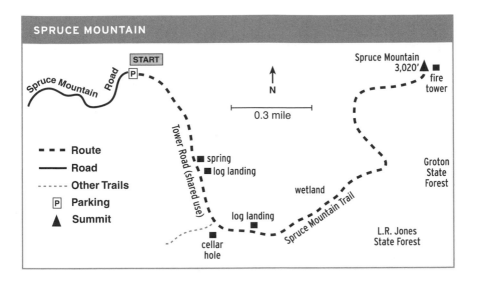

right side of the trail. Shortly after that, about 1.0 mile from the trailhead, enter a larger log landing where evidence of other roads leads off through overgrown grass. This is the end of the multiuse section of the trail. Stay straight, following the path into a forest with dense conifer walls and a hardwood canopy overhead.

Occasional faded blazes—some white, some blue—mark the route, though it is not difficult to follow the path as it narrows and climbs gradually. Rocks begin to stud the previously flat dirt trail as it curves northeast, and shortly the trail is paved with rocks. This path leads past a wetland on the left.

From here, gradual and almost flat terrain leads to a sharp left turn to the north, where the character of the hike changes significantly. Now the trail narrows as it weaves around jumbles of boulders and climbs over angled ledges lying across the slope. The woods shift to a higher-mountain spruce/fir forest.

The forest suddenly opens again after the trail climbs up and across many stretches of sloped ledge. The final leg of the hike ascends a ridge, with sky visible through the thick forest on either side of the trail.

The summit clearing is ringed with tall trees and dominated by the legs of the fire tower. In 1919, a wooden tower was constructed here to allow people to watch for fires caused by the drying debris left from intense forest-clearing activities. The legs of the tower formed the four corners of the caretaker's cabin, which squatted beneath an open lookout platform. After a dozen years, a taller wood tower was constructed with an enclosed lookout room, or "cab."

Looking east over the trees from high in the tower, you will see a rumpled landscape of peaks and ponds that is largely within the borders of Groton State Forest. Signal Mountain (3,323 feet) is the tallest of the cluster of peaks to the

The fire tower elevates hikers above the tall conifers on Spruce Mountain's summit.

south, with Burnt (3,100 feet), Butterfield (3,123 feet), and Knox (3,064 feet) mountains beyond it. To the west, the ridge of the highest Green Mountains marches across the horizon, from Killington Peak (4,235 feet) in the southwest, across the distinct two-tiered summit of Camel's Hump (4,083 feet) due west, to the long summit ridge of Mount Mansfield (4,393 feet) in the northwest.

Return downhill the way you hiked up.

DID YOU KNOW?

Spruce Mountain's current steel tower began its career on Bellevue Hill in Saint Albans and was relocated here in 1943, where it was staffed until the early 1970s.

MORE INFORMATION

L. R. Jones State Forest is managed by the Vermont Department of Forests, Parks and Recreation, 5 Perry Street, Suite 20, Barre, VT 05641; 802-476-0170; vtfpr.org.

NEARBY

The seven state parks within Groton State Forest offer camping, swimming, a rail trail, and hiking trails, 20 to 25 miles from the Spruce Mountain trailhead via US 302 or US 2. Plainfield has restaurants and shops along Main Street and US 2.

TRIP 29
OWL'S HEAD

Location: Peacham, VT
Rating: Easy to Moderate
Distance: 3.8 miles round-trip
Elevation Gain: 210 feet
Estimated Time: 2 hours
Maps: USGS Marshfield; vtstateparks.com/pdfs/groton_trails.pdf

Pass through lovely fern meadows on your way to the open granite summit and unique stone octagon shelter of Owl's Head.

DIRECTIONS
From the junction of US 302 and VT 232 (State Forest Road) in Groton, go north on VT 232 for 9.3 miles (passing Owl's Head Road). Turn right into New Discovery State Park. Pay a day-use fee at the gate and proceed to a fork; go right. Pass through a metal gate and immediately go left at another fork. Owl's Head trailhead parking is a shallow pullout (space for about 4 cars) a short distance down the road on the right. (Winter hikers park at the gate at New Discovery's entrance and add 1.3 miles round-trip to the hike.) *GPS coordinates:* 44° 18.70′ N, 72° 17.28′ W.

TRAIL DESCRIPTION
Owl's Head (1,958 feet), a low but prominent and easily accessible peak with long views, is the knobby sentinel of Groton State Forest. A mile-long auto road (open during daylight hours when state parks are operating) ascends to within 0.25 mile of the summit and provides a good alternative for those who can't walk far. But the beautiful forests and gentle rise of the trail from New Discovery State Park make this one of the most enjoyable hikes in the area, suitable for kids about ages 7 and older.

An old road leads north from the parking area into a shady forest of tall, thin conifers. Follow the road 0.3 mile to the trail's register box at a junction just shy of a field with a campground maintenance building. Go left onto the blue-blazed Owl's Head Trail, turning almost 180 degrees to head south, parallel to the old road. Canada mayflowers and bunchberries sprout amid club moss alongside the path. The flat, rooty trail leaves the conifer forest that dominates the campground, shifting to beech and maple.

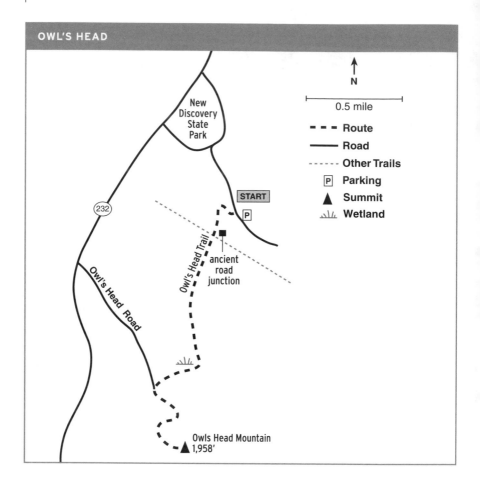

OWL'S HEAD

New Discovery State Park

232

Owl's Head Road

Owl's Head Trail

START

P

ancient road junction

Owls Head Mountain
▲ 1,958'

N

0.5 mile

- - - Route
—— Road
------ Other Trails
P Parking
▲ Summit
⎁⎁ Wetland

Ascending gradually, you will arrive at the junction of an ancient road. An old split sign off to the left seems to point to Lake Groton, though it is so weathered that it is barely legible. The area that is now Groton State Forest was one of Vermont's earliest Colonial settlements. Farming—never easy in the mountains—was especially difficult here where granite chunks are plentiful, so logging has long been a dominant activity in these woods. The state forest is managed for tree harvesting and recreation today. Go straight across the ancient road and up a gentle climb.

As the trail rolls gradually uphill, you are likely to hear white-throated sparrows, ovenbirds, and the distinct flutey calls of wood thrushes, hermit thrushes, and veeries. In light gaps where trees have fallen, the understory grows rapidly, narrowing the trail corridor in places. A series of gentle curves with easy climbing brings you to a remarkable sea of ferns stretching across the forest floor beneath widely spaced trunks, 1 mile from the trailhead.

The lovely, undulating trail to Owl's Head passes through two broad fern meadows spreading across the floor of the open, hardwood forest.

At 1.4 miles, the trail descends slightly to a small wetland, studded with ferns growing on hummocks. Owl's Head Trail curves right, crossing a lichen-crusted ledge 5 feet above the wet ground. Beyond the swamp, climb over a low knoll and begin a long, gradual descent into a hollow. A string of bog bridges brings the trail through a low spot, followed by a short climb into another airy fern meadow and the final rise to Owl's Head Road.

Go left on the road, turning left again onto the summit trail. The other, unmarked trail on the road leads to a picnic pavilion. Passing toilets, you will begin the steep, rocky final 0.2 mile. Rock steps lead into a boreal forest of paper birch, spruce, and fir. Blueberry bushes sprout between moss-covered rocks as you round the final curve to the stone octagon built on the summit by Civilian Conservation Corps crews in the 1930s (see page 241). Granite ledge rolls away below the octagon, giving views west and south, most notably of Kettle Pond pointing west to the distant peak of Camel's Hump (4,083 feet).

Return downhill the way you climbed up.

DID YOU KNOW?

At more than 26,000 acres, Groton State Forest is the second-largest landholding of the state, with only the 43,049-acre Mount Mansfield State Forest eclipsing it in size.

MORE INFORMATION

Hiking trails in Groton State Forest (designated with blue blazes) are for foot travel only. State parks within Groton State Forest open for the season on Memorial Day. New Discovery, Kettle Pond, and Ricker Pond state parks are open through Columbus Day; Boulder Beach, Big Deer, and Stillwater state parks are open through Labor Day. Day use of the parks is 10 A.M. to official sunset. Seyon Lodge State Park operates year-round with seasonal closures and is open for day use 6 A.M. to official sunset. New Discovery State Park, 4239 Route 232, Marshfield, VT 05658; 802-426-3042; vtstateparks.com/htm/newdiscovery.htm.

NEARBY

The seven state parks (New Discovery, Kettle Pond, Big Deer, Boulder Beach, Stillwater, Ricker Pond, and Seyon Lodge) in Groton State Forest provide abundant swimming, paddling, camping, and picnicking options in addition to many more hiking trails. Bike or ski on the multiuse Montpelier Wells River Rail Trail, which hosts the Cross-Vermont Trail through Groton State Forest. Restaurants and shops are limited along US 2 in Marshfield, 6 miles northwest, and Plainfield, 12 miles west, with more variety in Barre, 22 miles west, or Montpelier, 23 miles west.

IS IT A SWAMP OR A BOG?

You round a bend on the trail and see an opening in the forest. Shrubby plants grow on hummocks, surrounded by still water. A few scraggly tree trunks poke up, and decaying logs lie in the muck. The ground becomes squishy under your boots, and you hear a faint splash as a small animal takes cover. This is clearly wetland, but is it a swamp or a bog? How can you tell?

"Wetland" is a general term for the many types of soggy natural communities that exist somewhere between open water and terra firma. Vermont has 300,000 acres of wetlands, including marshes, swamps, bogs, and fens.

Freshwater marshes are wide-open, water-on-the-surface places: They are the grass-choked corridors you paddle through when a slow river spreads out over a wide area. They are the reedy edges of ponds and lakes where frogs and dragonflies hang out. Marshes have many herbaceous plants, such as grasses, cattails, and pond lilies, but because water is usually present year-round, there are no trees.

Swamps are the slightly less wet version of marshes; in a swamp, trees survive seasonal flooding. At lower elevations, swamps are dominated by hardwood trees such as maple and ash. Higher in the mountains, softwoods dominate the swamps: cedar, tamarack, spruce, and fir.

While marshes and swamps have water flowing through them, bogs and fens develop where water collects and stagnates. Thick mats of vegetation may cover the entire surface of the water. Bogs and fens differ in the chemistry of their water. Bogs have acidic water, very few dissolved nutrients, and very low levels of oxygen in the water. This is a tough place for plants to live, and only a few thrive: sphagnum moss, heath shrubs, and the adaptable black spruce. Fens have water more accommodating to life; fen water ranges from slightly acidic to slightly basic, and has more dissolved nutrients, minerals, and oxygen than bog water does. Fens may have some of the same plants as bogs, but they have many more as well, including goldenrod, red osier dogwood shrubs, cattails, and sedges.

All of these soupy places are important parts of healthy ecosystems. Wetlands provide important habitat, and their absorbent soils help recharge water tables, slow floodwaters, stabilize shorelines, and filter out sediments, pollutants, and nutrients. (For more details, read *Wetland, Woodland, Wildland*, by Elizabeth H. Thompson and Eric R. Sorenson, published by The Nature Conservancy and the Vermont Fish and Wildlife Department).

TRIP 30
WRIGHT'S MOUNTAIN

Location: Bradford, VT
Rating: Easy to Moderate
Distance: 2.7 miles round-trip
Elevation Gain: 326 feet
Estimated Time: 1.5 hours
Maps: USGS East Corinth; uvlt.org/docs/trails/Wrights_2011_trailMap.pdf.

Spectacular views of pastoral Vermont and a vernal pool are highlights of this gentle mountainside loop hike.

DIRECTIONS
From the junction of US 5/VT 25, head west for 5.2 miles. Turn right onto Wright's Mountain Road and go 2.3 miles to the parking area (space for 8 cars) on the right at the height-of-land. *GPS coordinates:* 44° 03.22′ N, 72° 10.02′ W.

TRAIL DESCRIPTION
Wright's Mountain (1,800 feet) is not as well known as some Vermont day-hike destinations, but it's a nature lover's gem with 800-plus acres of conserved woods. The height-of-land, with its reward of long views, is gained early in the hike; a shelter at the lookout rocks is just 0.8 mile from the trailhead, making Wright's Mountain an ideal first backpacking trip for children.

Wright's Mountain Trail begins just beyond a gate on a wide woods road lined with tall red pines. The trail is not blazed, but all of the trail junctions—and there are many—are clearly signed. A short distance from the parking lot, a pit toilet perches off the left side of the trail, and not far beyond that the yellow-blazed Appreciation Trail leaves to the right. The trail then climbs more noticeably into a deciduous forest.

At 0.4 mile, Sylvia's Trail departs to the left (part of your return route). Wright's Mountain Trail curves southwest and climbs to the ridge, where the top of Appreciation Trail appears on the right and a spur trail leads left to a wooden bench with a view of the Connecticut River valley and distant New Hampshire hills. The brushy understory of this ridgeline supports ruffed grouse. If you come across a mother with chicks, she will limp and moan to attract your attention, giving the young time to scurry to safety. The male

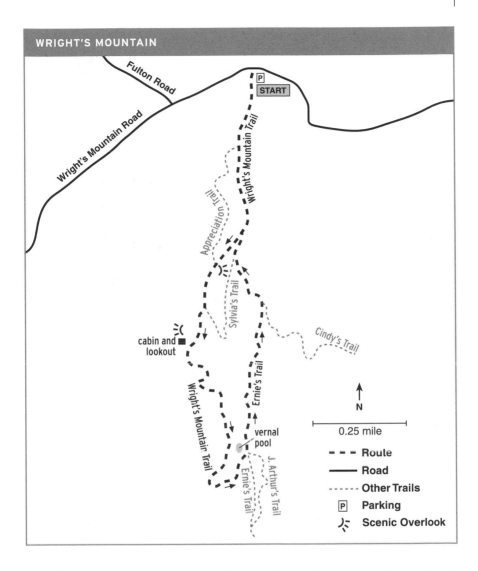

WRIGHT'S MOUNTAIN

ruffed grouse's wing drumming is frequently heard in Vermont's woods, its deep, thumping tempo sounding like a heartbeat rapidly increasing.

The top of Sylvia's Trail joins on the left as you make your way around the forested summit. At 0.8 mile, descend to a clearing with spectacular views west over the hilly farmland and forests of the Waits River valley. A large, airy shelter perches dramatically over the ledges. The outlook rocks are a natural lunch spot, even though they're barely a third of the way into the hike.

Wright's Mountain Trail, now marked with yellow blazes, exits the clearing along a notable wall of rock jutting up from the forest floor. Heading south, pass two smaller viewpoints before swinging east and descending into oak

Early on the loop around Wright's Mountain, an overlook with a large, airy shelter makes a scenic picnic spot in any weather.

and maple woods. When an abandoned leg of trail heads left, stay right and descend along a rope railing. The trail makes S curves back and forth across the ridge, passing through dark, fragrant spruce/fir stands and clambering over mossy rock outcrops. Given the short ascent to the lookout, you lose more elevation on this side of the mountain than you'd expect. As you approach the southernmost part of your loop, views appear through tall white pines and the land drops away in front of you. Now the trail crosses onto the eastern slope of the mountain and swings north, entering a damp deciduous forest. Shortly, a depression that hosts a vernal pool in spring and early summer diverts the trail onto a low ridge. This shallow seasonal pond not only provides breeding habitat for wood frogs and spotted salamanders but also serves as a watering hole for mammals and birds. Wright's Mountain Trail ends at a four-way junction in a narrow gully just below the pool.

Go left onto Ernie's Trail and follow this old two-track north. The ground can be soggy, providing not only an impressionable surface for animal tracks but also good habitat for mosquitoes. The path gets drier as it ascends gradually through thick woods. After about 0.5 mile, Cindy's Trail descends to the right. Stay straight on Ernie's Trail to the junction of Sylvia's Trail. Go right and follow the bottom leg of Sylvia's Trail to its junction with Wright's Mountain Trail. From here, go right, returning the way you came.

DID YOU KNOW?

The brightly colored red eft you may see moving at the speed of a sloth is the juvenile stage of the eastern, or red-spotted, newt. As larvae, they have gills and live in the pond where they hatched; as adults they return to aquatic life as olive-green salamanders. In between, they spend up to seven years wandering on land.

MORE INFORMATION

Wright's Mountain trails are managed by the Bradford Conservation Commission, P.O. Box 339, Bradford, VT 05033; bradfordconservation.org. Conservation easements on the Wright's Mountain/Devil's Den Town Forest are held by the Upper Valley Land Trust, 19 Buck Road, Hanover, NH 03755; 603-643-6626; uvlt.org.

NEARBY

The Waits and Connecticut rivers are popular for paddling and bird-watching; a boat launch near their confluence in Bradford is part of the 240-mile Connecticut River Paddlers' Trail. Several riverside parks in Bradford provide picnic spots; dining can be found on US 5 (North Main Street), just north of its junction with VT 25. The Montshire Museum of Science in Norwich, Vermont, 24 miles south, has indoor and outdoor exhibits geared toward kids but entertaining for all ages.

TRIP 31
MOUNT HORRID'S GREAT CLIFF

Location: Goshen, VT
Rating: Moderate
Distance: 1.6 miles round-trip
Elevation Gain: 630 feet
Estimated Time: 1.5 hours
Map: USGS Mount Carmel

Rare plants and wide views await hikers on this rugged cliff top in the Joseph Battell Wilderness.

DIRECTIONS
US 7 and VT 73 coincide through the village of Brandon. From the southern junction of these two roads, head east on VT 73 for 7.7 miles to the U.S. Forest Service Brandon Gap parking area (space for 20 cars) on the right. *GPS coordinates: 44° 17.78′ N, 72° 17.67′ W.*

TRAIL DESCRIPTION
Mount Horrid's Great Cliff (2,600 feet) supports a remarkable diversity of life, including rare and uncommon plants as well as peregrine falcon nesting sites. Some years, depending on where the falcons nest, the cliffs may be closed between March 15 and August 1 to protect the chicks. Check with Audubon Vermont (vt.audubon.org) or the Green Mountain National Forest (fs.usda.gov/greenmountain) for details. The hike to the cliffs is relatively short but steep and rocky. Use caution on the cliff, because the edge is sudden and unprotected.

From the parking area, cross VT 73 and follow a dirt path through chokecherries to a cluster of signs and kiosks. Beyond the signs, you enter the Joseph Battell Wilderness, an L-shaped tract bounded by Brandon Gap to the south and Middlebury Gap to the north. While the north–south leg of the L surrounds the Long Trail, the east–west leg of this Wilderness encompasses Monastery Mountain (3,224 feet) and Philadelphia Peak (3,203 feet), which together make up the longest roadless and trailless ridgeline in the Green Mountain National Forest. (Note: Wilderness areas are designated by Congress to provide retreats from civilization, where humans are visitors and nature takes precedence. Natural conditions dominate the character of the landscape, so travel may be slower as you encounter downed trees, few signs,

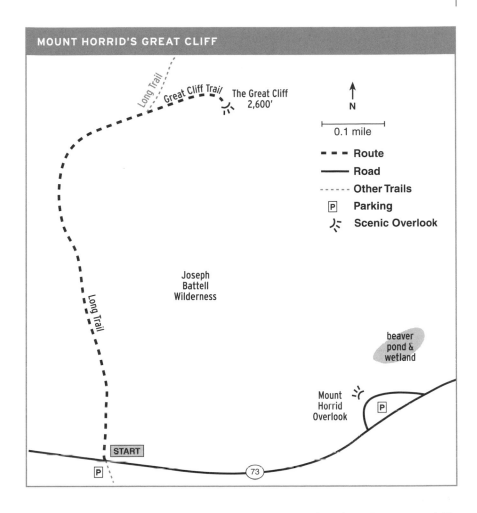

or a lack of bridges across streams. This section of trail to the Great Cliffs, however, has clear signage at the single junction and no large streams to cross.)

The trail is blazed in white, the sign of the Long Trail (see page 29). The hike starts steeply on a rock-choked trail through boulders and skinny striped maples (also called goosefoot maples for their large leaves' resemblance to a webbed foot). The trail switches back and forth across the steep slope as it ascends from the road, and then heads up the west side of the hill.

The climb moderates as the trail crosses to the east side of the hill and follows a smooth bedrock path through a grassy birch forest. After a short distance, the side of the Great Cliff rises from the soil on your right and the climbing gets steep again. Multiple rock staircases pass the ledge and ascend to the junction of the Long Trail and Great Cliff Trail. Go right onto the blue-blazed Great Cliff Trail, which climbs a short distance before flattening out.

Exiting the forest, you pass through a band of ferns and goldenrod before stepping onto a narrow ledge with an uneven surface. Between the rocks, in pockets where soil has accumulated, mats of three-toothed cinquefoil grow.

Directly in front of you, a ridge running east–west rises steeply, cresting into several summit points; Goshen Mountain (3,292 feet) is the peak on the right. In the southeast, Round Mountain (3,342 feet) lifts its pointed summit skyward before sloping north over Corporation Mountain (3,142 feet). If you're lucky, you might spot beaver or moose in the wetland directly below your perch.

Seventeen rare, threatened, or endangered plants have been reported on Mount Horrid over the years, many of them on and around Great Cliff. Sitting on the lookout, you are amid a number of interesting plants. Northern single-spike sedge (sometimes called scirpus-like sedge in Vermont) is rare in the state, but widespread on Great Cliff. Among the common American mountain ash growing around Great Cliff is some uncommon showy mountain ash, with more-rounded leaf tips and larger fruits. The best treat to stumble across here may be blueberry bushes. Black bears, finding good habitat in the remoteness of Joseph Battell Wilderness, would agree.

Return the way you hiked up.

DID YOU KNOW?

The black bear is the smallest of the three North American bears, and the only kind living in Vermont. While you are unlikely to see one of these elusive creatures, if you do, alert it to your presence by clapping, waving your arms, and talking; then back away slowly.

MORE INFORMATION

No personal property may be left in the Joseph Battell Wilderness area, and wheeled devices of any kind are not allowed. Green Mountain National Forest, 99 Ranger Road, Rochester, VT 05767; 802-767-4261; fs.usda.gov/greenmountain. The Long Trail is maintained by Green Mountain Club, 4711 Waterbury–Stowe Road, Waterbury Center, VT 05677; 802-244-7037.

NEARBY

Branbury State Park on Lake Dunsmore provides swimming and paddling 10.8 miles northwest of here. Both Brandon, 7.5 miles west, and Rochester, 9.9 miles east, have restaurants and shops.

3

NORTHWESTERN VERMONT

THE IMMENSE, SHINING MARVEL OF NORTHERN LAKE CHAMPLAIN dominates the landscape of Northwestern Vermont. Sometimes referred to as the country's sixth Great Lake, its long shorelines, large tributary deltas, and varied depths and temperatures support a range of natural communities. After the last ice age, while the land was still compressed from the weight of the recently melted glacier, the Atlantic Ocean poured into this valley. For a time, until the land rebounded and the salt water drained, whales and seals swam here and the Green Mountain slopes descended directly into the Champlain Sea. Remnants of the ocean are still in the area: Endangered Champlain beach grass grows along sandy beaches and dunes, which are themselves difficult to find. Most of the big lake's shoreline is rocky, and many of those rocks are vertical, creating a landscape that is strikingly beautiful, if recreationally challenging.

The many islands in the northern half of the lake are known as the flattest land in the Green Mountain State. Their jaw-dropping views of the surrounding water and mountain ranges, as well as their own inherent pastoral beauty, make the islands a popular destination for visitors. Many of the smaller islands, including Burton (Trip 37), have the added attraction of being a refuge from cars, accessible only by boat. Agricultural use of the land has declined in recent years—abandoned farm buildings and homesteads on smaller islands are not uncommon sights—but farming and orchards are still prevalent on the larger, more settled islands.

Three very large, very old rivers flow west through the Green Mountains and spill a constant stream of sediment and water into Lake Champlain: the Missisquoi in the north, the Lamoille emptying near South Hero, and the Winooski ending next to Burlington. Their deltas provide rich habitat for birds, amphibians, fish, and some mammals, and support some rare and uncommon species. Missisquoi National Wildlife Refuge (Trip 38) preserves acres of saturated ground around the bird-foot delta of that river, including some remarkable natural communities found in the sprawling Maquam Bog.

Burlington and surrounding Chittenden County are densely developed by Vermont standards, but farmlands and wooded areas are the norm just a few miles from the city. South of Burlington, the most northerly Taconic Mountains jut from the farmland in small, steep knobs—most notably, Mount Philo (Trip 32). For a small hiking effort, these cliffy little peaks give spectacular views of the dramatic Northwestern Vermont landscape.

TRIP 32
MOUNT PHILO STATE PARK

Location: Charlotte, VT
Rating: Moderate
Distance: 2.4 miles round-trip
Elevation Gain: 580 feet
Estimated Time: 2 hours
Maps: USGS Mount Philo; vtstateparks.com/pdfs/philo.pdf

Trek beneath a dramatic cliff band to breathtaking views of the Champlain valley and surrounding mountains.

DIRECTIONS
From the junction of US 7 with Ferry Road and Church Hill Road, travel 2.5 miles south on US 7. Turn left onto State Park Road and follow it 0.6 mile to its end at Mount Philo Road and the park entrance, where there is a parking lot (space for 70 cars). *GPS coordinates:* 44° 16.68′ N, 73° 13.32′ W.

TRAIL DESCRIPTION
Mount Philo (968 feet) is a small peak packed with pleasant surprises. The hill rises steeply from gently rolling farmland, visible for miles across the Champlain valley. Though the climb is not long, the steepness and the occasionally rough terrain make it most suitable for kids ages 6 and up.

House Rock Trail begins where the paved road to the summit leaves the parking lot. The wide, needle-covered trail climbs steeply at first, following blue blazes through hophornbeam, sugar maple, and tamarack. After a few minutes, the trail's massive namesake boulder looms above a flight of rock steps. House Rock is one of many glacial erratics that traveled south in glaciers during the last ice age and dropped to the ground on Mount Philo when the ice melted about 12,000 years ago. Climb beneath House Rock's shady overhang and skirt its left side. The slope is more gradual from here to the auto road.

Turn right onto the road and follow it a short distance to the continuation of the footpath on the left. Climb up around a curve to a junction; go right onto Devil's Chair Trail. Follow the base of an impressive cliff band that runs around the south side of the mountain, zigzagging between boulders that have splintered away from the main ledges. Near the beginning of the trail, look for grooves etched into trailside boulders. These ridges were formed by water

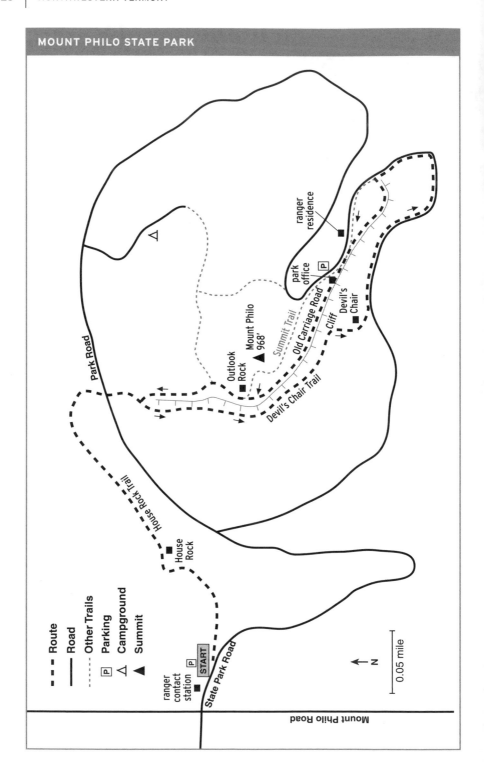

MOUNT PHILO STATE PARK

eroding cracks in the rock, and they help identify these rocks as dolomite, different from the harder, more erosion-resistant quartzite that dominates Mount Philo.

The cliffs rise higher the farther you walk, with ferns and white cedars growing vertically out of cracks in the rocky face. After you pass the tallest of the cliffs, a gradual ascent leads to an intersection: A blue blaze on your left seems to indicate that the trail turns left and climbs steeply between the cliffs where metal poles indicate an old railing. Do not climb this abandoned trail; continue straight on the more developed footpath. As the cliffs recede, the trail enters thick woods and begins a short descent along a ridgeline. The chair-shaped rock that gives the trail its name perches on this hill.

Devil's Chair Trail ends at the auto road; go left along its edge for 0.2 mile. Vehicle traffic is one-way; be aware of cars approaching from behind during the park's operating season. In winter, the closed road makes a fun ski trail. After a long left curve, turn left onto Old Carriage Road Trail, following the top of the cliffs. Pass close to the park office and summit parking lot before wending through grassy picnic areas.

Old Carriage Road Trail ends at a grassy lawn where Adirondack chairs offer a commanding view of Lake Champlain and the Adirondacks. Climb the rocky knob on the right side of the lawn (somewhat hidden by trees) for a higher vantage point to see the Vermont peaks. Stretching south in line with Mount Philo, similar lone hills rise up from the valley floor: Shellhouse, Buck, and Snake mountains. Along with Mount Philo, these small peaks are the northern extent of the Taconic Mountains.

The descent trail begins on the north side of the outlook rock amid clumps of honeysuckle, raspberry, and sumac. Follow switchbacks down a steep hillside to complete your loop at the junction of Devil's Chair Trail. Go right, following the same trail down that you walked up.

DID YOU KNOW?

Poison parsnip burns the skin similarly to poison ivy, but its toxin is photosensitive. If you encounter poison parsnip on a cloudy day, you may never know it, but if the sun comes out, you will likely develop a rash. Identify the clump growing behind the ranger's booth at Mount Philo's entrance so you will know what to avoid.

MORE INFORMATION

Mount Philo State Park is open Memorial Day weekend through mid-October, 10 A.M. to official sunset, though hikers and skiers can use the trails year-

Mount Philo has served as a lookout since the arrival of the ancestors of the Abenaki thousands of years ago; today, bird-watchers gather here to watch seasonal migrations.

round. A day-use fee is charged when the park is open; a campground with tent sites and lean-tos has a separate fee. Picnic areas, water, and restrooms are available on the summit during the open season. Mount Philo State Park, 5425 Mount Philo Road, Charlotte, VT 05445; 802-425-2390. For campsite reservations, contact Vermont State Parks Reservation Center: 888-409-7579; vtstateparks.com.

NEARBY
Swim and paddle at Kingsland Bay State Park, 10.4 miles southwest. Rokeby Museum, 4.6 miles south on US 7, is a National Historic Landmark with walking trails and one of the country's best-preserved stops on the Underground Railroad. Dining can be found along US 7 north into Shelburne and on VT 22A, 7 miles south in downtown Vergennes.

TRIP 33
WILLIAMS WOODS

Location: Charlotte, VT
Rating: Easy
Distance: 1.2 miles round-trip
Elevation Gain: Minimal
Estimated Time: 1 hour
Maps: USGS Charlotte; TNC map at trailside register box

Wander through "pillows and cradles," ancient oaks, and tall pines in this mature valley clayplain forest, a rare natural community in the Champlain valley.

DIRECTIONS
From the junction of US 7 and Ferry Road in Charlotte, drive west on Ferry Road for 0.3 mile. At the stop sign, turn left onto Greenbush Road (County Road 22K). After 1.9 miles, bear left where Thompsons Point Road goes right. Follow Greenbush Road another mile to a small dirt pullout (space for 3 cars) alongside the road on the right. *GPS coordinates:* 44° 16.21′ N, 73° 15.10′ W.

TRAIL DESCRIPTION
Williams Woods Natural Area is a 63-acre island of mature forest surrounded by open, active farm fields. It harbors two of the largest swamp white oaks in Charlotte—each estimated to be more than 200 years old—and offers a rare opportunity to see how the Champlain valley looked before agricultural clearing left few stands of the native valley clayplain forest. The lollipop-loop trail rolls over undulating ground, making it a pleasant cross-country ski outing. This hike is suitable for all ages; dogs are not allowed.

Descend from the roadside onto a curving string of bog bridges. Fifty feet into the woods, The Nature Conservancy (TNC) maintains a registration box with maps and interpretive brochures. The tall, shady white-pine-and-hemlock canopy is interspersed with bright holes left where big trees fell. In this wet environment, trees keep their roots close to the surface to avoid drowning, making for an unstable anchor in the wind. Logs in various states of decomposition are scattered thickly over the forest floor throughout Williams Woods. Look for saplings growing on top of downed trees called nurse logs—the logs'

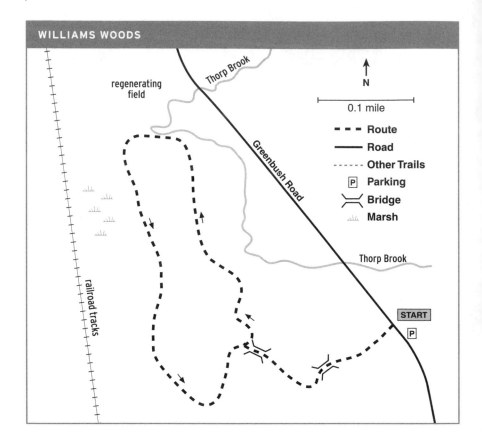

WILLIAMS WOODS

Thorp Brook

regenerating field

N

0.1 mile

- - - Route
—— Road
----- Other Trails
P Parking
Bridge
Marsh

Greenbush Road

Thorp Brook

railroad tracks

START

P

additional height above the water table provides better growing conditions than the saturated ground does.

Curving around conifers, cross a narrow gully on a bridge, using caution on the awkwardly spaced treads. A slight rise brings you near the edge of the woods, with an open farm field visible beyond. Following white blazes, the trail curves sharply to the right along the small stream. In early spring, look for the small white, pink, or lavender flowers and fuzzy stems of hepatica. As spring warms to summer, tiny yellow blooms of barren strawberry appear. Bog bridges over low spots give way to root-covered humps as you approach the second bridge at 0.2 mile. On the far side of the bridge, the trail splits, forming a loop. Go right.

The path bumps along over clusters of roots, passing from shady hemlocks into hardwoods interspersed with tall white pines. Thorp Brook appears in a gully on the right, winding its way slowly toward Lake Champlain. Decomposing trunks of blowdowns—trees that have fallen in the wind—give plentiful opportunity to examine insect activity, woodpecker holes, mosses, and fungi.

The hike through Williams Woods is a mostly flat ramble beneath the multi-layered canopy of white pines, red maples, white oaks, and hophornbeam in what is known as a clayplain forest–the original and now rare forest of the Champlain valley.

Turkey tail mushrooms—with their fluted, striped edges—are particularly striking.

The trail dips slightly downward toward the regenerating field on the northern border of Williams Woods. When the path curves left, look downhill to the right to find a very large swamp white oak—about 3.5 feet across—on the edge of the field. Along the northern end of the trail loop, the pine canopy blocks so much light that there is almost no undergrowth, just a blanket of orange needles on the forest floor. Among all the thin young spires, a massive white pine stretches its branches horizontally into the forest. This old tree was probably a "wolf tree"—left standing when the forest was harvested, giving it plenty of sun and space to grow wide as well as tall.

Curving back to the south, the trail edges along a marsh. In sunny patches, watch for garter snakes sunning on the bog bridges. The trail can be difficult to discern as it passes through hemlock stands and weaves over mossy ground (prevalent TNC trail markers clarify the route).

A mile into your walk, you will arrive back at the trail junction, completing the loop portion of the hike. Turn right, descending to cross the bridge, and return the way you walked in.

DID YOU KNOW?

The humpy-bumpy landscape of hemlock and pine stands is called "pillows and cradles." Cradles are the pits left when trees fall over and pull soil up with their roots; pillows are the mounds of soil left after those upturned roots decay.

MORE INFORMATION

Williams Woods Natural Area is limited to passive recreational activities such as hiking, snowshoeing, cross-country skiing, bird-watching, photography, and nature study. Remove no plants, animals, artifacts, or rocks; do not build fires. The Nature Conservancy, 27 State Street, Montpelier, VT 05602; 802-229-4425; nature.org/vermont.

NEARBY

Go to Kingsland Bay State Park, 10 miles southwest, for swimming and paddling, and to Mount Philo State Park, 2.5 miles east, for camping. The Lake Champlain Maritime Museum provides tours to historical shipwrecks 15 miles southwest. A couple of restaurants and markets are on the Ferry Road in Charlotte, 3 miles north, with more variety in Shelburne Village, 9 miles north.

TRIP 34
ALLEN HILL

Location: Shelburne, VT
Rating: Easy
Distance: 1.9 miles round-trip
Elevation Gain: 120 feet
Estimated Time: 1.5 hours
Maps: USGS Burlington; shelburnevt.org/departments/339.html

This hike along Lake Champlain passes through a rare cedar/pine forest and offers plenty of opportunities for swimming.

DIRECTIONS

From the traffic light at US 7 in Shelburne Village, go west on Harbor Road for 1.6 miles and turn right onto Bay Road. Drive 0.5 mile to Shelburne Bay Park on the left. Pass the parking lot closest to the road and drive to the lot next to the lake (space for about 50 cars). *GPS coordinates:* 44° 24.08′ N, 73° 14.23′ W.

TRAIL DESCRIPTION

Allen Hill (220 feet) is a steep, rocky knob on the edge of Lake Champlain that supports a limestone-bluff cedar/pine forest that is rare in Vermont. Three parallel trails in Shelburne Bay Park lead to the hill, making hiking loops possible. The most scenic route follows Clarke Trail along the shore to the Allen Hill Trail loop and returns via Clarke Trail. The other two trails leading to Allen Hill Trail are wooded, without the regular views and lake access that make Clarke Trail so appealing. Cross-country skiers and hikers of all ages will enjoy the combination of woods and shore along the 0.5-mile Clarke Trail; kids about ages 4 and older will be able to complete the 0.9-mile loop over Allen Hill. In winter, the loop is better suited to snowshoes than it is to skis. Lookout ledges near the summit perch on tall cliffs; use caution. Dogs must be leashed.

Clarke Trail begins where the parking area and grassy lawn border the woods. Initially, it follows a wide gravel path through a dark stand of cedar, hemlock, and white pine. Numerous short side trails lead to smooth rock ledges that slide gently into Shelburne Bay. After the third side trail to the lake, Clarke Trail becomes narrower and more rugged. Bog bridges over a damp area lead to a short climb up slanted bedrock, followed by more bog bridges.

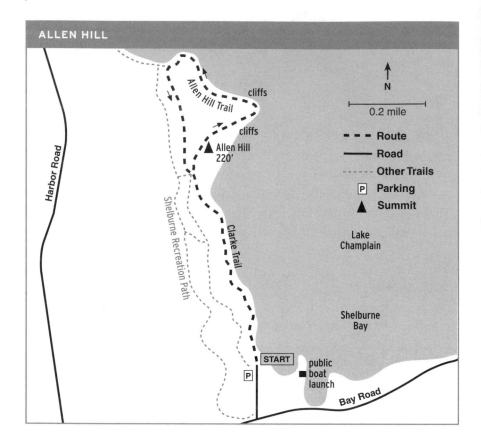

Following the shoreline north, you wander through open grassy areas, dark conifer stands, and muddy spots where water trickles from the ledgy hillside.

Descend from the bluff onto a shaded, gravelly beach where a stream enters the lake, then climb through red oaks and trout lilies to arrive at a five-way junction on the hillside. The left trail leads through the woods back to the parking lot. Straight ahead, a connector trail leads to the wide, graded Shelburne Recreation Path. The two right legs are the beginning and end of Allen Hill Trail. Take the first right turn—which is actually a couple of steps back downhill toward the lake—and follow the east leg of Allen Hill Trail 0.2 mile up a steep slope to the summit. Trillium and hepatica grow between oaks on the dry, rocky sides and flat top of Allen Hill. Look for chestnut oaks here, with their deeply grooved bark and toothed—rather than lobed—leaves.

Leaving the high point, Allen Hill Trail descends gradually, skirting the cliffy edge of the limestone bluffs; use caution here. Northern white cedars line the top of these headlands, giving way to white pine and hemlock as you drop to lake level. Rounding the northern tip of this peninsula, a sandy beach

The diverse landscapes of Allen Hill—lake shore; deep, shady forests; high bluffs—make this short hike a fun and interesting outing for the whole family.

appears on your right, and Allen Hill Trail turns left where a short connector trail leads straight ahead to the Recreation Path. Turn left, leaving the lakeshore for a shady pine forest full of big old trees, some hollow and some pocked with the rectangular holes of pileated woodpeckers. A short climb over the shoulder of Allen Hill brings you beneath steep, mossy cliffs—look up to see the summit you were just on. In early spring, bloodroot blooms in these woods, opening its white petals in the sunlight and closing them up at night.

A gradual descent brings you back to the five-way junction. Go left, returning to the parking lot via Clarke Trail.

DID YOU KNOW?

Northern white cedars, also called arbor vitae—"tree of life"—dominate in environments with difficult conditions: coniferous swamps and dry, rocky cliffs.

MORE INFORMATION

Shelburne Bay Park is managed by the Town of Shelburne Parks and Recreation Department, P.O. Box 88, Shelburne, VT 05482; 802-985-9551.

NEARBY

An interpretive paddle trail exploring Shelburne Bay begins at the boat launch next to the park. Shops are in Shelburne Village, 2 miles southeast.

TRIP 35
COLCHESTER POND

Location: Colchester, VT
Rating: Easy to Moderate
Distance: 3.2 miles
Elevation Gain: 150 feet
Estimated Time: 2 hours
Maps: USGS Essex Center and Colchester; wvpd.org/colchesterpond. htm

Walk through open farm fields and shady woods as you circle the quiet waters of this mile-long pond.

DIRECTIONS
From the junction of US 2 (also US 7) and VT 2A in Colchester, go east on VT 2A for 0.8 mile to the center of Colchester Village. Turn left onto East Road and proceed 1.0 mile, then turn right onto Depot Road. Drive 2.3 miles to a fork and bear left onto Colchester Pond Road. In 2.2 miles, bear right into the Colchester Pond parking area (space for 18 vehicles). *GPS coordinates:* 44° 33.05′ N, 73° 07.50′ W.

TRAIL DESCRIPTION
Colchester Pond Natural Area is a quiet refuge in a busy part of Vermont. With Indian Brook Reservoir Park on its eastern border and Milton Town Forest to the north, the pond lies within a tract of more than 1,600 acres of contiguous forest. Walking the circumferential trail brings you through different stages of land use and forest succession, from hayfields to abandoned orchards to young forests growing over old pastures.

Colchester Pond's loop trail begins next to a kiosk. Leash your dog before heading down the grassy slope past the boat launch for paddle craft on the water's edge. The trail turns left and follows the shoreline northward. Pass through small stands of shagbark hickory, basswood, and sumac between hayfields that rise to a scenic barn on your left. Sections of bog bridges keep your feet out of the soggy soil.

The trail enters woods halfway up the length of the pond. At first it stays close to the shore, curving through white pines and passing clearings with access to the water. Then it begins a gentle climb into a mixed hardwood forest, stay-

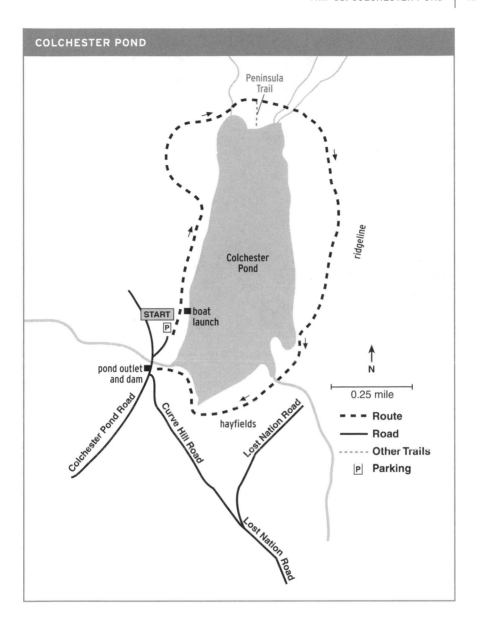

COLCHESTER POND

ing high on the hillside for a short time before descending again to water level. As you approach the top of the pond, a rocky opening in the trees reveals a picturesque view southward across the water, providing an opportunity to spot ducks swimming or—if you're lucky—a bald eagle soaring. Colchester Pond attracts many species of birds and has been designated an Important Birding Area by the Lake Champlain Birding Trail. Canada geese, mallards, great blue herons, and common and hooded mergansers are some of the more frequent

Colchester Pond's loop hike features fields, pond and marsh shores, woods, and a walk along the crest of a ridge.

visitors. If you visit at dusk, you may be treated to barred owls calling *who-cooks-for-you?*

The trail rounds the damp north end of the pond on a series of step stones and bog bridges; it then climbs a small hill to the junction of Peninsula Trail. This path leads south 425 feet down a gentle slope to a clearing and water access. This promontory provides the last good swimming opportunity until you return to the trailhead. Continue straight on the main trail, descending to cross several threads of inlet streams.

After this soggy area, clamber up rocky ledges and switchbacks on the steep hillside. By the time you've mounted the ridge that follows the eastern side of the pond, thick woods prevent any views of the water below. Walk south along the relatively flat height-of-land on the remains of a narrow road. This area was once cleared of woods and used agriculturally—probably as pasture—but it's difficult to imagine a farmer driving anything with wheels across this rough rocky road. Watch for red efts (the juvenile stage of the eastern, or red-spotted, newt), which gravitate to these muddy, mossy areas.

The trail becomes smoother and the woods drier as you descend to walk a long string of bog bridges and emerge in a meadow with views of the pond. Cross several hayfields on your way to the marshy south end of the pond, where the trail returns to the shoreline. As the trail curves northward over bog bridges, tall cattails sprout up amid thick shoreline vegetation on one side, and a fence, grown over with honeysuckle and raspberries, lines the other. At the end of this verdant corridor, the trail hits dirt again and climbs to the road next to the pond's outlet. Turn right onto the road and walk onto a bridge. Look down from its left side to see the 25-foot-tall dam that controls the pond's water level. Continue across the bridge to the trailhead parking area.

DID YOU KNOW?

Invasive species such as common buckthorn don't get eaten by Colchester Pond's wildlife, so they have an advantage over species that are a source of food. As invasive species overtake habitat, animals in search of food are displaced and whole food chains are disrupted. Winooski Valley Park District actively removes invasive species to encourage native ones to thrive here.

MORE INFORMATION

Colchester Pond Natural Area is open dawn to dusk. Dogs must be leashed. Motorized boats, motorized vehicles, bicycles, and campfires are not permitted. Winooski Valley Park District, Ethan Allen Homestead, Burlington, VT 05408; 802-863-5744; wvpd.org.

NEARBY

Some dining options are available on Main Street and Blakely Road (VT 127) in Colchester, with more just south in Winooski. Niquette Bay State Park has a sandy swimming beach 7 miles west on US 2. Camping is available near Mallets Bay in Colchester and at North Beach in Burlington, 9 miles south.

TRIP 36
EAGLE MOUNTAIN

Location: Milton, VT
Rating: Easy
Distance: 2.1 miles round-trip
Elevation Gain: 200 feet
Estimated Time: 1 hour
Map: USGS Georgia Plains

A peaceful hike through woods rich with wildflowers leads to the highest point on Vermont's Lake Champlain shoreline.

DIRECTIONS
From I-89 Exit 17, go west on US 2 for 2.4 miles. Turn right onto Bear Trap Road and travel 1.8 miles to a fork. Bear left toward the barn and then turn left at the T onto Cadreact Road. Follow Cadreact Road for 2.0 miles to a stop sign. Go straight onto Beebe Hill Road and drive 0.9 mile. Turn left onto Henry Road and drive a little over 0.1 mile to the parking lot at its end. (Note: The Henry Road trailhead was built in 2012 to replace the Cold Spring Road trailhead.) *GPS coordinates: 44° 40.28′ N, 73° 12.08′ W.*

TRAIL DESCRIPTION
Eagle Mountain (578 feet) was a pasture and sugar bush not too many years ago, but today it is a forest of rich variety. The limestone-bluff cedar/pine forest found here is increasingly rare in Vermont, and the 226-acre natural area encompasses a remarkable diversity of wildflowers, including trillium, hepatica, false Solomon's seal, jack-in-the-pulpit, bloodroot, white baneberry, and blue cohosh. Eagle Mountain's trails are appropriate for hikers of all ages. Hoyt Lookout is a good destination for cross-country skiers, while the summit's slightly steeper, rockier slope may be more easily climbed with snowshoes.

From the parking area, Blue Trail follows diamond-shaped markers across a field, bears left between two rows of trees, and climbs gradually to arrive at the edge of the woods at 0.25 mile. Enter a forest of cedar, maple, and hophornbeam, with large, blocky, moss-covered rocks. Curving left, cross over an old stone wall. At 0.3 mile, you will arrive at a T junction where Blue Trail descends left toward Hoyt Lookout and the 0.2-mile Yellow Trail goes right to the summit. Blue and Yellow are the new (as of 2012) names for what were

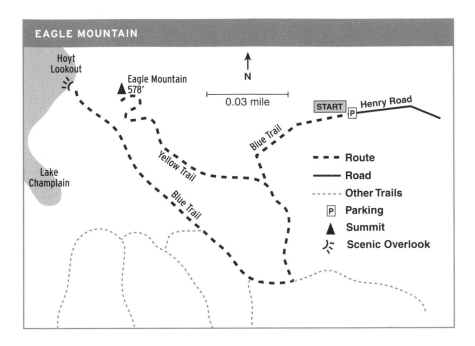

previously called Trail 1 and Trail 2. Turn right on Yellow Trail and ascend a moderate pitch. Look for the red-and-black segmented bodies and numerous tiny red legs of millipedes crawling across rotting birch trunks here.

In a short distance, Yellow Trail turns sharply right where a discontinued trail continues straight. Cross a rocky hillside and curve left up the hill. In spring, this slope supports a patch of large-flowered trillium, which blossom white and then turn pink as they age and wither. When Eagle Mountain was farmed, this wooded hillside sheltered animals such as the horses that helped with the sugaring operation. Today, the horses have been replaced by white-tailed deer, porcupines, mink, fishers, foxes, and bobcats. At 0.5 mile, you will arrive on the thickly wooded summit, which is marked by four rock cairns and is the highest point along the Lake Champlain shoreline in Vermont. The views are not at Eagle Mountain's summit, despite its elevation, but a little farther down the trail at Hoyt Lookout.

Return down Yellow Trail to the junction with Blue Trail and continue straight, descending on Blue Trail to another T junction in a clearing. The discontinued trail to Cold Spring Road is on the left. Turn right, staying on Blue Trail, and notice a large rock outcrop on your right. This dolomite bedrock leaches calcium into the soil, part of the reason these woods are so hospitable to a wide variety of wildflowers and plants. Walk through a large, flat field of

Hoyt Lookout gives a view of Lake Champlain's islands and the Adirondacks. Turkey vultures often soar over the lakeshore here.

goldenrod, milkweed, and Queen Anne's lace and reenter the woods. Climb gradually for about 0.3 mile to Hoyt Lookout and its tree-framed view west.

Lake Champlain's Inland Sea—its eastern arm—opens in front of you. The small islands of Lower and Upper Fishbladder are centered in your view, while Savage Island stretches to the north and Cedar Island is just visible to the south. What looks like mainland beyond these small islands is actually the broad expanse of Grand Isle; slivers of Main Lake are visible beyond it.

DID YOU KNOW?

The dolomite bedrock underlying Eagle Mountain was once the floor of an ocean. The calcium it provides to the soil is from seashells slowly dissolving.

MORE INFORMATION

Lake Champlain Land Trust donated Eagle Mountain Natural Area to the Town of Milton and retains a conservation easement (One Main Street, Burlington, VT 05401; 802-862-4150; lclt.org).

NEARBY

Swim and picnic at Sand Bar State Park, 7 miles southwest. Camp at Grand Isle State Park, 15 miles west. Food is along US 7 in Milton, 7 miles southeast.

TRIP 37
BURTON ISLAND

Location: Saint Albans, VT
Rating: Easy
Distance: 2.8 miles round-trip
Elevation Gain: Minimal
Estimated Time: 2 hours
Map: USGS Saint Albans Bay

This island hike passes through woods and fields teeming with wildflowers and along rocky shorelines with astounding views and plenty of swimming.

DIRECTIONS

From US 7 (South Main Street) in downtown Saint Albans, turn west onto Lake Street (VT 36). Go 2.9 miles (Lake Street becomes Lake Road) to Saint Albans Bay, and stay on Lake Road as it swings right along the bay. After crossing the bay's inlet, turn left onto Hathaway Point Road. After 2.8 miles, Hathaway Point Road runs directly into Kill Kare State Park (space for about 100 cars). Ferry service runs in season from Kill Kare to Burton Island ($4 per person round-trip), or you can boat the approximately 0.8 mile in your own craft. Off season, park on the side of Hathaway Point Road, being careful not to block the gate, and carry your boat in about 0.2 mile. Winter explorers will need to have a dependable craft or reliable ice thickness to get to Burton Island. *GPS coordinates:* 44° 46.74′ N, 73° 10.89′ W.

TRAIL DESCRIPTION

Burton Island has 253 acres of nearly flat woods, fields, and marshes ringed by rocky Lake Champlain shoreline. A campground, swimming beach, and marina are at the north end, but most of the rest of the island is undeveloped. Several trails link to make a beautiful 2.8-mile hike around the edge of the island.

From the marina, follow the campground road along the north shore, keeping right at all junctions to stay near the water. Where the road ends, North Shore Self-Guided Nature Trail departs into a tunnel of staghorn sumac. Numbered posts along this 0.4-mile stretch to Eagle Bay correspond to an interpretive brochure available at the campground office. The trail winds generally along the water's edge, the forest shifting between dark, dry cedar and

BURTON ISLAND

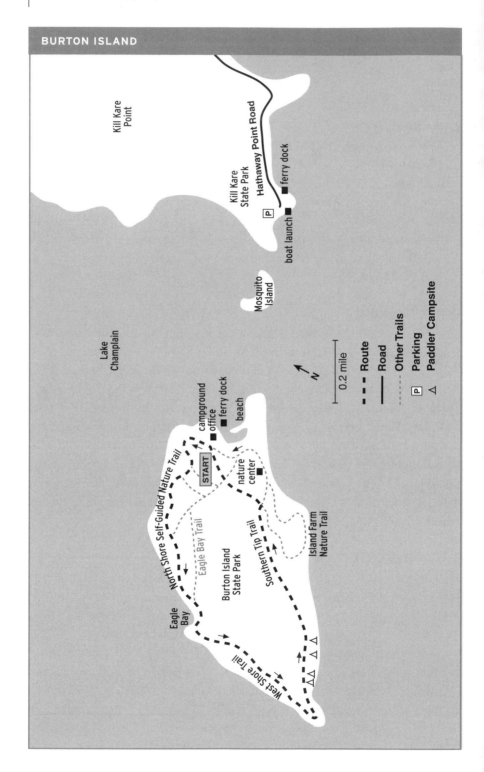

Burton Island's circumferential trail offers one exceptional view after another while passing through a variety of terrain and natural communities.

hemlock stands that are common on the rocky, thin-soiled shores to lighter, greener stands of poplar, paper birch, and ash where farm fields stood not long ago. Canada anemone, goldenrod, milkweed, dame's rocket, daisy fleabane, and bedstraw are just a few of the wildflowers that sprout in sunny, open spots around the island.

At 0.3 mile, Eagle Bay Trail leaves to the left. Continue through the trees to a curved cove. The rare sandy beach here is a treat for bare feet, making this one of the best swimming spots on the island. Startling spikes of wild red columbine sprout from pebbly ground high on the beach. A narrow peninsula defines the southern edge of the cove, giving wide views across the lake's Inland Sea. Grand Isle and North Hero lie to the west, and the low profiles of Woods and Knight islands are visible to the north.

Passing Eagle Bay, continue southwest along the shore and find the fainter, unsigned West Shore Trail climbing into the woods. The path stays mostly within the trees for the next 0.5 mile, passing a wetland before emerging on the rocky shore near the island's southern tip. Walk along the water and climb a trail to a grassy bluff with picnic tables, benches, and spectacular views south to the distant Adirondack Mountains beyond nearby Ball Island.

On the eastern side of the promontory, find the mowed two-track of Southern Tip Trail, which leads 0.7 mile back to the developed east side of the island. An outhouse perches in the woods on your left as a boardwalk leads past four paddler campsites on the right. From there the wide, grassy path meanders through sumac until it reaches its end in a field. Continue northeast on a campground road. As you approach the marina, the path to the nature center diverges to the right across a grassy lawn. From the nature center, Island Farm Nature Trail leads through a pretty marsh of sweet flag; a brochure guide is available at the campground office.

DID YOU KNOW?

During much of the past 8,000 years since Abenaki moved into this area, the lake was lower and Burton Island was part of the peninsula stretching from the mainland. By the time Europeans arrived, the lake level had risen enough to isolate this spot as an island.

MORE INFORMATION

Burton Island State Park operates Memorial Day to Labor Day; the island is open to the public year-round, but no facilities are available in the off-season. Burton Island State Park, P.O. Box 123, Saint Albans, VT 05481; 802-524-6353; vtstateparks.com/htm/burton.htm. The ferry and boat launch are operated by Kill Kare State Park, 2714 Hathaway Point Road, Saint Albans, VT 05481; 802-524-6021; vtstateparks.com/htm/killkare.htm. A day-use fee is charged unless you're camping on Burton Island. Kill Kare is open for day use only, 10 A.M. to official sunset, Memorial Day to Labor Day. Pets are not allowed in Kill Kare except en route to Burton Island.

NEARBY

Camp and swim here on Burton Island or more remotely at state parks on neighboring Woods and Knight islands. A small store and grill provide food near the marina; more food options are in Saint Albans, 6 miles east. Paddling on the lake can be difficult due to wind and waves, but the Missisquoi National Wildlife Refuge (Trip 38), 13 miles north, has a slow river and excellent wildlife watching.

TRIP 38
MISSISQUOI NATIONAL
WILDLIFE REFUGE

Location: Swanton, VT
Rating: Easy
Distance: 3.0 miles round-trip
Elevation Gain: Minimal
Estimated Time: 1.5 hours
Map: USGS East Alburg

Birds swoop, call, and float around as you pass through fields, woods, and wetlands on this flat hike to the shore of Lake Champlain.

DIRECTIONS

Follow VT 78 west from its intersection with US 7 in downtown Swanton. At 0.3 mile, cross the Missisquoi River and turn right at the stop sign, staying on VT 78. Go 5.4 miles, entering the Missisquoi National Wildlife Refuge and passing several trailheads. Turn left onto Tabor Road and travel 1.0 mile, passing the refuge headquarters and visitor center and turning left into the trailhead parking lot (space for 10 cars). *GPS coordinates:* 44° 57.24′ N, 73° 12.32′ W.

TRAIL DESCRIPTION

Missisquoi National Wildlife Refuge is an important migratory stopover for birds on the Atlantic Flyway between Canada and South America. Encompassing 6,729 acres of the Missisquoi River's bird-foot delta—so termed due to its webbed-foot appearance from above—the refuge hosts a diversity of natural communities. In addition to migratory birds, it supports many resident species, including the state-threatened spiny softshell turtle, and has Vermont's largest great blue heron rookery, on Shad Island. Old Railroad Passage Trail takes advantage of the height of an abandoned railroad bed to visit four natural communities in the refuge: field, wetland, pitch-pine bog, and lakeshore.

From the trailhead kiosk, follow the mowed path across an open field. In summer, bobolinks and savannah sparrows may be hopping about, eating insects and seeds, and tending nests hidden in the grass.

A thin line of trees on either side marks the beginning of the trail's path along the old railroad bed. In 1883, the Lamoille Valley Extension Railroad was built from what is now Swanton Town Beach to Rouses Point, New York,

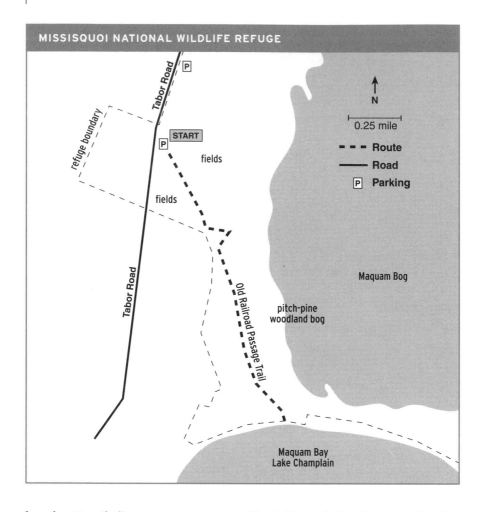

but the 11-mile line was not commercially viable and closed six months after opening. The field vegetation beyond the narrow band of trees shows its increasing sogginess with the appearance of cattails, red osier dogwood, alders, winterberry holly, and a variety of willow species. You are walking through the edges of an 890-acre open peatland called Maquam Bog.

After 0.5 mile, Old Railroad Passage Trail diverges from the rail bed on an S-curved path through a slightly elevated woodland. In the middle of it, a couple of ancient maples raise thick, gnarled limbs amid oak and beech saplings. The path passes through a stand of paper birch as it returns to the railroad bed. Ahead, the corridor stretches straight for as far as you can see; you are entering Maquam Bog—the only pitch-pine woodland bog in Vermont. In addition to many bird species, several mammal species—including the white-tailed deer, meadow vole, and red squirrel—call the bog home. The ebb and

A lakeside floodplain forest, with ferns and broadly spaced trees, is one of several interesting places this trail passes through in the Missisquoi National Wildlife Refuge.

flow of annual flooding is critical to maintain the flora and fauna here. Fires, whether caused naturally or by humans, allow the shrub understory to thrive, producing large quantities of fruits and berries—especially blueberries, which feed both wildlife and people.

The surface of the bog is peat, ranging in depths from 2 to 8 feet. Peatland water is acidic, so only a few trees can live here besides pitch pine: gray birch, black spruce, and red maple. Most of the peat is covered with low shrubs; the dominant one here is rhodora, which adorns the bog in late May with pink flowers. Other common shrubs are bog laurel, Labrador tea, leatherleaf, and sheep laurel.

Approaching Lake Champlain, the trail curves southeast and enters a lakeside floodplain forest, with silver maple, green ash, red maple, and cottonwood creating a towering canopy. Beyond the trees, Maquam Bay opens south to the Inland Sea, the northeastern arm of Lake Champlain. Look for herons wading and spearing fish along the shore, and osprey and the occasional bald eagle soaring overhead.

Retrace your steps to return to the trailhead.

DID YOU KNOW?

Before the explorer Samuel de Champlain named this lake after himself, it was called Bitawbagok, "the lake between." The lake is the western edge of the Wabanaki homeland, which extends across northern New England and the Canadian Maritime Provinces. Swanton remains a center of Wabanaki population and culture.

MORE INFORMATION

Portions of the Missisquoi National Wildlife Refuge are closed to hikers and boaters to protect sensitive habitat. Fishing, berry picking, and hunting are permitted in specific areas; obtain details at the visitor center. Camping, open fires, removal of plants or animals, snowmobiles, off-road vehicles, and overnight parking are not allowed. Dogs must be on a leash no longer than 10 feet. Missisquoi National Wildlife Refuge, 29 Tabor Road, Swanton, VT 05488; 802-868-4781; fws.gov/northeast/missisquoi.

NEARBY

The Missisquoi, Lamoille Valley, and Alburg rail trails are multiuse recreational paths exploring this region. The Northern Forest Canoe Trail's route includes Lake Champlain and the Missisquoi River. Alburg Dunes State Park, 13.4 miles southwest, has interesting geologic history and vegetation, as well a picnic area and beach for swimming. The Abenaki Tribal Museum has a small exhibit on US 7 in Swanton, 4.5 miles southeast. Food is available along VT 78 in Swanton.

4

NORTH-CENTRAL VERMONT

NORTH-CENTRAL VERMONT IS ALMOST EXCLUSIVELY MOUNTAINOUS, and a certain toughness is associated with the northern Greens. They are rugged and tall, standing more in individual peaks than in long ridges. Vermont's highest peak, Mount Mansfield (Trip 45), is recognized for its long, rocky crest, which spills over the steep walls of Smugglers' Notch in avalanches and landslides. Jay Peak (Trip 51) is known for being bare, windy, and the snowiest place in Vermont. Despite these reputations, this region has some very pleasant day hikes that are not necessarily the most strenuous in the state.

A concentration of big peaks occurs between the western-flowing Winooski and Lamoille rivers. The tall, main range of the Green Mountains forms a dramatic landscape here, leading the Long Trail and Catamount cross-country ski trail across some of its most challenging terrain. A short distance to the east, the parallel Worcester Range has steep sides and rocky summit domes, shown characteristically on its most well-known peak, Mount Hunger (Trip 41).

From the Lamoille River north to the Missisquoi River along the Canadian border, the mountains are a little lower and more spread out, with ranges less frequently explored by hikers. That relative isolation gives places like Burnt Mountain (Trip 50) a feeling of remoteness, even given the prevalence of dairy farms across the lower terrain.

TRIP 39
HUBBARD PARK

Location: Montpelier, VT
Rating: Easy to Moderate
Distance: 3.5 miles round-trip
Elevation Gain: 250 feet
Estimated Time: 1.5 hours
Maps: USGS Montpelier; montpelier-vt.org/group/246.html

Explore the deep forests, open fields, and steep ravines surrounding a stone lookout tower perched above Vermont's capitol building.

DIRECTIONS

From I-89, Exit 8, enter Montpelier on Memorial Drive. At the second traffic light, turn left onto Bailey Avenue (US 2). At the next traffic light, turn right onto State Street and drive past the statehouse, turning left onto Governor Davis Avenue. The trailhead is at the top of Governor Davis Avenue, where it meets Court Street and Greenwood Terrace. Parking on Court Street and most downtown streets is metered on weekdays from 9 A.M. to 5 P.M. but is otherwise free. *GPS coordinates:* 44° 15.74′ N, 72° 34.74′ W.

TRAIL DESCRIPTION

Hubbard Park forms the backdrop to Vermont's capitol building: a steep, wooded hillside that is emblematic of the Green Mountain State. From there, the park spreads across almost 200 acres of undulating high ground, supporting a variety of forest types and recreational pursuits, including 7 miles of hiking and skiing trails. The network of trails in the park is dense and not always clearly marked; it's a good idea to bring a map. The route described here is best suited to hikers about ages 6 and older, and is only one of countless ways to explore the landscapes of the park.

Follow Greenwood Terrace uphill about 100 feet to the trailhead on the left, where steps lead into the woods. Statehouse Trail follows a series of switchbacks that ascend through an open pine forest behind the capitol building. Nearing the top of the 0.5-mile climb, Tower Circle crosses the trail; continue straight and emerge at the base of the 54-foot stone tower. Built to resemble a crumbling castle, the tower is actually very sturdy and provides a year-round observation platform. Climb the staircase inside for views of Camel's Hump

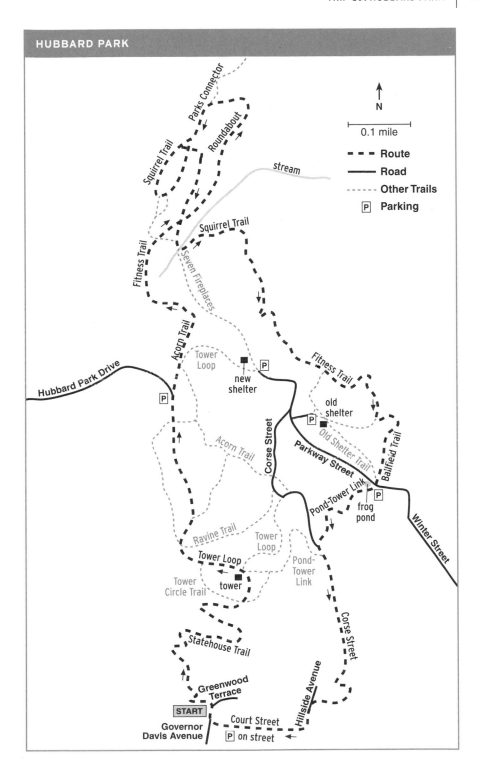

HUBBARD PARK

Hubbard Park's stone tower lets hikers climb above the trees for a view of the mountains around Montpelier, the nation's least-populous capital city, with about 8,000 residents.

(4,083 feet), Mount Hunger (3,539 feet), White Rock (3,194 feet), and the Granite Hills. Tall trees limit the view of Montpelier immediately below, but this land was mostly open fields when it was given to the city in 1899 by John E. Hubbard, a local businessman who also helped create the public Kellogg-Hubbard Library on Main Street.

From the front steps of the tower, turn left onto the wide gravel road of Tower Loop, which is shared with bikers. Descending gradually, enter a shady deciduous forest and pass several trails forking off the road in either direction. A short distance beyond the gate at Hubbard Park Drive, turn left onto Acorn Trail and descend gradually through a stand of large, older deciduous trees surrounded by young, shade-tolerant conifers. When Acorn Trail ends at Fitness Trail, bear left and pass several workout stations on a gently curving path.

You will arrive on the gravel Seven Fireplaces road, 0.7 mile from the tower. Cross the road onto Roundabout Trail. In 200 feet, cross Squirrel Trail (your return path) and walk downhill along the stream. Roundabout Trail slabs the hillside, staying high as the stream descends. After 0.3 mile, a long curve left passes two trails descending into a deer yard on the right; dogs must be leashed here in winter. In a red-pine plantation, cross Squirrel Trail at a four-way junction and emerge onto the grassy Seven Fireplaces field, with its picnic tables, stone grills, and outhouse.

At the gravel road loop, head right and immediately turn right again onto Squirrel Trail, descending into a shady hemlock forest. Mounds of moss-covered rocks lie in an intermittent streambed on the left, and crumbling logs crisscross the otherwise bare ground. Hemlocks give way to red pines at the four-way junction; go straight, staying on Squirrel Trail, and cross the steep slope of the ravine high above the stream. Cross Roundabout Trail and emerge onto the gravel road. Turn left, cross the stream, and turn left again onto the continuation of Squirrel Trail. Climb gradually for 0.2 mile and rejoin Fitness Trail. Head left, traversing a knoll and crossing a small field to enter a stand of red pines. Rise and descend a couple of times, passing behind the Old Shelter before emerging in a broad, hilly field.

Passing old apple trees, follow the path back into the woods, where it veers sharply left and drops to the grassy expanse of a ballfield. Cross it and turn right, following Ballfield Trail downhill to the frog pond at the Parkway Street gate. Cross a wide bridge at the head of the pond and climb Pond-Tower Link. At a fork just below the road, bear left and climb onto Corse Street. Turn left and exit the park, following Corse Street downhill steeply. Turn left onto Cliff Street, with its view of Montpelier, and continue downhill, merging onto Hillside Avenue before arriving on Court Street. Turn right and walk 0.6 mile on Court Street to return to the trailhead.

DID YOU KNOW?

The lookout tower was constructed using rocks salvaged from old stone walls in the area.

MORE INFORMATION

Hubbard Park is open 7 A.M. to 9 P.M. daily. Gates may be locked after dark and during mud season. Montpelier Parks, 39 Main Street, Montpelier, VT 05602; 802-223-7335; montpelier-vt.org/department/81/Montpelier-Parks.html.

NEARBY

North Branch Park has a mountain-bike trail and more walking trails, 1.5 miles north. Swim and boat at Wrightsville Reservoir, 4.5 miles north. The capitol building's lawn is a popular picnic spot. Restaurants and shops are in downtown Montpelier, 0.3 mile east.

TRIP 40
WHITE ROCK MOUNTAIN

Location: Middlesex, VT
Rating: Moderate to Strenuous
Distance: 4.6 miles round-trip
Elevation Gain: 1,558 feet
Estimated Time: 3.5 hours
Maps: USGS Middlesex; USGS Stowe

The rugged spire of White Rock provides an adventurous hike and exhilarating views.

DIRECTIONS

From downtown Montpelier, follow VT 12 north 5.3 miles and turn left onto Shady Rill Road. Go 2.1 miles and turn right onto Story Road. At 0.5 mile, stay straight to get onto Nellie Chase Road; 0.1 mile farther, bear left onto North Bear Swamp Road. Drive 1.9 miles to the parking lot (space for 15 cars) on the right. *GPS coordinates: 44° 22.31′ N, 72° 38.41′ W.*

TRAIL DESCRIPTION

White Rock Mountain (3,194 feet) is a ledgy peak off the south shoulder of Mount Hunger (3,539 feet). Open, flat terraces with panoramic views circle its summit, and the hand-over-hand scrambling required to get to the tip-top makes this one of Vermont's more exciting summits to attain. The top third of the trail up White Rock is particularly rugged, steep, and often wet, but the payoff is worth muddy feet.

From the parking lot, Middlesex Trail follows a 500-foot, blue-blazed connector trail to a dirt road; turn left and follow the road north past a metal gate. Martin's Brook gurgles mostly unseen on the left as the road climbs gradually through a mixed hardwood forest. At 0.8 mile, just after a cascade tumbles out of the woods, turn left off the road onto a footpath.

The footpath climbs moderately, curving through birches and maples and traversing occasional rock steps. After crossing a wide brook on rocks, the trail becomes wider, reminiscent of its early days as a carriage road.

After a gradual climb, the trail levels. A logged clearing can be seen through a strip of trees on the right, and the trail curves west and enters a tunnel of young beech trees.

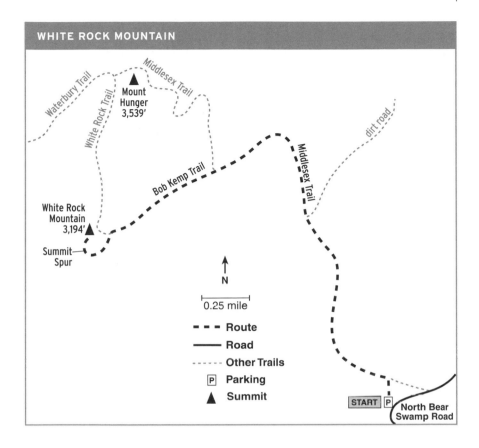

WHITE ROCK MOUNTAIN

Middlesex Trail alternately crosses and climbs a damp, ledgy hillside. At 1.6 miles, a small clearing marks a junction (Middlesex Trail turns right here toward Mount Hunger). Go straight onto the blue-blazed Bob Kemp Trail. The next 0.5 mile is steeper and more rugged than Middlesex Trail, with numerous ledges and rock steps to mount and muddy saddles to cross. After two stream crossings, a long rock escarpment slices down through the forest. Follow the trail up into a cleft in the cliff, then climb through an airy stand of paper birch with long, slightly obstructed views as the mountainside drops away on the right. The trail then climbs steeply into balsam firs, where thick mosses blanket the forest floor.

After a short scramble that requires hands as well as feet, two log bridges lead across a foamy, copper-colored pool. Tannic acid from decomposing conifers gives the water its dark color. A short distance above the pool, climb a bare rock slope into a gully and emerge onto flat, open rock with views eastward. The bald summit of Mount Hunger rises behind you, to the north. Although the views are magnificent here, they get better as you circle and

Climbing to the tip-top of White Rock Mountain is a fun scramble over rugged outcrops. Broad, flat rock terraces surrounding the summit are easier destinations with the same spectacular views.

ascend the peak. Weave through small clumps of trees across broad terraces of rock and climb to a trail junction. (Bob Kemp Trail goes right, becoming White Rock Trail as it heads north to meet Waterbury Trail just below the summit of Mount Hunger.) Go left on the 0.15 mile spur to the White Rock summit.

Cross an open rocky area with a view of Camel's Hump (4,083 feet), then climb a tricky rock pitch, where a long crack makes the best toeholds. Ascending this kind of slab using a combination of friction and balance is characteristic of hiking in the Worcester Range. Around the next curve, dramatic western views appear. The dark waters of Waterbury Reservoir snake through the hills, and the notch of the Winooski River valley points west to distant Adirondack peaks. As you continue around the curve, the profile ridge of Mount Mansfield (4,393 feet) and the pointed summit of Whiteface Mountain (3,714 feet) come into view. Hoist yourself through a crack in the boulders to clamber onto the little bare summit of White Rock.

Return the way you came up.

DID YOU KNOW?

When settlers cleared farms in Middlesex in the 1760s, White Rock and Mount Hunger were covered with trees. Later, forest fires left the peaks in their current bald state.

MORE INFORMATION

White Rock is within the C. C. Putnam State Forest, managed by the Vermont Department of Forests, Parks and Recreation; vtfpr.org. To minimize erosion along fragile, high-elevation terrain, the state closes Worcester Range trails between mid-April and Memorial Day. Green Mountain Club helps maintain trails in the Worcester Range. Green Mountain Club, 4711 Waterbury–Stowe Road, Waterbury Center, VT 05677; 802-244-7037; greenmountainclub.org.

NEARBY

Swimming holes along Shady Rill Road are well marked by a dirt road pull-off with picnic shelters, 4 miles southeast. Wrightsville Reservoir also has a public beach and boat launch, 5.2 miles southeast. Groceries, shops, and restaurants are in Montpelier, 10 miles southeast.

VERMONT'S ANCIENT, ILLOGICAL RIVERS

Logic says that water takes the path of least resistance: Rain and snowmelt flow downhill off mountains and continue downhill to the sea. The ridge of highest mountains divides the watersheds: As in the Continental Divide in the Rocky Mountains, the Green Mountains' high peaks shed water from their east side easterly and from their west side westerly. Why, then, do some rivers start on one side of a mountain range and, instead of continuing downhill to the ocean, cut through those high hills to drain on the other side?

Look at three of Vermont's big rivers: the Missisquoi, the Lamoille, and the Winooski. Each rises on the eastern side of the Green Mountains and slices through the highest ridgeline to empty into Lake Champlain on the western side. How did the water come to take such an illogical path?

The simple answer is that these three rivers have been flowing since before the Green Mountains were born. Their ancient routes were established and continued as continental plates crashed into each other and thrust mountains up around them. The Acadian Orogeny—the mountain-building period in which the Greens arose—was immensely disturbing to the landscape, but it was also immensely slow, uplifting, folding, thrust-faulting, and deforming the hills over 40 million years. During this time, the rivers continued down their paths and cut into the new mountains as they heaved upward.

Ancient rivers that predate and cut through mountain ranges are known as antecedent drainages, and there are many across North America (as well as in other mountainous parts of the world). In the Appalachian Mountains, the Potomac and Delaware rivers are prime examples. Both rivers have water gaps—places where the river slices through a ridge. Similarly, the Columbia River cuts a deep canyon through the Cascade Mountains on the Washington—Oregon border as it flows westward to the Pacific.

Since they provide passage through steep terrain, antecedent rivers are natural routes for people finding their way through the mountains. Abenaki used the relatively slow flows of the Missisquoi River for upstream canoe travel into the Green Mountains and the more rollicking descent of the Lamoille River to return through the mountains to Lake Champlain. Today, four parallel roads and a railroad take advantage of the Winooski River's mighty erosive power as it plows its illogical route through the Green Mountains' highest peaks.

TRIP 41
MOUNT HUNGER

Location: Waterbury Center, VT
Rating: Moderate to Strenuous
Distance: 4.0 miles round-trip
Elevation Gain: 2,290 feet
Estimated Time: 3.5 hours
Map: USGS Stowe

"The mountaintop is one of the pleasantest places of earth, and will be visited so long as people inhabit the country." Mount Hunger's rocky domed top was a favorite with hikers even before Middlesex resident William Chapin penned this thought in 1880, and has remained so ever since.

DIRECTIONS
From I-89, Exit 10, follow VT 100 (Waterbury–Stowe Road) north for 1.2 miles and turn right onto Guptil Road. Travel 2.0 miles to the green in Waterbury Center and bear right onto Maple Street. Go 0.2 mile and turn right onto Loomis Hill Road. Drive up Loomis Hill Road for 1.9 miles; here it curves left and becomes Sweet Road. Go 1.5 miles north on Sweet Road to the trailhead parking lot on the right (space for about 12 cars). *GPS coordinates:* 44° 24.14′ N, 72° 40.52′ W.

TRAIL DESCRIPTION
Mount Hunger (3,586 feet at the treed north summit, though the south summit where most hikes end is 3,539 feet) is a rounded bald spot at the southern end of the Worcester Range. Its rocky top is a fun place to explore, in addition to providing immense views. Waterbury Trail is moderate, but the final 0.5 mile becomes progressively steeper, with ledges to scramble up. Most older kids will enjoy doing so if they're prepared for the distance and steepness. Dogs and winter hikers may struggle to climb the steep slab.

A rocky, rooty trail leads east from the parking lot past a register box into a hardwood forest sprinkled with a few hemlocks. The climb begins gently. As the trail curves southeast, it becomes moderate. Pass between mossy boulders and climb rock steps. Listen for hermit thrush, Vermont's state bird, trilling short ethereal phrases that almost sound like they have their own echo. Named

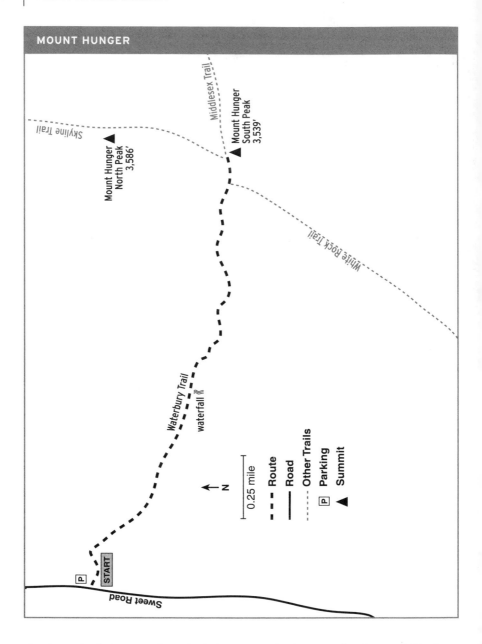

MOUNT HUNGER

Middlesex Trail

Mount Hunger
South Peak
3,539'

Skyline Trail

Mount Hunger
North Peak
3,586'

White Rock Trail

Waterbury Trail

waterfall

0.25 mile

N

— Route
— Road
·········· Other Trails
P Parking
▲ Summit

P

START

Sweet Road

for their shy behavior, these little brown-and-white songbirds are difficult to spot in a thick forest, but their haunting song is the soundtrack of many summer hikes.

Waterbury Trail climbs steadily but easily for about half a mile, then descends gradually to cross two small streams. After the second stream, the trail becomes steep and climbs to the edge of a boulder-filled stream. A scenic

Mount Hunger's rocky dome is well loved for its 360-degree views.

waterfall tumbles from above during wet weather. Continue up the eroded slope on the left side and cross the stream above the waterfall. The trail continues moderately or steeply up a rocky slope that is loose and eroded in places. Following a streambed, you will enter the boreal forest of the upper mountain. Canada mayflowers, bunchberries, and blue-bead lilies cover the forest floor beneath spindly sprigs of hobblebush, and the first steep ledge appears. Zigzag up it and continue uphill for another couple tenths of a mile to the next set of ledges. Climb cautiously on this steep rock, which may be especially slick on wet or humid days.

At 1.9 miles, between two vertical scrambles, the trail to White Rock Mountain heads right. Continue straight uphill, skirting small stands of wind-stunted trees to arrive on the rock summit. Skyline Trail leads north into the trees, passing over Hunger's forested north peak. The south peak of Mount Hunger was also treed before a fire left the rock bare. Middlesex Trail leads straight ahead, down the eastern side of the mountain, joining the trail from White Rock Mountain (3,194 feet; Trip 40).

Views from Mount Hunger are vast and unencumbered, justifying this small peak's popularity. To the south, along Hunger's descending ridgeline, are the rocky terraces and pointy summit of White Rock Mountain. To the west, the long ridge of the Green Mountains' highest peaks stretches as far as you can see south and north. The Winooski River cuts a deep gouge between Camel's Hump (4,083 feet) and Bolton Mountain (3,725 feet). Waterbury Reservoir shines in the foreground, and the craggy profile of Mount Mansfield (4,393 feet) dominates the ridgeline heading north. The eastern side of the Worcester Range is mostly low foothills, with the exception of the Granite Hills in the southeast. Mostly encompassed by Groton State Forest, this cluster of tall peaks is related to the White Mountains in New Hampshire, which are also visible on a clear day.

Return the way you came.

DID YOU KNOW?

In 1878, a road ascended the eastern side of Mount Hunger. It was broad and smooth enough to accommodate six horses pulling a carriage of 20 people to within half a mile of the summit.

MORE INFORMATION

Mount Hunger is within the C. C. Putnam State Forest. To minimize erosion along fragile, high-elevation terrain, the state closes Worcester Range trails between mid-April and Memorial Day. Vermont Department of Forests, Parks and Recreation, 5 Perry Street, Suite 20, Barre, VT 05641; 802-476-0184; vtfpr. org. The Green Mountain Club helps maintain trails in the Worcester Range. Green Mountain Club, 4711 Waterbury–Stowe Road, Waterbury Center, VT 05677; 802-244-7037; greenmountainclub.org.

NEARBY

Waterbury Center State Park, 4 miles west, has swimming and boating on Waterbury Reservoir; the Winooski River also has good paddling. Camp on the reservoir at Little River State Park, 12 miles west, or at Smugglers' Notch State Park, 12.5 miles northwest. The Green Mountain Club's Hiker Center is along VT 100 in Waterbury Center, 4.5 miles west. Food is along VT 100 in Waterbury, 7 miles south, or in Stowe, 7 miles northwest.

TRIP 42
MOSS GLEN FALLS

Location: Stowe, VT
Rating: Easy
Distance: 0.8 mile round-trip
Elevation Gain: 150 feet
Estimated Time: 45 minutes
Maps: USGS Stowe; USGS Mount Worcester

Hike alongside one of Vermont's tallest cascades as it spills through a deep scenic gorge.

DIRECTIONS

From the junction of VT 108 and VT 100 in Stowe, follow VT 100 north 3.0 miles and bear right onto Randolph Road. Travel 0.4 mile and turn right onto Moss Glen Falls Road. Go 0.5 mile to the trailhead and a pullout (space for about 10 cars) on the left. *GPS coordinates:* 44° 29.11′ N, 72° 37.62′ W.

TRAIL DESCRIPTION

Moss Glen Falls reveals itself to hikers in small doses. When you first reach the base of the falls and spy the lower cascade around the corner of a rock wall, you'll feel like you've discovered a small treasure. You will view the upper falls higher on the trail and think you've experienced its full grandeur, but above that, a slot canyon directing the upper river to the precipice is a remarkable sight on its own. In all, the tiered waterfall drops 125 feet, making it one of the tallest in Vermont. While the hike is short and easy enough for most ages, the trail follows close to the edge of the gorge in places; warn young hikers, and keep them close by as you climb.

From the trailhead, you will cross wet ground on bog bridges and step stones. The trail curves through shrubby vegetation a short distance from Moss Glen Brook and then follows its bank, passing through yellow and paper birch. After walking alongside a brushy clearing, look for a beaver dam impounding the stream. Dams are remarkably durable due to beavers' vigilance in inspecting and repairing them, and they serve an important role in the succession of wetlands. Beavers remove a lot of the woody plants in the area of their pond, and then when nearby food runs out, they move on. The dam

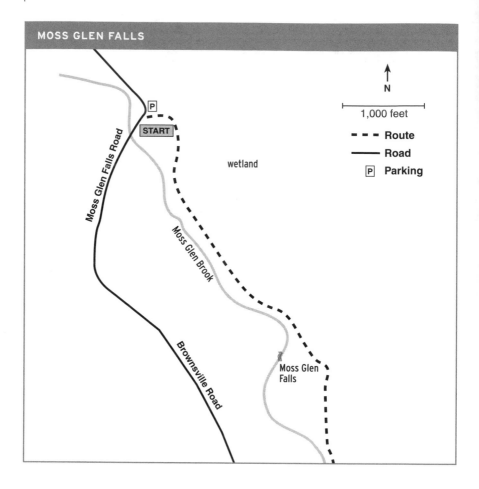

MOSS GLEN FALLS

P

START

Moss Glen Falls Road

Moss Glen Brook

Brownsville Road

wetland

Moss Glen
Falls

N

1,000 feet

- - - Route

——— Road

P Parking

eventually fails and mud flats are left, providing a variety of changing habitats as the area becomes vegetated again.

Enter a dimmer, more mature forest with yellow birch, maple, and hemlock. A stony beach gives access to the stream and views of the scenic tall forest on the steep opposite bank. The trail begins to climb, and after the first, short pitch, a side trail leads right; head down it for a view of the lower falls. Pick your way upstream to a place where the steep ravine opens enough to give you a view of the base of the waterfall.

Return to the main trail and turn right, climbing steeply. The trail becomes indistinct when the understory vegetation disappears in the shadows of the thick hemlock canopy. The route up the ledge can be accomplished in switchbacks or by going more directly up the hill; however you go, be aware of the steep drop on your right and, after cresting this pitch, directly in front of you. Leash your dog if you haven't done so already. As you climb onto a flat shelf,

Moss Glen Falls' 125-foot-tall cascade is a stunning sight after a short, pretty walk from the road.

the midpoint of the hike, the upper falls appear between tree branches. The highest part of the drop plummets from a narrow canyon into a pool, followed by the longest drop of the falls, spilling down a rock face directly in front of you. Rock walls rise above and drop out of sight below.

Continue uphill over mossy rocks along the edge of the cliff. As the ground levels, you can walk along the canyon that leads the stream to the top of the waterfall. It's easy to see why a hydropower dam once spanned this narrow, deep gorge, though there's no sign of it today. In a short distance, the cliffs recede and the environment changes character dramatically: The stream winds lazily through a relatively flat meadow and an open hardwood forest with an old dirt road on the left. This bucolic setting is a relaxing place to sit and have a snack.

Descend the way you hiked up.

DID YOU KNOW?

The top of Moss Glen Falls is called a plunge: The water drops over an edge and loses contact with rock. Below that is a horsetail, where the waterfall contacts the rock for part of the drop, then plunges off it. The bottom is a fan, where water spreads horizontally across rock as it descends.

MORE INFORMATION

No camping or fires are allowed at Moss Glen Falls Natural Area, which is within the C. C. Putnam State Forest, managed by the Vermont Department of Forests, Parks and Recreation; vtfpr.org/lands/vtna.cfm.

NEARBY

Waterbury Center State Park off VT 100 in Waterbury Center, 11.3 miles south, provides swimming, boat rentals, and boat access to Waterbury Reservoir. Food is available in Stowe, along VT 100 and VT 108 (Mountain Road). The Vermont Ski and Snowboard Museum has exhibits chronicling the evolution of winter sports in Vermont, 4.3 miles south on VT 100. The Green Mountain Club Visitor Center and Headquarters is just north of the village of Waterbury Center, 9.6 miles south on VT 100.

TRIP 43
WIESSNER WOODS

Location: Stowe, VT
Rating: Easy
Distance: 1.5 miles
Elevation Gain: 100 feet
Estimated Time: 1 hour
Maps: USGS Stowe; USGS Sterling Mountain; Stowe Land Trust map, stowelandtrust.org/fileadmin/slt/docs/Wiessner_Trail_map_new.pdf

Tall hemlocks and bubbly brooks characterize this leisurely loop walk to a bench with a quintessential Vermont view.

DIRECTIONS

From the junction of VT 100 and VT 108 in Stowe Village, take VT 108 (Mountain Road) 3.3 miles and turn right onto Edson Hill Road. Drive 0.5 mile and, just past Stowehof Inn, turn right into a drive. Parking is in a lot on the left (space for 8 cars). *GPS coordinates:* 44° 29.81′ N, 72° 43.62′ W.

TRAIL DESCRIPTION

Wiessner Woods is a lovely, shady forest sprawling over 79 acres near Stowe Village. Its network of wide trails is inviting for hikers of all ages as it ambles over rolling ground, passing through stands of mature trees and crossing small brooks.

From the parking area, cross a private driveway and a grassy lawn to a kiosk at the trailhead. Enter Wiessner Woods on a broad dirt path and immediately cross a wide bridge over a stream. Blue pawprint trail markers let you know that you're on a section of the Catamount Trail, a 300-mile cross-country ski and snowshoe trail that extends the length of Vermont (see Appendix). Follow the flat path through birch, maple, and broad patches of jewelweed, a native plant that sends up soft leggy stems in spring and dangles a small orange or yellow open-mouthed flower between June and September.

Around a bend, white pines surround the Four Corners junction at 0.1 mile. Meadow Trail, your return route, rises gently to the left; Main Street continues straight ahead. Go right, following the Catamount Trail, also called Hardwood Ridge Trail here. The path narrows and crosses a long line of bog bridges before entering a lovely, mature hemlock forest. The thick canopy of these large trees blocks so much sun that few plants grow in the understory;

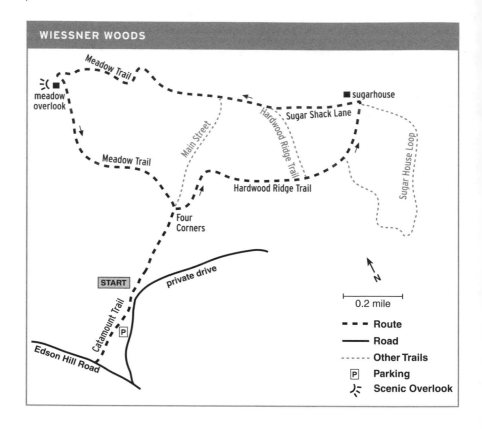

the ground is covered with copper needles and the soft, mossy remains of rotting logs. Dip through a stream valley before climbing out of the conifers. At 0.4 mile, by the Gnome Home (you'll recognize it when you get there), Hardwood Ridge Trail goes left; stay straight on the Catamount Trail. Pass the junction for Sugar House Loop on your right and reach the boundary of Wiessner Woods. The large, metal-roofed sugarhouse (actually a privately owned warming hut) stands in a clearing here. Check the mailbox for a surprise; if the flag is up, a bag of dog treats is probably stuffed inside.

Reenter Wiessner Woods and turn right, following Sugar Shack Lane over bog bridges along a wide, rolling trail. As you pass through this moist area, watch for patches of wood sorrel, which looks much like clover growing low to the ground. Its heart-shaped leaves have a thirst-quenching lemony flavor, but eat just a couple; the sourness comes from oxalic acid, which is toxic in large amounts. Delicate white flowers veined with dark pink bloom above the leaves between June and August.

After crossing the Bridge of Si's, Sugar Shack Lane gives way to Hardwood Ridge Trail, continuing in the same, northwesterly direction. You will pass

Catamount Trail, a long-distance cross-country ski trail stretching the length of Vermont, uses the gentle paths of Wiessner Woods on its route through Stowe.

several junctions where private trails lead to the right and Main Street departs left (returning to Four Corners). After the junction with Main Street, the trail is called Meadow Trail, and it passes into a stand of relatively young conifers. Unlike in more mature forests, these smaller trees let some sunlight through to the forest floor, encouraging thick undergrowth. Meadow Trail dips through a stream valley and climbs out the other side to a wooden bench alongside a stone wall. A large field rolls away on the other side of the wall below the gently rounded Dewey Mountain (3,323 feet).

From the bench, follow Meadow Trail downhill through a mixed hardwood forest. After crossing a stream, enter the widely spaced pine forest once again and soon arrive at Four Corners. Turn right to follow the Catamount Trail out to the trailhead.

DID YOU KNOW?

Jewelweed is also commonly called spotted touch-me-not for its tendency to burst and fling seeds when disturbed late in the season. It can be used to soothe itching from poison ivy, poison oak, and stinging nettle: Break open the stem and rub it on the affected area; the juice inside the stem can help stop the itch.

MORE INFORMATION

Wiessner Woods is for day-use hiking, skiing, and snowshoeing only; no camping, fires, mountain bikes, horses, or hunting. Please respect surrounding private property by parking in the designated lot and observing No Trespassing signs. Keep dogs under control and clean up after them. Please stay on the marked trail to protect plants, nesting sites, and fragile habitats. Wiessner Woods is owned and managed by the Stowe Land Trust, P.O. Box 284, Stowe, VT; 802-253-7221; stowelandtrust.org.

NEARBY

Swim and paddle at Waterbury Center State Park, 11 miles south. The Winooski and Lamoille rivers both have whitewater and flatwater paddling. Camp near a scenic waterfall and swimming hole at Smugglers' Notch State Park, 4 miles northwest. Food and shops are along VT 100 and VT 108 in Stowe, 4 miles southeast.

WHERE ARE THE CATAMOUNTS?

Catamounts seem to be everywhere in Vermont. The big, tawny-colored mountain lion is the unofficial state animal (the official one is the Morgan horse), appearing as the mascot of the state university and in the names of local companies and organizations. But you'll look in vain for a live catamount—also called eastern mountain lion, cougar, puma, or panther. The last confirmed one in Vermont was killed in 1881.

Nowadays, hikers (and, more often, drivers) see other animals—white-tailed deer, moose, beaver, turkey, loon, and osprey—that were scarce or missing from Vermont in the last century. So where is the catamount?

When colonists arrived in Vermont in the seventeenth century, they cleared forests for farms. According to the Vermont Fish and Wildlife Department, the state was at its barest in the 1840s, with 60 percent cleared. This loss of habitat led to dwindling numbers or the complete disappearance of many native animals. A cultural zeal to exterminate predators completed the job, driving catamounts out of the northeastern United States altogether. Over the past century, changing economies led to regrowth of the region's vast woods—today Vermont is 78 percent forested—and changing attitudes about wildlife and the value of complete ecosystems supported the return of many native species.

But the road back has been more challenging for the big cat that—at more than 100 pounds and 7 feet long from nose to tip of tail—towers over its 35-pound, 3½-foot-long kin, the bobcat and lynx. Female catamounts don't move far from where they were born, so it takes a long time for populations to spread.

Many people believe, however, that the catamount is back. Dozens of sightings are reported each year to the Vermont Fish and Wildlife Department. Biologists who investigate catamount sightings agree that some may be big cats, but believe that observers have spotted escaped or intentionally released exotic pets. No one has yet found any "field evidence" of a breeding population, such as tracks, scat, kill remains, scent mounds, or a body.

In March 2011, the U.S. Fish and Wildlife Service declared the catamount extinct. Despite that, the Vermont Fish and Wildlife Department maintains a "Vermont Catamount Sighting Form" on its website. Apparently, members of the department, like many other Vermonters, hope to find that elusive cat back in the wild—rather than just on a sports jersey.

TRIP 44
STOWE PINNACLE

Location: Stowe, VT
Rating: Moderate
Distance: 2.8 miles round-trip
Elevation Gain: 1,520 feet
Estimated Time: 2.5 hours
Map: USGS Stowe

The Pinnacle's rocky knob provides dramatic close-up views of the Worcester Range and the pastoral Stowe Valley.

DIRECTIONS

From the junction of VT 100 (Main Street) and VT 108 (Mountain Road) in Stowe, head north on VT 100 and take your third right onto School Street. After 0.2 mile, when Taber Hill forks left, bear right onto Stowe Hollow Road. After 0.8 mile, at the junction with Covered Bridge Road, go left to stay on Stowe Hollow Road. After another 0.7 mile, when Stowe Hollow Road turns right, stay straight to get onto Upper Hollow Road. Follow this 0.6 mile to the parking lot (space for about 9 cars) on the left, just past Pinnacle Road (also on the left). *GPS coordinates: 44° 26.19′ N, 72° 40.04′ W.*

TRAIL DESCRIPTION

Stowe Pinnacle (2,651 feet) is a rocky bald spot poking out of the side of the Worcester Range, giving hikers unrivaled views of the high peaks of north-central Vermont. The steepness of the climb makes the short hike vigorous, and the open summit is a good picnic spot. This is a popular hike in a popular resort town, so don't expect solitude, but you can look forward to the wide-open skies and long views usually reserved for higher summits.

Stowe Pinnacle Trail starts through an overgrown field before entering woods. Blue blazes mark the route as it ascends gradually over bog bridges and large step stones through maples, white pine, and paper birch. An over-grown rock cairn, continuously built up by hikers over the years, sprawls in the middle of the trail at the point where the climb becomes more sustained.

Stowe Pinnacle Trail takes the most direct route up a steep, wooded ridge between two stream valleys. Rock staircases provide a relatively flat treadway on this highly angled route; they prevent erosion and gullying of the trail. At

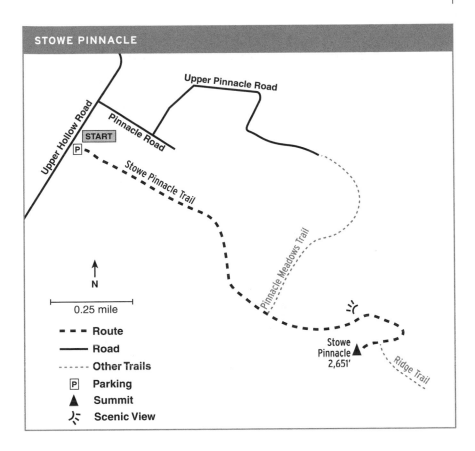

1.0 mile, catch your breath in a clearing where Pinnacle Meadows Trail leaves to the left. Climb rock steps out of the clearing and follow the blazes to the right, where an old footpath veers left.

More climbing, more ledges, and flight after flight of rock steps lead, finally, to a small saddle between two steep slopes. A spur trail leads up the left slope to a view of the ridgeline between Camel's Hump (4,083 feet) and Mount Mansfield (4,393 feet), and of the farm fields and rolling hills of Stowe. The trail to the summit continues straight ahead, curving through beech, hobblebush, and striped maple as it circles behind Stowe Pinnacle. Rock steps lead down briefly before the trail levels across the contour of the hill and then begins to climb again. A hard right turn brings you into woods full of fragrant balsam fir. Wide wooden ladders help with the scramble up vertical ledges. Just before the summit, Ridge Trail (also called Hogback Trail) departs left. Then the trees open and the views take over.

The long ridge of summits ranges from Monroe Skyline in the south, over Camel's Hump, Bolton Mountain (3,725 feet), Mount Mansfield, Whiteface

Stowe Pinnacle combines a lower-elevation hike with the long views found on Vermont's higher mountaintops. Looking south, the bumpy Northfield Mountains run parallel to the Green Mountains' highest range.

Mountain (3,714 feet); and north, past Belvidere Mountain (3,360 feet) to Jay Peak (3,858 feet) on the Canadian border.

Looming overhead to the east, the steep ridge of the Worcester Range stretches 18 miles between the Lamoille River in the north and the Winooski River to its south. Elmore Mountain (2,608 feet) is the somewhat isolated peak on its northern end. Rising steeply from there, the rocky tip of Mount Worcester (3,293 feet) is one end of the high, densely forested Skyline Trail, which traverses the spine over Hogback Mountain (3,642 feet) and the wooded north summit of Mount Hunger (3,586 feet), to Hunger's bald, south summit (3,539 feet), not visible from Stowe Pinnacle. A short distance south of Mount Hunger, a thrust of rocky ledges makes up White Rock Mountain (3,194 feet). The Worcester Range's large tracts of red spruce and balsam fir subalpine forest support the inconspicuous spruce grouse, the elusive Bicknell's thrush, and one of the boreal forest's savviest hunters, the fisher. On lower slopes, red-oak forests feed black bears, and the dense cover of mixed

Spotted joe-pye weed grows on tall stalks in damp fields, such as the open area at the beginning of Stowe Pinnacle Trail. Its pink flower clusters bloom from July through September.

hardwoods provides protection and food for breeding neotropical songbirds such as wood thrushes.

Return downhill the way you hiked up.

DID YOU KNOW?

Gold Brook Covered Bridge, just down the slope from Stowe Pinnacle's trailhead, is reportedly haunted by the ghost of a lovelorn nineteenth-century girl. Read Tim Simard's *Haunted Hikes of Vermont* for the spooky details.

MORE INFORMATION

The C. C. Putnam State Forest is managed by the Vermont Department of Forests, Parks and Recreation; vtfpr.org. The Green Mountain Club helps maintain trails in the Worcester Range. Green Mountain Club, 4711 Waterbury–Stowe Road, Waterbury Center, VT 05677; 802-244-7037; greenmountainclub.org.

NEARBY

Swim and paddle at Waterbury Center State Park, 8 miles south. The Winooski and Lamoille rivers have popular whitewater and flatwater paddling. Camp near a scenic waterfall and swimming hole at Smugglers' Notch State Park, 9.5 miles northwest. Food and shops are along VT 100 and VT 108 in Stowe, 4 miles northwest.

TRIP 45
MOUNT MANSFIELD

Location: Underhill, VT
Rating: Strenuous
Distance: 6.2 miles round-trip
Elevation Gain: 2,543 feet
Estimated Time: 4.5 hours
Map: USGS Mount Mansfield

The exceptional Sunset Ridge hike to Vermont's highest summit rises above treeline quickly for vistas, and includes a visit to the remarkable Cantilever Rock.

DIRECTIONS

From VT 15 east in Underhill Flats, bear right onto River Road, following a sign for Underhill State Park. After 2.7 miles, go straight at the stop sign in Underhill Center onto Pleasant Valley Road. In 0.9 miles, turn right onto Mountain Road, which ascends 2.5 miles to the entrance of Underhill State Park, which can accommodate 60 day-hiker vehicles in addition to overnight campers. (Winter hikers park at the Mountain Road gate and add 3 miles round-trip to the hike.) *GPS coordinates:* 44° 31.78′ N, 72° 50.52′ W.

TRAIL DESCRIPTION

Mount Mansfield's easily recognizable summit ridge appears like a profile in repose. From the Forehead (3,940 feet) at the south end, over the craggy Nose (4,060 feet), sprouted with antennae, to its highest point at the Chin (4,393 feet), and down to the Adam's Apple (4,060 feet) at the north end, the ridge stretches 2.5 miles. The high-elevation ridgeline supports the biggest patch of rare alpine tundra (see page 184) in Vermont, but to the peril of those delicate plants, more than 40,000 visitors explore Mansfield each year.

Sunset Ridge is a favorite of day-hikers for good reasons: It is one of the easier ascents (its "strenuous" rating comes more from overall distance and time than from hiking difficulty), and its relatively quick arrival on open rock means the awe-inspiring views are part of the hike, not just the reward at the summit. While this hike may be too ambitious for kids younger than about 10, the shorter trips to Cantilever Rock or onto the open rock of lower Sunset Ridge are excellent destinations on their own merits.

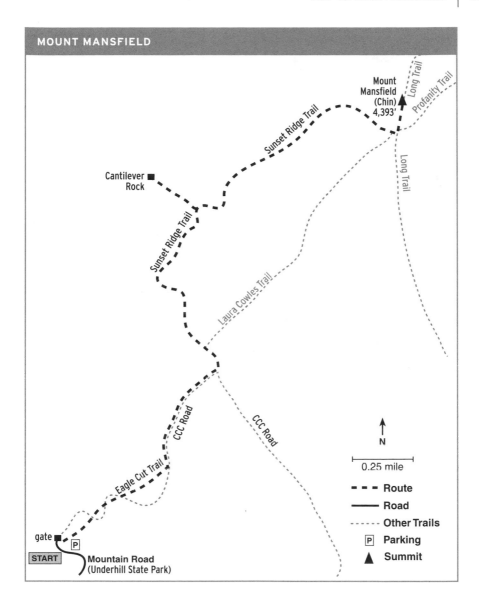

After paying a day-use fee and finding out the high-elevation weather forecast at the ranger station, follow the blue-blazed Eagle Cut Trail up a gentle pitch for 0.3 mile, crossing the CCC Road three times before turning left onto the road at your fourth encounter. Follow the CCC Road 0.4 mile to a clearing with a kiosk; turn left and cross a bridge to begin up Sunset Ridge Trail. After 0.1 mile, Laura Cowles Trail departs to the right; stay left. The wide, rocky trail heads north across the flank of the mountain, climbing moderately. After pass-

Hikers crossing Mount Mansfield's long, rugged, above-treeline ridge help protect delicate, rare tundra plants by walking only on rock or on wood bridges.

ing a small clearing, the trail gets steeper, passing cascades and a whale-sized glacial erratic.

At 0.7 mile, the spur trail to Cantilever Rock heads left. Follow it into a damp, dense conifer forest, scrambling between moss-covered boulders. In 0.2 mile, a cliff towers over a narrow canyon. Stuck in a high crack, the namesake rock juts 30 feet into open air over your head. This schist column likely ended up here due to ice and water eroding fractures in the cliff, causing occasional and sometimes drastic movement. Climb the huge boulder beneath the rock to get a view of Camel's Hump.

Return to Sunset Ridge Trail and continue climbing; you will encounter a more challenging section weaving through boulders and rocky gullies. The fragrance of balsam fir marks your arrival in the primarily coniferous forest above 2,700 feet.

Climb from a narrow gully onto open rock. The view is incredible, especially the long ridge of Mansfield looming steeply above. Minuscule hikers pick their way across the rocks between the Nose and the Chin. A large bulb of rock ahead appears to be the top of Sunset Ridge. This is the West Chin, which is closed to hiking for alpine revegetation; the summit proper is behind it. Crossing bands of rock and stunted, bent trees, you may notice lengths of thin white string at ankle height. These subtle guides help define the route and keep bootsoles off fragile vegetation; please respect the tenuous existence of rare alpine plants by stepping only on rock.

After traversing beneath the West Chin, Sunset Ridge Trail passes the top of Laura Cowles Trail and continues to the ridgeline, ending at the Long Trail. Turn left, following the Long Trail north. Pass Profanity Trail—a steep, 0.5-mile, bad-weather bypass of the Chin—on your right and climb up a rock gully to the summit. The views from here are in all directions, as you might expect when standing on the highest point in Vermont. The Adirondacks cut a jagged line across the western horizon high above Lake Champlain. Camel's Hump (4,083 feet) is the tallest point in a sea of high peaks to the south. The Worcester Range stretches across the valley to the east, while just north of the Chin, across the rugged gap of Smuggler's Notch, Spruce Peak (3,320 feet) leads northward over Madonna Peak (3,668 feet) to Whiteface Mountain (3,714 feet).

Return the way you came up.

DID YOU KNOW?

You may hear occasional loud booming while you are hiking here. Some say that's Wampahoofus, the legendary creature who lives only on Mount Mansfield and whose legs evolved to be shorter on one side of its body due to its always walking across the steep hillside. (Others say that the booming is from the Ethan Allen Firing Range in nearby Jericho.)

MORE INFORMATION

In the alpine zone, walk only on rock and keep dogs on a leash. Underhill State Park office is open Memorial Day to mid-October, 9 A.M. to 9 P.M. daily; use self-pay envelopes prior to 9 A.M. Underhill State Park, 352 Mountain Road, Underhill, VT 05490; 802-899-3022; vtfpr.org/parks/htm/underhill.htm. The Long Trail is maintained by the Green Mountain Club, 4711 Waterbury–Stowe Road, Waterbury Center, VT 05677; 802-244-7037; greenmountainclub.org.

NEARBY

Underhill Center has a small store; more dining options are on VT 15 in Jericho, 10 miles west. The Bentley Museum in Jericho exhibits some of the 5,000 snowflake photographs made by Wilson "Snowflake" Bentley after 1885, when he discovered how to photograph a single snow crystal.

THE SPARSE TUNDRA OF VERMONT

Most hikers know that climbing a mountain is similar to traveling north: The air gets cooler, the winds get stronger, and the trees get shorter and then disappear altogether as the tundra begins. The word "tundra" conjures images of arctic places—Alaska, perhaps, or Canada. But peaks that rise higher than 4,000 feet in New England exhibit the same extreme conditions. Vermont has three of these special arctic alpine zones: one each on Mount Mansfield, Camel's Hump, and Mount Abraham.

The plants you will most often see on Vermont's highest windswept peaks are grassy-looking sedges, lichens spreading over the rocks, and dwarf wildflowers adding splashes of color in spring. The word "krummholz" ("crooked wood") refers to the dense mats of stunted, bent spruce and fir trees that look more like creeping shrubs than proper trees.

Some of the plants that live above treeline in New England are arctic plants that don't occur anywhere else in the contiguous United States. They are therefore designated rare and, in some cases, threatened or endangered. These plants are adapted to the harsh life above treeline: They grow low to the ground in clusters that are designed to retain warmth and moisture; they absorb water from fog as well as from precipitation; and they photosynthesize in low light to make the most of the brief season when they aren't under a cap of snow and ice. That these plants are hardy is obvious; what isn't so easily observed is how fragile they are. While tundra plants have adapted to withstand harsh conditions, they are not equipped to contend with being trod on by 150-pound people wearing hiking boots. Imagine a lawn of Bigelow's sedge, a grassy alpine plant that can form appealing-looking meadows across open summits. When a patch of sedge is killed, its roots no longer stabilize the thin soil, and strong summit winds blow the soil away. This hole in the vegetation is now susceptible to further erosion at its exposed edges, and what started as a small patch of damage can quickly spread.

Be sensitive to the challenges of life on these harsh summits, and keep your footsteps on the rocks or the trail. If you're hiking on Mount Abraham (Trip 25), Camel's Hump (Trip 27), or Mount Mansfield (Trip 45), take time to speak with the Green Mountain Club's summit caretakers to learn more about the fragile natural communities on the summits.

TRIP 46
STERLING POND

Location: Cambridge, VT
Rating: Moderate
Distance: 3.1 miles round-trip
Elevation Gain: 1,040 feet
Estimated Time: 3 hours
Map: USGS Mount Mansfield

This scenic hike leads around a high-mountain lake perched above the steep cliffs of Smugglers' Notch.

DIRECTIONS

From the junction of VT 100 and VT 108 (Mountain Road) in Stowe, turn onto VT 108. Go 9.5 miles to parking areas on either side of the road (space for 20 cars) just beyond the height-of-land in Smugglers' Notch. (Note: The final mile is a narrow roadway with switchbacks around enormous boulders and is not passable by recreational vehicles or buses. VT 108 is closed beyond the ski area in winter; add 4 miles round-trip for a winter hike.) *GPS coordinates:* 44° 33.39′ N, 72° 47.63′ W.

TRAIL DESCRIPTION

Sterling Pond rests in a thickly forested alpine basin between Spruce Peak (3,320 feet) and Madonna Mountain (3,668 feet), both of which host ski areas. The spring-fed lake is a small refuge of beauty between these high-mountain developments. The hike to Sterling Pond Shelter is relatively short and quite popular, but looping around the far side of the pond, you are likely to find solitude on the craggy slopes before descending. Although the watery destination is appealing to children of all ages, the climb is steep in places and most enjoyable for kids about ages 8 and older.

Sterling Pond Trail ascends the east wall of Smugglers' Notch. A steep flight of rock steps climbs directly up, then turns north to cross a gully. Blue blazes lead to a break in the trees and a view of 1,000-foot cliffs across the narrow valley. These awe-inspiring crags were exposed by mile-thick glaciers that plowed through the notch for thousands of years, gouging and scraping their massive way southward until about 15,000 years ago. Today, landslides and toppling

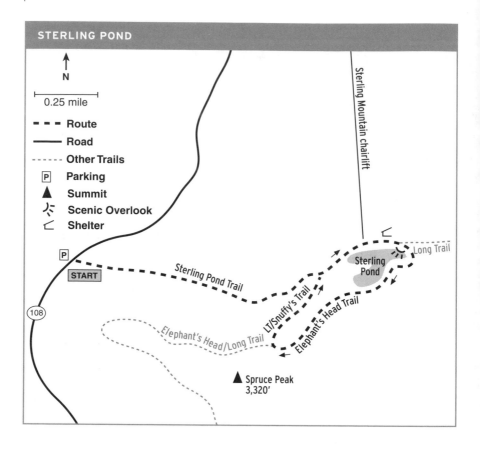

rocks are part of the normal, sometimes drastic geomorphic activities shaping the notch.

For a short distance, Sterling Pond Trail traverses the steep hillside above the notch, then turns up a drainage. Moderate pitches of rooty dirt trail are interspersed with sections of steep rock steps and stream crossings. In the dense spruce/fir forest on the upper section of Sterling Pond Trail, look and listen for high-mountain inhabitants. Red squirrels erupt in sudden annoyed chatter and leave piles of plucked spruce-cone scales, while white-throated sparrows call *old Sam Peabody-Peabody-Peabody*. In winter, snowshoe hares leave oblong tracks in the snow and fisher prints show five distinct toes.

At 0.9 mile, Sterling Pond Trail tops out at a wide swath of cleared forest. This is Snuffy's, a service road and ski trail as well as the Long Trail. Turn left, following the Long Trail's white blazes north 0.1 mile to Sterling Pond. Rock-studded soil rims this western shore, giving an open view across the water to the ridge of Madonna Mountain. Leash dogs in this sensitive area.

High above Smugglers' Notch, Sterling Pond's quiet waters reflect the northern shoulder of Mount Mansfield. Sterling Pond is Vermont's highest-elevation trout pond, supporting brook trout and the wildlife that fish for them.

Continue north on the Long Trail, crossing a log bridge at the pond's outlet and climbing onto a ridge above the water. The trail weaves through thick shoreline woods, then climbs away from the pond to cross a wide, grassy opening. Stay straight, reentering the woods and climbing to the top of the Sterling Mountain chairlift. Find white blazes on the opposite side of the lift and continue through the woods to Sterling Pond Shelter at 1.2 miles. From the shelter's southeast corner, pick up the blue-blazed Elephant's Head Trail and follow it downhill to a fork. Go right for a view across the pond to Mount Mansfield's steep ridge; return and take the left fork to continue your hike. This would be a good turnaround point for hikers who are losing steam, as there is a fair bit of climbing in the next 0.7 mile.

Elephant's Head Trail circles the eastern end of the pond and follows the southern shore over rough, rooty terrain before climbing away from the pond, weaving through huge mossy boulders, and crossing over slabs with footholds chipped into the rock. After scrambling beneath an overhang and through a narrow notch of rock, the ascent finishes steeply on an eroded trail. Pass through a hollow before meeting the Long Trail again. Elephant's Head Trail continues straight and descends steeply into Smugglers' Notch. Go right, following the Long Trail north and downhill for 0.3 mile of easy walking to the top of Sterling Pond Trail. Turn left here, descending the way you came up.

DID YOU KNOW?

Old debris slides may be recognized where stands of paper birch grow, because these trees colonize disturbed soil. Sterling Pond Trail passes through a white birch stand that is believed to have taken root after the destructive 1938 hurricane.

MORE INFORMATION

Sterling Pond's trails and shelter are maintained by the Green Mountain Club, 4711 Waterbury–Stowe Road, Waterbury Center, VT 05677; 802-244-7037; greenmountainclub.org.

NEARBY

Camp at Smugglers' Notch State Park, 3.1 miles south, across the road from the scenic Bingham Falls, which is a good spot for a picnic and a swim. The Lamoille River, 8 miles north, has whitewater and calmwater paddling options. Shops and restaurants are along VT 108 south and on VT 100 in Stowe, 9.5 miles south.

TRIP 47
ELMORE MOUNTAIN

Location: Elmore, VT
Rating: Moderate
Distance: 4.4 miles round-trip
Elevation Gain: 1,450 feet
Estimated Time: 2.5 hours
Maps: USGS Morrisville; vtstateparks.com/pdfs/elmore.pdf

This short climb to a ridgeline walk has many attractions: rock outlooks, a historical fire tower, and an unusual balanced boulder.

DIRECTIONS

From the junction of VT 12 and Beach Road in Elmore, head north on VT 12 for 0.2 mile. Turn left into Elmore State Park, where a day-use fee is charged in season. Follow the road through the campground to a parking area (space for about 15 cars) by a picnic pavilion and a metal gate. (Winter hikers follow Beach Road 0.1 from VT 12 to the park's day-use parking lot on the right. Walk through the campground to the trailhead, adding 0.7 mile round-trip to the hike distance.) *GPS coordinates: 44° 32.68′ N, 72° 32.02′ W.*

TRAIL DESCRIPTION

Elmore Mountain (2,608 feet) is a low peak at the north end of—and slightly detached from—the higher peaks of the rugged Worcester Mountain Range. Elmore's solitary location and many outlooks afford spectacular views in all directions and make rewarding destinations short of the full 2.2 miles to Balancing Rock. Lake Elmore spreads across 219 acres at the foot of the mountain, offering especially scenic views, as well as a refreshing swim afterward. This hike is appropriate for kids about ages 7 and older.

From the parking area, walk past the metal gate to follow a multiuse dirt road uphill. The road climbs gradually as it heads first west, then south, paralleling the ridge of the mountain high above and the western shore of the lake below. Catamount Trail shares this route along the flank of the mountain; a short distance from the parking lot, Beaver Trail departs right.

At 0.5 mile, Elmore Mountain Trail turns right off the road and climbs rock steps into the forest. Blue blazes mark the route through hobblebush and ferns as it continues southward along a stream. Climbing moderately, the trail

ELMORE MOUNTAIN

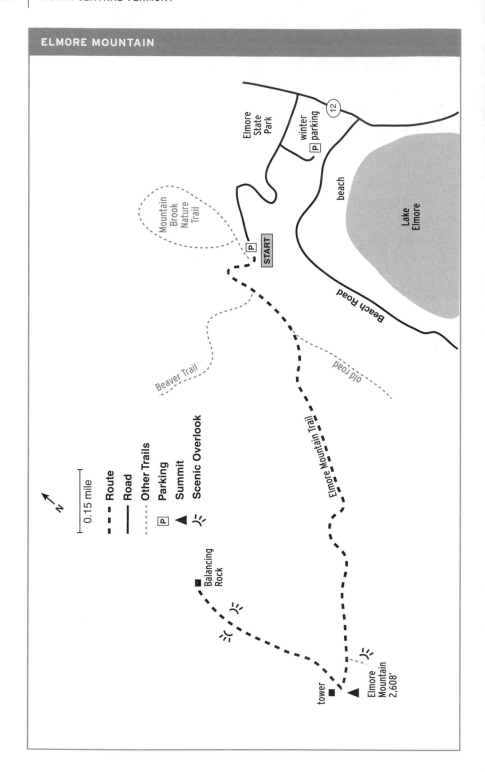

Elmore Mountain's long ridge features several rock outcrops, providing plentiful views east over Elmore Lake and west to Mount Mansfield.

crosses patches of bare bedrock and occasional step stones. A switchback to the right leads onto a rugged, rocky path through a tall maple forest. After several more switchbacks, the path flattens and the forest becomes noticeably shorter due to the elevation and exposure here. At 1.4 miles, where the trail bends right, an opening straight ahead beckons. Follow this short side trail onto rocks with an old foundation and a view east. Look up to the ridgeline to spot the 60-foot-tall fire tower above the trees. From 1938 (when the present tower was erected to replace one destroyed by that year's infamous hurricane) through 1974, a fire lookout lived in a cabin here on the ledge and hiked to the summit each day to work.

Return to the main trail and go left, continuing uphill. This final quarter-mile to the summit is steep, with scrambles over rooty sections and up steps blasted into the bedrock. A T intersection marks the top of the climb; go left to the fire tower for extensive views in all directions. The spine of the Worcester Range stretches south, and the tallest Green Mountains lie to the west, including Mount Mansfield's 4,393-foot Chin, the highest point in Vermont. Lamoille River valley farmlands spread across the landscape north of Elmore, and boats are visible on the lake beneath the eastern slope.

Return to the T intersection and follow the blue-blazed Balancing Rock Trail north 0.5 mile along the ridge. Rocky outcrops provide occasional views east and west. Around 0.4 mile, use caution exploring a prominent east-facing ledge with wide cracks and intriguing cavelike spaces. Follow the trail to its end, where a whale-sized boulder raises its mighty bulk from a precarious-looking perch on a bed of ferns. Known as a glacial erratic, this rock was left here when the glacier transporting it melted about 12,000 years ago.

A new trail connecting Balancing Rock with Beaver Trail below, which leads back to Elmore Mountain Trail, was due to be completed in late 2012, making this hike into an appealing loop. Until the new trail is constructed, return to the trailhead by retracing your path along the ridge to the fire tower and heading downhill from there.

DID YOU KNOW?

A turn-of-the-twentieth-century hotel hosted guests on the eastern slope of Mount Elmore. It was the only building on the mountain when the Civilian Conservation Corps arrived in 1934, and it was removed during development of the recreation area that became Elmore State Park in 1936.

MORE INFORMATION

Elmore State Park is open for day use from 10 A.M. to official sunset, Memorial Day through Columbus Day. Dogs are allowed except on the beach; bring proof of rabies vaccination. Elmore State Park, 856 VT Route 12, P.O. Box 93, Lake Elmore, VT 05657; 802-888-2982; vtstateparks.com/htm/elmore.htm.

NEARBY

Swimming, paddling, and camping are at the base of the mountain in Elmore State Park. The Lamoille River has good paddling as well, and mountain-bike trails can be found in Morrisville, 4.5 miles west, and Stowe, 13 miles southwest. A small general store is on VT 12 next to Elmore Lake; head to Morrisville for more food options.

TRIP 48
PROSPECT ROCK

Location: Johnson, VT
Rating: Easy to Moderate
Distance: 2.0 miles round-trip
Elevation Gain: 540 feet
Estimated Time: 1.5 hours
Map: USGS Johnson

A short, somewhat steep hike leads to panoramic cliff-top views of the braided channels of the Lamoille River and the high peaks rising steeply beyond it.

DIRECTIONS

From downtown Johnson, follow VT 15 west about 1.5 miles and turn right onto Hog Back Road. Drive 1.2 miles to the crossing of the Long Trail. Dirt pullouts are on either side of the road for parking (space for about 10 cars). *GPS coordinates:* 44° 39.11′ N, 72° 43.72′ W.

TRAIL DESCRIPTION

Prospect Rock (1,040 feet) is an open ledge jutting out of the trees above the pastoral Lamoille River valley. The hike passes through a lovely diverse forest, and the rock is broad enough to accommodate numerous picnic blankets. The ascent is vigorous, but short enough for kids about ages 8 and older to accomplish.

Start at the Long Trail crossing on Hog Back Road. The impressive hiker suspension bridge just over the bank was built in 2005 to reroute the Long Trail from a couple miles' walk along the shoulder of local roads. Head north on the white-blazed Long Trail, uphill away from the river. The first pitch is a steep climb on a wide trail through mixed hard- and softwoods, leading to a couple of switchbacks across the hill and another climb. The trail continues in this pattern of climbing steeply, crossing the hill, and climbing again for most of the distance.

The craggy southwest-facing hillside supports a diverse forest at this elevation. As you climb, you will pass hemlock, red oak, spruce, fir, birch, black cherry, red pine, red maple, and striped maple. Some striped maples have grown large here, meaning about 8 inches in diameter and 30 feet tall for this species, which grows very slowly. Striped maples are shade-tolerant, so

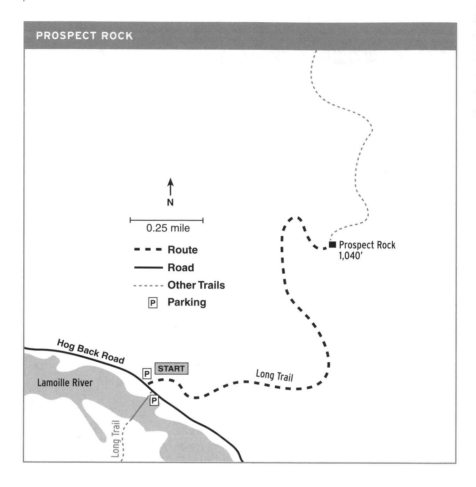

they often form the understory in mixed hardwood forests in the northeast. Because they grow mostly in the shade, their leaves are large—5 to 7 inches long and wide—which allows them to catch as much sunlight as possible. The leaves have a rounded, web-footed appearance that lends this tree the nickname "goosefoot maple." Look for striped-maple trunks with sections of their pretty green-and-white bark missing. Moose eat the bark (giving rise to the nicknames "moosewood" and "moose maple"), as do rabbit, porcupine, and deer.

Climbing into a broad saddle, follow the faint remnants of an old road along the side of Prospect Rock before turning right to switchback up the slope onto drier ground. A flat wooded area leads onto the open terraces, where a view opens broadly to the southwest and through small trees to the south. Use caution near the edges of the rock, which is steep enough and high enough to attract rock climbers. Below, the Lamoille River meanders west through

Prospect Rock overlooks the valley floodplains of the Lamoille River and the mountains of the Sterling Range.

its floodplain, which is largely cultivated. The river extends 85 miles from its headwaters in Glover to its delta in Milton, on Lake Champlain. The long ridge of the Sterling Range rises steeply from the river and points southeast to Whiteface Mountain (3,714 feet).

If you were standing on Prospect Rock about 13,000 years ago, you would have looked out over a lake formed by melting glaciers. At one point, Glacial Lake Winooski would have lapped at the edges of Prospect Rock. The massive lake was dammed by retreating glaciers; as the ice continued to melt, the lake drained partially, creating a series of subsequently lower-elevation glacial lakes. One of these, Glacial Lake Vermont, stretched across the Champlain Valley with a surface 500 feet higher than Lake Champlain's is today. Long watery arms extended high into the Green and Adirondack mountains until a sudden catastrophic failure of the ice dam released the water and the lake dropped 300 feet in just a few hours or days. The Lamoille River valley would have been revealed at that time, covered with muddy lake-bottom sediment.

Return to the trailhead the way you hiked up.

DID YOU KNOW?

Just beyond the Sterling Range, Smugglers' Notch is a narrow, cliffy gap through Vermont's highest mountains. Embargoed cattle were sneaked through the notch to markets in Montreal (which were closer than legal American markets) in the early nineteenth century. Later, fugitive slaves headed north through the gap en route to Canada, and Prohibition-era liquor headed south.

MORE INFORMATION

The Long Trail is maintained by the Green Mountain Club, 4711 Waterbury–Stowe Road, Waterbury Center, VT 05677; 802-244-7037; greenmountainclub.org.

NEARBY

The Lamoille River is popular for paddling, and the multiple waterfalls along the Gihon River in Johnson, 2.5 miles east, give steep-creek kayakers a wild run. Jeff Falls on the Brewster River along VT 108 in Jeffersonville, 9 miles west, is a clear, pretty swimming hole (public access on private property). Smugglers' Notch State Park has camping 16.7 miles southwest. Smugglers' Notch Resort has outdoor activities year-round, 13.5 miles southwest. Food and other shops are along VT 15 in Johnson, 1.5 miles east.

TRIP 49
DEVIL'S GULCH AND BIG MUDDY POND

Location: Eden, VT
Rating: Moderate
Distance: 5.2 miles round-trip
Elevation Gain: 465 feet
Estimated Time: 4 hours
Maps: USGS Hazens Notch; USGS Eden

Two beautiful ponds, a boulder-strewn ravine, and a camp on a high perch keep this hike interesting from beginning to end.

DIRECTIONS

From the junction of VT 100 and VT 118, go north on VT 118 for 4.6 miles. Just after a left curve, turn right onto an unnamed dirt drive. A sign high on a tree partway down the drive reads "Long Trail Access." Go about 300 feet to the parking area at the end of the road (space for about 12 cars). *GPS coordinates:* 44° 45.84' N, 72° 35.27' W.

TRAIL DESCRIPTION

The Green Mountain landscape on the southwest side of Belvidere Mountain (3,360 feet) is rumpled and gullied, with pockets of water between steep-sided hills and heaps of boulders beneath the cliffs that calved them. The Long Trail (LT) and Babcock Trail make a lollipop loop through this enchanting area, traipsing through the canyon of Devil's Gulch, climbing to a lovely camp and overlook on Spruce Ledge, and traversing the shoreline of the more-scenic-than-it-sounds Big Muddy Pond. There is a lot to see in a relatively short distance, making this a fun hike for kids about ages 8 and older. Although many LT thru-hikers have traversed Devil's Gulch with their canine companions, scrambling over the slippery rock pile at the head of the ravine is challenging for most dogs.

From the parking lot, climb a short trail to VT 118 and cross carefully on this blind curve, heading slightly left to find the white-blazed continuation of the southbound LT. The path rises for 0.4 mile, then meanders along a pleasant wooded ridge for 0.5 mile, eventually descending along the right side of a stream ravine. As the path begins a more noticeable descent, Ritterbush Lookout appears at 1.3 miles, with a view of Ritterbush Pond beneath a steep

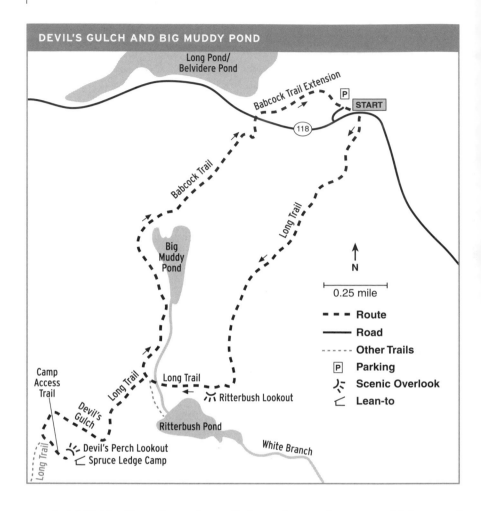

DEVIL'S GULCH AND BIG MUDDY POND

Long Pond/
Belvidere Pond

Babcock Trail Extension

P

START

118

Babcock Trail

Big
Muddy
Pond

Long Trail

N

0.25 mile

- - - Route

——— Road

------- Other Trails

P Parking

Scenic Overlook

Lean-to

Camp
Access
Trail

Long Trail

Long Trail

Devil's
Gulch

Long Trail

Ritterbush Lookout

Ritterbush Pond

White Branch

Devil's Perch Lookout

Spruce Ledge Camp

wooded hillside. From here, the trail descends steeply over multiple sets of rock steps, dropping to the hike's lowest point (1,100 feet) at the junction of Babcock Trail at 1.7 miles. The LT continues straight across this intersection, with Babcock Trail rising to the right and an unidentified extension of Babcock Trail dropping down a gully to the left.

Continue on the LT across the hillside, where the landscape gets really interesting. Approaching a stream plummeting from a mossy gully, the trail bends right and ascends a log ladder. The path snakes between boulders and ledges to the entrance of Devil's Gulch at 2.1 miles, where enormous slabs of rock lean against one another like a massive house of cards. Pass under this rock A frame and enter a mossy, drippy canyon. Sheer rock walls soar up to 70 feet high, undercut in large arcs where chunks of rock fell to the damp floor of the ravine. A line of bog bridges leads to the head of the short gully, which is

An A-frame tunnel marks the entrance to Devil's Gulch, a narrow, craggy canyon that is one of several highlights on this hike through varied terrain.

choked by rock fall. Navigate over the boulders, being aware of their slick surfaces. Suddenly, just over 0.1 mile after entering, you are out of the gulch and climbing gradually along the left side of a gentle valley. Curving left, the pitch steepens and follows a stream up to a junction. Turn left onto the spur trail to Spruce Ledge Camp, climbing over a ridgeline before dropping to an attractive little cabin at 2.6 miles. Just beyond, a log bench perches atop a steep drop—watch children and dogs here—giving a broad view of Belvidere Mountain and a slice of Ritterbush Pond.

From Spruce Ledge Camp, retrace your steps 0.9 mile back through Devil's Gulch to the Babcock Trail/LT junction. Go left on Babcock Trail, climbing steadily northward out of the valley along a rocky, blue-blazed path. The outlet of Big Muddy Pond appears through the trees 0.4 mile from the junction. As you skirt the western shore, look for signs of beaver. On the far end of the pond, Babcock Trail climbs out of the basin and crosses a narrow height-of-land. From here, 0.7 mile of mostly moderate descent leads to VT 118. Cross the road and continue northeast on the 0.4-mile Babcock Trail Extension, which passes a cellar hole and briefly follows a dirt road before returning to a footpath. The trail rises to parallel the dirt drive, then climbs to the parking lot.

DID YOU KNOW?

In the hollows deep under the boulders of Devil's Gulch, winter ice is sheltered and melts slowly through the spring and early summer, keeping the ravine pleasantly cooled. You may even feel cool breezes.

MORE INFORMATION

The Long Trail and Spruce Ledge Camp are maintained by the Green Mountain Club; 4711 Waterbury–Stowe Road, Waterbury Center, VT 05677; 802-244-7037; greenmountainclub.org. Babcock Trail is within Babcock Nature Preserve, owned by Johnson State College; College Hill Road, Johnson, VT; 800-635-2356; jsc.edu/ChangeYourWorld/BabcockNaturePreserve.aspx.

NEARBY

Paddle on Long Pond (also called Belvidere Pond), 0.5 mile west. Camp, paddle, and swim at Green River Reservoir State Park, 20 miles southeast. Food and shops are in Johnson, 14 miles south.

TRIP 50
BURNT MOUNTAIN

Location: Montgomery, VT
Rating: Moderate
Distance: 4.8 miles round-trip
Elevation Gain: 1,600 feet
Estimated Time: 3 hours
Maps: USGS Hazens Notch; hazensnotch.org/Winter-Trail-Map.htm

Pass beaver ponds and an orchard on the way to a remote, rocky ridgeline with long views.

DIRECTIONS

From the junction of VT 118 and VT 58 (Hazens Notch Road), go east on VT 58 for 2.1 miles. Turn right onto Rossier Road, then stay right at a fork. Drive about 0.5 mile from VT 58 to the High Ponds Farm trailhead parking area (space for about 10 cars) at the end of the road. VT 58 is maintained in winter from Montgomery, but not from Lowell. (Winter hikers park and buy a trail pass at the Hazen's Notch Association Welcome Center on VT 58, 1.4 miles from the VT 118 junction; add 2.2 miles round-trip to the hike. See special-use information below.) *GPS coordinates:* 44° 51.68′ N, 72° 34.64′ W.

TRAIL DESCRIPTION

Burnt Mountain (2,800 feet) offers a relatively new hiking adventure in Vermont, its trail established in 1990 and maintained by Hazen's Notch Association (HNA), a nonprofit organization dedicated to conservation, education, and land restoration. The route up this wild peak is within a 500-acre private conservation area that is open to the public and that includes a variety of landscapes, including native mixed-species forest, a spruce plantation, old pastures and hayfields, orchards, beaver ponds, and the craggy mountaintop. The hike has a pleasant, gradual ascent over the first mile and the final 0.6 mile, with a steep, challenging 0.8-mile climb in between. The first mile past beaver ponds to picnic tables in High Meadow is a fun short hike for small kids. Dogs must be leashed on all trails.

Follow a gravel road south from the parking area, skirting the edge of a beaver pond before the Window Rock Trail junction at 0.1 mile. Stay right on Beaver Ponds Trail for 0.2 mile to its junction with High Meadow Trail. Go left

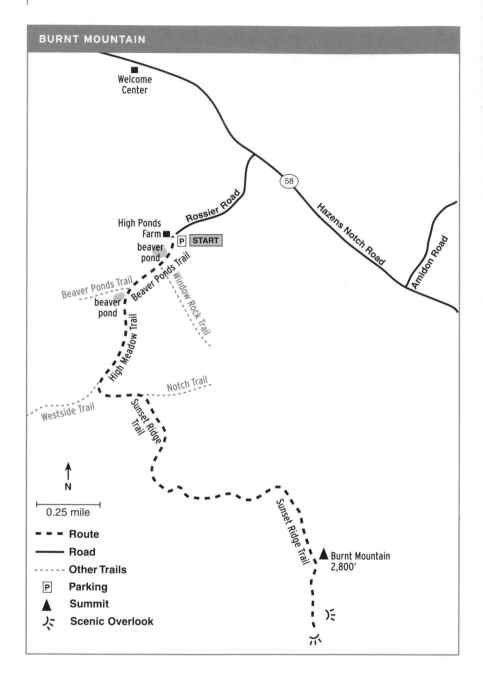

BURNT MOUNTAIN

Welcome Center

Rossier Road

58

Hazens Notch Road

Amidon Road

High Ponds Farm

P START

beaver pond

Beaver Ponds Trail

Beaver Ponds Trail

Window Rock Trail

beaver pond

High Meadow Trail

Notch Trail

Westside Trail

Sunset Ridge Trail

Sunset Ridge Trail

Burnt Mountain 2,800'

N

0.25 mile

- - - Route
— Road
----- Other Trails
P Parking
▲ Summit
⅃ᒣ Scenic Overlook

and pass beneath a wetland restoration area, where a peek over the bank may reward you with a beaver sighting.

Walk another 0.2 mile along the gradually rising road and enter the wide, grassy High Meadow. Burnt Mountain rises above the apple trees dotting this

The rugged, boreal crest of Burnt Mountain affords a view of one of the northernmost stretches of the Green Mountains, dominated by Jay Peak and Big Jay.

large field, and wildflowers such as milkweed, morning glory, meadowsweet, meadow rue, and daisy fleabane grow along the edges of the road. Cross High Meadow to the junction of Westside Trail and turn left toward Burnt Mountain. Picnic tables with a dramatic view of Jay Peak (3,858 feet) offer a rest spot before you leave High Meadow. From here, the mowed path passes the junction of Notch Trail (stay right) before arriving at the foot of Burnt Mountain. Proceed onto the rocky Sunset Ridge Trail and begin climbing.

Sunset Ridge Trail ascends moderately and then steeply under a tall maple canopy, its first pitch ending at a bench at a woods-road junction. Heading left, the trail mounts the steep hill in rising switchbacks until, 0.6 mile from the base of the mountain, you arrive on the ridge. Now hobblebush, club moss, and lilies fill in the understory beneath stout paper birches. Sunset Ridge Trail continues to rise more moderately to the northern end of the mountain, where it turns right and traverses the length of Burnt Mountain's ridge. Pass over the treed summit in the middle of the ridge, and descend gradually through blueberry bushes and over ledges to outlook rocks at the southern end. Big Green Mountain peaks are visible to the southwest, including Whiteface (3,714 feet), Madonna (3,668 feet), and Mansfield (4,393 feet). To the west, the Cold Hollow Mountains rise above the Trout River valley, and a distant sliver of Lake

Champlain is visible. The knob of Haystack Mountain (3,223 feet) is prominent to the east, crossed by the Long Trail on its northward trek over the cliffs of Hazen's Notch.

Return the way you hiked up.

DID YOU KNOW?

Heart-leaved paper birch grow around the northern tip of Burnt Mountain. Look for the notch at the stem that gives the leaf a heart shape, and look for the dark-pink color on the underside of peeling strips of bark—but leave bark on live trees.

MORE INFORMATION

Trails are open during daylight hours. Large groups should contact Hazen's Notch Association ahead of time to ensure adequate parking. Trails are maintained for skiing and snowshoeing in winter; dogs and hiking (without snowshoes) are not allowed December 15 through May 15. Trails are closed April 15 through May 15 for mud season; trails may be closed at other times, depending on conditions. Skiing is not allowed off trail or on Burnt Mountain. Winter trail users must park, register, and pay a fee at the Welcome Center on VT 58. Hazen's Notch Association, P.O. Box 478, Montgomery Center, VT 05471; 802-326-4799; hazensnotch.org.

NEARBY

The Northern Forest Canoe Trail traverses northern Vermont and southern Quebec along the nearby Missisquoi River and Lake Memphremagog. The Green River Reservoir State Park has remote campsites on a pristine lake, 32 miles south, while Lake Carmi's more developed campground includes a beach, 22 miles northwest. Food is in Montgomery, 2.5 miles east.

TRIP 51
JAY PEAK

Location: Westfield, VT
Rating: Moderate
Distance: 3.4 miles round-trip
Elevation Gain: 1,638 feet
Estimated Time: 3 hours
Map: USGS Jay Peak

This boreal forest hike to the summit of Vermont's northernmost ski area features sweeping views of northern Vermont, New Hampshire, and New York, as well as southern Quebec.

DIRECTIONS
From its junction with VT 101 in Jay, take VT 242 west 6.5 miles, passing through the village and past the entrance to the ski area. At the height-of-land, the Long Trail crosses VT 242. Park on the southern shoulder of the road (space for about 15 cars). *GPS coordinates:* 44° 54.46′ N, 72° 30.15′ W.

TRAIL DESCRIPTION
Jay Peak is a quintessential peak: high and solo, with a distinct profile and incredible summit views. Its ardent fans are numerous, from skiers and snowboarders who cherish its rugged terrain and famously deep snowfalls to Long Trail hikers for whom the singular summit is a milestone at the beginning or end of a journey. The hike from Jay Pass is short and steep, and rocky and beautiful. Snowshoers can expect to share some of their hike with skiers on the upper mountain.

Find the trailhead on the north side of VT 242, where the white-blazed Long Trail enters the trees and immediately encounters Atlas Valley Shelter. (This roofed resting area was built in 1967 by a plywood company and is not intended for overnight use. For campers, Jay Loop spur trail departs on the left here, leading to the bunks at Jay Camp, and rejoins the Long Trail 0.2 mile uphill.) The climb begins gradually through a deciduous forest. By the upper junction with Jay Loop, the trail has narrowed and steepened; within minutes, the forest becomes distinctly more boreal.

The trail ascends steadily along the southwest-facing slope of the ridge.

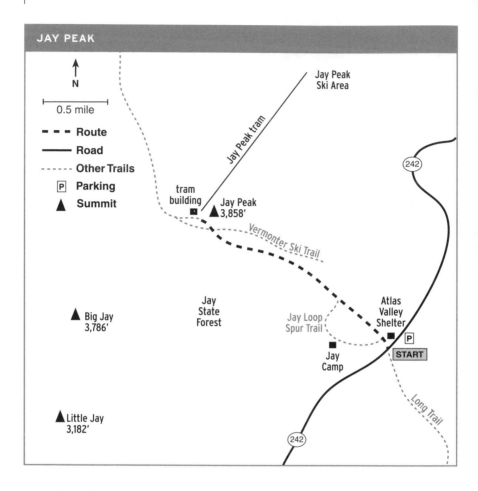

Where the Long Trail crests the ridge and traverses the top of it, an informal path leads right a short distance onto a ski slope. The Long Trail then curves to the west and continues climbing through a dense conifer forest. Moderate pitches are interspersed with scrambles up rocky ledges, and moss grows thickly on the forest floor. At 1.5 miles the Long Trail crosses steel snowmaking pipes onto the Vermonter ski trail. To the left, the summit building of the tram is visible a short distance up the open slope. The hiking trail continues directly across the ski slope, climbing steep ledges onto the ridgeline for the final 0.2-mile ascent. Walk on the rocks, weaving between spruce and fir krummholz—crooked wood, stunted and deformed by wind and snowpack. Passing a stone bench, arrive at the top next to the tram summit station.

The views from here are unparalleled in North-Central Vermont. Big Jay (3,786 feet) hulks close by to the southwest, rising opposite a glacial cirque that connects it with Jay Peak. Little Jay (3,182 feet) is a short distance down

Jay Peak's famous snowfall depths and northern location create a relatively short season for snowless hiking.

Big Jay's southern shoulder. The high ridge of the Green Mountains leads your eyes southwest over the distinct point of Mount Mansfield's Chin (4,393 feet) to Camel's Hump (4,083 feet), which is 46 miles away. To the west, beyond the low, rolling landscape of Franklin County's dairy farms, narrow slivers of Lake Champlain reflect the sky. Look southwest for the famed Adirondack High Peaks. You know you're about as far north as you can go in Vermont when the big peaks of the Adirondacks (and, looking southeast, the White Mountains) are south of you.

To the north, Quebec's Sutton Mountains continue where the Green Mountains leave off at the international border. Bear Mountain and Owl's Head (with ski trails) perch on the western edge of the transborder Lake Memphremagog. Much of the Sutton Mountain massif due north has been conserved by groups such as Ruiter Valley Land Trust, which maintains hiking trails through their lands, and Appalachian Corridor, which works with Vermont's Green Mountain Club and other American organizations to ensure that conservation strategies are developed on both sides of the border, linking important ecological areas to each other.

Descend the way you came up. To give your knees a brief respite, head down the wooden stairway to the top of Vermonter Ski Trail and follow its gentle grade downhill to rejoin the Long Trail.

DID YOU KNOW?

The 27-mile-long Lake Memphremagog hides curiosities beneath its surface. At least one car loaded with Prohibition-era whisky rests in the murky depths, and divers have surfaced with still-corked jugs of hooch. A sea serpent called Memphre has been spotted numerous times in the lake since 1816—most recently in 2005.

MORE INFORMATION

Jay Peak is within Jay State Forest, managed by the Vermont Department of Forests, Parks, and Recreation, St. Johnsbury Regional Office, 1229 Portland Street, Suite 201, St. Johnsbury, VT 05763; 802-751-0116; vtfpr.org/lands/bigjay.cfm. The Long Trail is maintained by the Green Mountain Club, 4711 Waterbury–Stowe Road, Waterbury Center, VT 05677; 802-244-7037; greenmountainclub.org.

NEARBY

The Missisquoi River and Lake Memphremagog are part of the 740-mile Northern Forest Canoe Trail. The multiuse Missisquoi Valley Rail Trail extends 26 miles between Richford and St. Albans. Big Falls State Park in Troy, with the state's largest undammed cascade and gorge, is a scenic picnic spot, 10 miles northeast. For food, head to Jay, 5.5 miles east, or to Newport, 21.0 miles east. The Newport State Office Building on the lakefront houses an interesting exhibit about Memphremagog history.

5

NORTHEASTERN VERMONT

COMMONLY CALLED THE NORTHEAST KINGDOM—or just the Kingdom—
Northeastern Vermont is just slightly a land apart. It has been called "Vermont's loneliest and loveliest corner," and it is a place where—even more than
in other parts of the state—the landscape and wildlife overshadow any human
creations such as towns or farms. As in other regions of Vermont, the landscape is mountainous and heavily forested, but unlike them, the Kingdom is
dotted with lakes and ponds, such as Wheeler Pond (Trip 57) and Little Averill
Lake, spreading beneath the cliffs of Brousseau Mountain (Trip 60) on the
Canadian border.

Covering high ground, the temperatures are generally a little lower here
than elsewhere in Vermont, and therefore the forests are more commonly
coniferous. Accordingly, moose, spruce grouse, and other denizens of the
boreal forest live here in greater numbers than in other parts of the state. Once
primarily logged, large tracts of forest have been conserved in recent years;
the 1999 purchase and conservation of the 132,000-acre Champion Lands was
Vermont's largest conservation project, stretching over 14 Northeast Kingdom
towns. The extensive basin of the Nulhegan River watershed is protected as a
National Fish and Wildlife Refuge.

In a region of dramatic landscapes, perhaps the most spectacular in the
Kingdom are the cliffy slopes of Mount Pisgah (Trip 54) and Mount Hor (Trip

55) rising 1,000-plus feet from the narrow, dark waters of Lake Willoughby. The mountains and lake together form Lake Willoughby Natural Area, which has been designated a National Natural Landmark. Just south of the Willoughby area, Burke Mountain (Trip 52) stands taller than anything else in the vicinity and is a hub of recreational activity, including Vermont's (and maybe New England's) premier mountain-bike trail system, Kingdom Trails.

On the eastern border of the state, another solo peak, Monadnock Mountain (Trip 58), towers over the fields and forests of the Connecticut River valley. The beginnings of this 407-mile-long river tumble southward, quick and shallow at first, then slow through S curves across broad floodplains before filling the 7-mile-long Moore Reservoir. The Connecticut River and its environs provide critical bird habitat and are an important bird migration flyway. Herons and mergansers are common along the edges, while osprey, various hawks, and bald eagles fish the river's waters. Common loons may occasionally visit the river but are more likely swimming in nearby Maidstone Lake (Trip 53).

TRIP 52
BURKE MOUNTAIN

Location: Burke, VT
Rating: Strenuous
Distance: 6.2 miles round-trip
Elevation Gain: 2,080 feet
Estimated Time: 4 hours
Map: USGS Burke Mountain

This remote trail passes through a stand of enormous ash and maple trees on its way to spectacular views from the summit of a popular skiing and mountain-biking destination.

DIRECTIONS
From VT 114 in East Burke Village, follow Mountain Road 1.1 miles to Sherburne Lodge Road on the right. Parking for the trailhead is at the far end of the large lower lot. *GPS coordinates: 44° 35.25′ N, 71° 55.08′ W.*

TRAIL DESCRIPTION
Burke Mountain (3,267 feet) rises steeply from the gently sloping Passumpsic River valley. Its northern slopes and summit are a beehive of activity during ski season, but the challenging hiking trail up its western ridge is surprisingly insulated.

From the trailhead kiosk, Red Trail follows a dirt two-track into the woods and curves through tamarack, maple, and overgrown log landings as it gently rises. After 0.6 mile, Red Trail turns left, departing the road. In 500 feet, the trail turns right, joining Kirby Connector, a mountain-bike trail. The two trails coincide for 0.2 mile; be aware of bikers and give them room to pass. The open understory here allows for long views beneath the canopy, a rare treat in eastern forests. At a register box, turn left off Kirby Connector and continue up Red Trail, entering Darling State Park.

Enormous tree trunks make this section of trail interesting. The largest are ash and maple, while bigger-than-usual yellow and paper birch also make an appearance. Look as well for jumbo-sized shelf mushrooms growing off the huge trunks.

The undergrowth thickens as the slope steepens. Red Trail turns sharply left to climb alongside a steep ravine and then to cross a saddle at its top. The

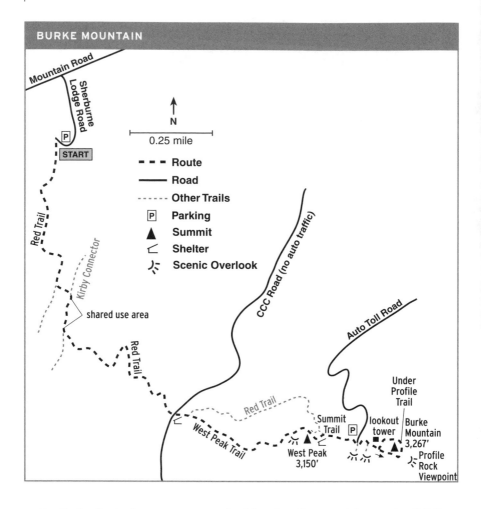

path climbs from there onto a maple ridge, heading straight up the fall line. After passing through a dark spruce/fir stand, cross the Civilian Conservation Corps (CCC) Road, which no longer bears vehicle traffic, at 1.7 miles.

Straight ahead, Red Trail enters a clearing with the junction of West Peak Trail and a CCC-era log lean-to and stone fireplace that are still used by campers and skiers. Turn right in this clearing and head up the scenic, blue-blazed West Peak Trail.

Climb steeply through paper and yellow birches for 0.2 mile, then enter a shallow ravine thick with bushy chokecherry and maple. Passing that, the trail ascends through stunted birch trees and mountain ash, traverses across the gully, and climbs out. Now on a high ridge, the hiking alternates between scrambling up ledges draped in thick moss and crossing benches where small pockets of fern glades open between fragrant softwood thickets. After several

Mossy, boreal forests along Burke Mountain's summit ridge lead to numerous craggy lookouts with long views over the Northeast Kingdom.

rising switchbacks, West Peak Trail emerges from the tree canopy, passes along the bottom of a steep rock face, and then climbs up the far side. On top of this promontory, views extend west across the broad Passumpsic Valley and south, over the shoulder of nearby Kirby Mountain (2,500 feet). The wooded summit of West Peak (3,150 feet) is just 0.1 mile farther and is marked by another log lean-to. Go right, staying on West Peak Trail, which ends at a five-way junction. Stay right to follow Summit Trail along the undeveloped south edge of the mountaintop, passing remnants of CCC campsites and shelters. After passing the top edge of a ski trail and parking lot, reenter the woods and find two successive spur trails leading to viewpoints. After that, the trail winds through the forest to the junction with Under Profile Trail (a.k.a. Profile Trail). Summit Trail heads left to the fire tower, but go right, continuing along the ridge to pass beneath the jutting rock overhang before circling to climb on top of Profile Rock (via the Profile Vista spur trail) for the most expansive views yet. Use caution: Surrounding trees can disguise cliff edges. To the northeast, East Haven Mountain (3,020 feet) rises in the foreground. Beyond it, an abandoned Cold War–era radar station is visible on East Mountain (3,420 feet).

Leaving Profile Rock, continue west across the rocky open area of Burke's true summit. Just beyond it, climb the metal tower for 360-degree views, including Willoughby Gap to the northwest, a remarkable notch formed by Mount Hor on the west, and Mount Pisgah on the east. From the tower, follow Summit Trail downhill and return the way you came.

DID YOU KNOW?

Burke Mountain is one of several Vermont monadnocks: isolated mountains that, due to their erosion-resistant rock, rise abruptly from gently sloping surroundings.

MORE INFORMATION

Darling State Park is managed by the Vermont Department of Forests, Parks and Recreation, 1229 Portland Avenue, St. Johnsbury, VT 05819; 802-751-0110; vtfpr.org. Trails are maintained by the NorthWoods Stewardship Center, P.O. Box 220, East Charleston, VT 05833; 802-723-6551; northwoodscenter.org.

NEARBY

East Burke's Kingdom Trails Association is a renowned mountain-biking center whose trails are open to hiking, running, skiing, and snowshoeing as well. Groceries and dining options are found on VT 114 in East Burke or on US 5 in Lyndonville, 5.7 miles southwest.

TRIP 53
MAIDSTONE STATE PARK

Location: Maidstone, VT
Rating: Easy
Distance: 1.5 miles round-trip
Elevation Gain: Minimal
Estimated Time: 1 hour
Map: USGS Maidstone Lake

Hike along an inlet of Maidstone Lake where loons—until recently an endangered species in Vermont—are frequently spotted.

DIRECTIONS

From the junction of US 2 and VT 102 in Guildhall, head north on VT 102 for 17.7 miles. Turn left onto Maidstone Lake Road and drive about 6 miles to its end at Maidstone State Park. Pass the day-use area and pay a fee at the campground office. Inquire there about the best place to park for Loon Trail, which will likely be at a vacant campsite. The trailhead is in Camping Area B, between sites 33 and 35. (Off season, park at the gate at the office and walk through the campground, adding 1.8 miles round-trip to your hike.) *GPS coordinates: 44° 38.01′ N, 71° 39.50′ W.*

TRAIL DESCRIPTION

Several trails traverse the heavily wooded south shore of Maidstone Lake. The most pleasant route is the aptly named Loon Trail, which follows the shoreline of a narrow inlet, affording frequent views of the water. Since the 1980s, when only seven breeding pairs of loons were counted in Vermont, efforts to protect nesting areas and educate people have led to the slow, steady return of the magnificent black-and-white bird. The loon was removed from the state's Endangered Species List in 2005, and its graceful profile may be spotted in summer on many Vermont lakes and deep ponds, particularly in the Northeast Kingdom. Loon Trail is mostly flat after crossing a short, steep ridge at the beginning of the hike. That ridge and a narrow inlet stream bridge may provide small challenges for cross-country skiers. The footing is rooty and uneven, but otherwise the trail is suitable for all ages.

Find the sign for Loon Trail and Moose Trail between campsites 33 and 35, and climb about 200 feet to a junction. Moose Trail goes left; stay straight

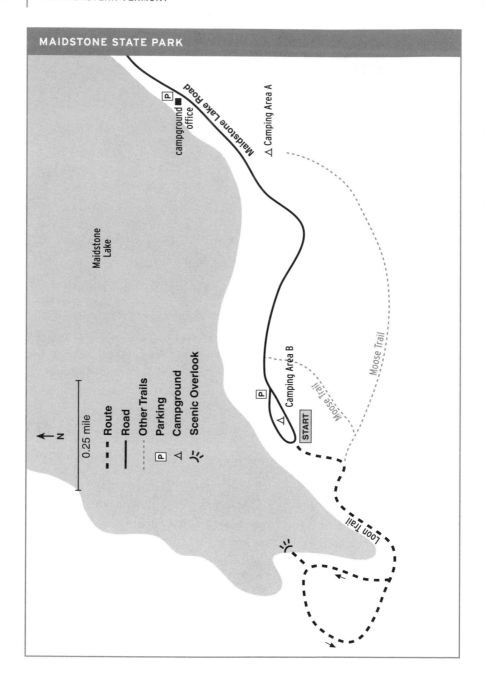

MAIDSTONE STATE PARK

Maidstone Lake Road

campground office

Camping Area A

Maidstone Lake

Camping Area B

Moose Trail

START

Loon Trail

0.25 mile

- - Route
—— Road
······ Other Trails
P Parking
△ Campground
Scenic Overlook

N

on Loon Trail. The narrow, leaf-littered path crosses the top of the ridge, then bends right and descends steeply through boulders, lilies, and wood sorrel to the water's edge. Curving left, the trail traipses over mossy rocks and roots, with a buffer of fir, spruce, yellow birch, and beech between the path and the

A shoreline hike along Maidstone Lake features loon sightings, wild flowers, swimming, and plenty of interesting terrain to explore.

shoreline. Loons nest and raise young close to the water's edge during prime lake recreation season—May through August—so they are particularly susceptible to disturbance from boaters and hikers. Remain at least 300 feet from nursery areas or nests, which may be a pile of vegetation on the ground or a shallow depression in the soil. Use binoculars to watch loons without alarming them.

In addition to waterfowl viewing, Loon Trail offers the chance to look for some uncommon wildflowers. In early summer, lady's slippers bloom abundantly in these woods, their delicate pink or white pouches drooping from a sturdy stalk that can be 15 inches tall. Look also for twin flowers, a pair of little pink or white bells dangling off either side of a thin stem.

Several bog bridges cross a damp area approaching the end of the cove, and a low log bridge spans the inlet stream. On the other side, at 0.5 mile, Loon Trail splits to begin its loop. Go right along the water. Rocky openings provide occasional viewing spots just off the trail, but the best lookout comes halfway around the loop. Rising to an unmarked junction, Loon Trail turns left, and on the right, a short, somewhat eroded slope drops to a clearing at the water's edge. Looking northeast across the water, Stoneham Mountain (2,143 feet) pokes above the wooded shoreline of Maidstone State Forest. The majority of

Maidstone Lake's 796-acre surface stretches north, out of sight. Formed 12,000 years ago when glaciers carved a depression and left a natural dam of rocks and sand at the outlet, the lake is deep, clean, and cold. Landlocked salmon thrive here, along with brook, rainbow, and lake trout.

Clamber back up to the main trail and follow it straight. The path passes through blueberry bushes and enters a thick forest where it curves left, descending gradually back to the start of the 0.5-mile loop. From there, follow Loon Trail back across the inlet stream, returning the way you walked in.

DID YOU KNOW?

The four distinct calls of the loon are the yodel, the tremolo, the wail, and the hoot. The yodel is a male's territorial call, while the tremolo—sometimes referred to as a laugh—is a warning or alarm. The long notes of the wail and the quiet hoot help the birds locate one another.

MORE INFORMATION

Maidstone State Park operates Memorial Day weekend to Labor Day weekend; day-use hours are 10 A.M. to official sunset. Pets are allowed, except at the beach. The area is open for day use in the off-season without staff or facilities; see the website for more information. Maidstone State Park, 5956 Maidstone Lake Road, Maidstone, VT 05905; 802-676-3930; vtstateparks.com/htm/maidstone.htm.

NEARBY

Camp, swim, and paddle here at the state park. The Connecticut River, 6 miles east, has leisurely paddling along the Northern Forest Canoe Trail and Connecticut River Paddlers Trail. Limited food is available 11 miles north in Bloomfield; more options are 23 miles south in Lancaster, New Hampshire.

IS THE WATER CLEAN?

Clear mountain streams tumbling over rocks alongside the trail; high-mountain lakes reflecting the sky: Pristine waters are part of the allure of hiking, and one of the signs that we're away from the garbage and pollution of developed areas. But is the water in the mountains really clean?

How you answer this question depends on why you're asking. If you're looking to swim or fish, chances are that the answer in Vermont will be yes, the water is clean enough. (Check healthvermont.gov for specific warnings.) If you're wondering about the health of the ecosystem, the answer is more complex. If you simply want to refill your water bottle, the answer to this question may surprise you: "Clean" may not mean "okay to drink."

New England's waterways suffered historically from industrial uses that involved mills and dams, and from erosion caused by extensive clearing of the trees. Today, most have recovered significantly due to decreased manufacturing and logging, as well as pollution-control standards such as the Clean Water Act of 1972. Some industrial-era dams have been dismantled, increasing the amount of free-flowing water that is crucial in the life cycles of some fish. But even with these improvements, Vermont's water quality is threatened. Power plants and factories emit chemicals that blow over New England and descend as acid rain or snow, altering the chemistry and thus the biology of streams, rivers, and lakes. Fertilizers washed into the water from farms and residential areas cause excessive growth of algae. Algae blooms are especially problematic in Lake Champlain, where they degrade habitat and limit boating and swimming opportunities. Lake Champlain receives water from so many feeder streams and rivers that any pollution problems upstream end up affecting the big lake as well.

So those clear, high streams and ponds are the place for you to refill your water bottle—but don't mistake clean water with healthy-for-you water. You still need to sterilize any surface water before you chug it down. Clean water has lots of microscopic organisms, and some of them can ruin your vacation and leave you sick for several weeks afterward. There are lots of ways to make clean surface water safe to drink, from boiling it, filtering it, or adding iodine, to the latest technology that zaps micro-organisms with electrically-charged brine or ultraviolet light. Staying hydrated is important to staying healthy while hiking, so head upstream with your treatment of choice and enjoy the clean water.

TRIP 54
MOUNT PISGAH

Location: Westmore, VT
Rating: Moderate
Distance: 4.8 miles round-trip
Elevation Gain: 1,395 feet
Estimated Time: 3 hours
Map: USGS Sutton

Outlooks atop Mount Pisgah's cliffs, which drop precipitously into scenic Lake Willoughby, provide sweeping views across the Northeast Kingdom.

DIRECTIONS
From the junction of US 5 and VT 5A in West Burke, travel north on VT 5A for 5.7 miles. Mount Pisgah's South Trail parking lot (space for about 15 cars) is on the right. An additional parking lot (space for about 12 cars) is on the left, at the bottom of the CCC Road. *GPS coordinates:* 44° 42.65′ N, 72° 01.44′ W.

TRAIL DESCRIPTION
Hikers climb Mount Pisgah (2,751 feet) not for its wooded summit, which you can pass over without realizing you're on it, but for the dramatic views from its west-facing ledges. The dark, deep waters of Lake Willoughby fill the narrow gap between Pisgah and its cliffy cousin, Mount Hor (2,648 feet). Together, these mountains and the lake are a National Natural Landmark. Mount Pisgah's cliffs are spectacular, but there are no restraints on them—not a railing or even a warning sign; use caution.

South Trail begins in the far right corner of the parking lot, where it descends several rock steps and enters the woods. A short distance from the road, step onto the first of two wide boardwalks that cross a beaver pond. Watch for great blue herons standing quietly amid the dead tree trunks and lily pads here. Cross the swamp and head north along a low ridge, passing a register box and beginning to climb gradually through a deciduous forest. Purple-flowering raspberry spreads its maple-looking leaves alongside the trail as it steepens. Hobblebush also thrives here, its flexible stems bending and taking root again where they touch the ground.

From high atop Mount Pisgah's sheer cliffs, hikers get a peregrine-falcon-eye's view of Lake Willoughby and the northern Green Mountains.

Glimpses of Lake Willoughby appear at intervals as the trail follows the edge of the steep western hillside. Be wary of this drop when exploring any of the informal footpaths that lead to lookout points alongside the trail. Pulpit Rock, a small overlook almost 700 feet above the lake, appears on your left at 0.9 mile. This popular destination provides a striking, if more limited, view of the south end of Willoughby and the cliffs of Mount Hor.

After passing an interesting tangle of two tree trunks leaning toward the precipice, the trail turns away from the ledges and heads into the woods, starting up the most sustained part of the climb. As you huff and puff up it, admire the artistry of many rock staircases built by the local youth crews of the North-Woods Stewardship Center. The forest changes here to firs and short, thick paper birches.

Just below the summit, South Trail emerges from the forest onto South Overlook, a rocky bald spot with a view of Burke Mountain's ski trails, which appear to be just a stone's throw away. The trail returns to the woods and without any fanfare passes over the summit of Pisgah on its way to the ledges. From the summit to the overlooks, you are on Mount Pisgah's North Trail. If you haven't already put a leash on your dog, do so now.

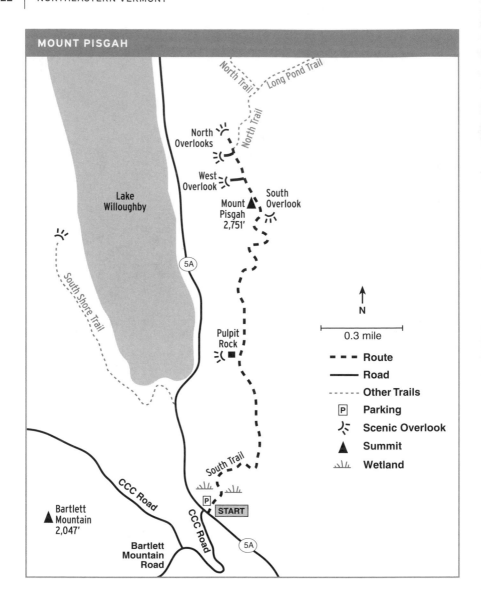

Three overlooks provide three slightly different angles from which to view the surrounding landscape, and each rocky sitting area is a little more spacious than the last. Spur trails to the ledges are marked inconspicuously by small, white, hand-lettered signs nailed high in trees along North Trail.

Below the ledges, the landlocked fjord of Lake Willoughby stretches long and narrow, its far shore an oddly straight line lacking coves and inlets. It's easy to imagine how southward-creeping glaciers of the last ice age pushed through this narrow valley, gouging the trough that eventually became the deepest lake (at 312 feet) within Vermont's borders. Look northwest over the woods to the cliffs of Wheeler Mountain for another example of the power of that grinding ice sheet. Beyond Wheeler Mountain, the spine of the Green Mountains etches the western horizon, with Mount Mansfield to the southwest and the distinctive point of Jay Peak to the northwest. In the far northwest, Lake Memphremagog stretches into Quebec.

Climb back up the overlook spur trail and turn right onto North Trail to return to the summit. Descend the way you came up.

DID YOU KNOW?

Mount Pisgah's nineteenth-century name was Mount Annance (or variants of that), after a local Wabanaki chief. When settlers of European descent began hosting tourists on the lake, the mountain was renamed, perhaps as clever marketing, to refer to the biblical Promised Land.

MORE INFORMATION

Willoughby State Forest is managed by the Vermont Department of Forests, Parks and Recreation, St. Johnsbury District Office, 1229 Portland Street, Suite 201, St. Johnsbury, VT 05819; 802-751-0110; vtfpr.org. Mount Pisgah trails are maintained by the NorthWoods Stewardship Center, P.O. Box 220, East Charleston, VT 05833; 802-723-6551; northwoodscenter.org.

NEARBY

Camping and swimming areas can be found at both ends of Lake Willoughby. Some dining options are found along the lake, with many more in East Burke or Lyndonville, each 20 miles south, or Newport, 20 miles north. Outdoor outfitters are in East Burke and Newport.

HIKER FOOTSTEPS (OR, THE PSYCHOLOGY OF TRAIL MAINTENANCE)

When you stop, panting, at the top of a flight of rock steps, are you more inclined to curse the steps or appreciate their flat surfaces? How you answer may indicate your awareness of erosion and trail maintenance techniques. Although some trail features are put in place to ease the way for hikers, such as a ladder up a rock face or a railing on a bridge, most trail work is done to prevent erosion.

Soil erosion is the biggest threat to the life of a trail. If you've ever hiked up a gullied path with tree roots suspended in midair, you know what the effects of erosion look like. Although erosion is a natural process of soils wearing away, it becomes a problem when it causes hikers to seek alternate routes, trampling plants and causing further damage. Trails that become too badly eroded have to be relocated, and relocation is an expensive, time-consuming activity that results in additional impact on the forest.

Trail maintainers assessing an eroded stretch of trail have two thoughts: "How can I drain the water off this trail and stabilize the soil?" and "How can I convince hikers to walk on the more durable path?"

There are many ways to drain and harden a trail—that is, to make it more durable. You've stepped in and out of countless shallow, rounded troughs that cross the trail; these dips guide downstream currents off the path. Dips reinforced with a slippery skinned log or a row of rocks are called water bars.

Step stones and bog bridges (also called puncheons) provide dry footing across persistently muddy areas while protecting soils and plants.

Log or rock steps stabilize steep trails and provide a durable and relatively flat surface for footsteps. Many hikers avoid steps and climb the dirt slope beside them, causing that to erode and undermine the stability of the staircase. To make the steps more appealing than the hill beside them, trail maintainers plant pointy, less stable-looking rocks called scree alongside the staircase.

You won't look at trails the same way after you start noticing the subtle ways maintainers guide your footsteps to prevent erosion. That log ladder helping you up a ledge controls erosion by keeping you on durable rock rather than on erodible soil around the edge. A railing makes the durable bridge route the most appealing way across a ravine. Trail maintainers focus on protecting the trail and its surrounding environment, benefitting hikers in the long term, even if occasionally making life a little more challenging.

TRIP 55
MOUNT HOR

Location: Sutton, VT
Rating: Easy to Moderate
Distance: 2.9 miles round-trip
Elevation Gain: 601 feet
Estimated Time: 1.5 hours
Map: USGS Sutton

A short hike through a lovely hardwood forest leads to lookouts with long views, including the dramatic vista of Lake Willoughby and the cliffs of Mount Pisgah.

DIRECTIONS
From VT 5A at the southern end of Lake Willoughby, go 0.5 mile south to the height-of-land and turn right onto the dirt CCC Road. After 0.5 mile, bear right at the fork and continue uphill. The unmarked parking area (space for 6 cars) is on the right at 1.7 miles. (The CCC Road is not maintained in winter; snowshoers park at the bottom and add 3.4 miles round-trip to the hike.) *GPS coordinates:* 44° 42.53′ N, 72° 02.83′ W.

TRAIL DESCRIPTION
Mount Hor (2,648 feet) is one of two peaks that create the National Natural Landmark of Willoughby Gap. Mirroring Mount Pisgah (2,751 feet) on the opposite side of the gap, Hor's sheer cliffs rise 1,000 feet from narrow Lake Willoughby, forming a canyonesque landscape. Although the hiking is appropriate for kids about ages 6 and older, children and dogs need to be carefully monitored at the outlook points.

Herbert Hawkes Trail begins up the road a short distance beyond the parking area. The wide path climbs briefly, following an old road, and then flattens out through an airy hardwood forest. After 0.4 mile, turn left off the old road and climb steadily on a narrow path. At 0.6 mile, you will arrive at a T junction on the ridge: to the left, the trail skirts Mount Hor's summit, offering a view southwest; to the right, the vistas north and east over Lake Willoughby are a little more than 0.5 mile along the ridge. Go left, ascending over rocks until the low curve of the summit appears above you on your right, at which point the trail flattens and curves around it. Straight ahead, down a short slope, a hole

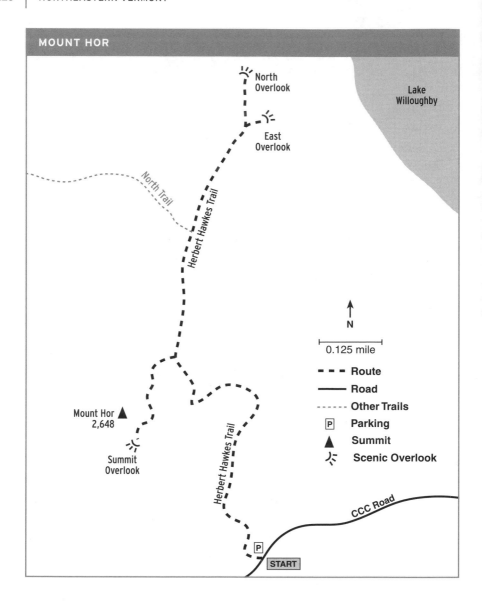

MOUNT HOR

North Overlook

East Overlook

Lake Willoughby

North Trail

Herbert Hawkes Trail

N

0.125 mile

- - - Route

——— Road

- - - - - Other Trails

P Parking

▲ Summit

Scenic Overlook

Mount Hor ▲
2,648

Summit Overlook

Herbert Hawkes Trail

CCC Road

P

START

in the forest frames a view over numerous small ponds to Norris Mountain (2,292 feet). The ponds are part of the 30-acre Marl Pond and Swamp Natural Area, a northern-white-cedar swamp with several rare plants.

Return to the trail junction and continue straight along the ridgeline. The 0.6 mile to East Overlook is mostly flat, passing the junction of North Trail on your left and crossing muddy areas where you're likely to see prints left by a moose, if not the hump-shouldered ungulate itself. A spur trail leads right down a short, eroded slope to a vista with limited views of the south cove of

The cliffs of Mount Pisgah across Lake Willoughby mirror the steep sides of Mount Hor. Together, they form a notch that is recognized as a National Natural Landmark.

Lake Willoughby and the end of the Mount Pisgah cliffs. For the best views on Mount Hor, head 0.1 mile farther to North Overlook, crossing the top of the ridge and descending to an open rock ledge. Immediately in front of you, Mount Pisgah's sheer face rises from the deep lake. If you snowshoed to this point, you may see the colorful gear of ice climbers ascending the rock walls. Peregrine falcons also gather here, as the combination of horizontal ledges to support nests (called eyries) and vertical drops for hunting dives make Mount Pisgah's cliffs ideal habitat for these raptors.

Lake Willoughby stretches 4.0 miles northwest from here, with the comparatively gentle slope of Goodwin Mountain rising from the water north of Pisgah. The village of Westmore sits along the lake beneath Goodwin, where the shoreline curves into the mountainside. The Westmore Association has long maintained an active role in developing trails, including this one, which is named for the Trails Committee chair who proposed building it in 1971.

Mount Hor sits at the heart of the approximately 8,000-acre Willoughby State Forest, which was established in 1928 with an initial 1,700 acres. The forest is managed for multiple uses, meaning that some areas are conserved for ecological reasons, such as Marl Pond and Swamp; some are maintained for recreation, such as the mountain summits; and some are managed for public timber harvest through a program that allows residents to cut wood for home heating. The forest also has a long history of work by various conservation corps programs (see page 241).

Return to the trail junction and go left, descending to the parking lot the way you came up.

DID YOU KNOW?

The peregrine falcon is the fastest animal in the world. These birds achieve horizontal cruising speeds of 40 to 65 MPH, and their hunting dives, called stoops, have been recorded at more than 200 MPH.

MORE INFORMATION

Willoughby State Forest is managed by the Vermont Department of Forests, Parks and Recreation, St. Johnsbury District Office, 1229 Portland Street, Suite 201, St. Johnsbury, VT 05819; 802-751-0110; vtfpr.org. Mount Hor trails are maintained by the NorthWoods Stewardship Center, P.O. Box 220, East Charleston, Vermont 05833; 802-723-6551; northwoodscenter.org.

NEARBY

Camping and swimming areas can be found at both ends of Lake Willoughby. Some dining options can be found along the lake, with more in East Burke or Lyndonville, each 20 miles south, or Newport, 20 miles north.

TRIP 56
WHEELER MOUNTAIN

Location: Sutton, VT
Rating: Easy to Moderate
Distance: 2.5 miles round-trip
Elevation Gain: 700 feet
Estimated Time: 2 hours
Map: USGS Sutton

Wheeler Mountain is one of Vermont's quickest hikes to panoramic views of the Northeast Kingdom landscape, including the spectacular fjordlike Lake Willoughby.

DIRECTIONS

From the junction of VT 16 and US 5 in downtown Barton, head south on US 5 for 4.7 miles. Turn left onto the dirt Wheeler Mountain Road (Sutton Town Road 15). Go 2.0 miles to a small parking area (space for 5 cars) on the left, under apple trees. Overflow parking is along the side of the road continuing uphill. *GPS coordinates: 44° 43.41′ N, 72° 05.46′ W.*

TRAIL DESCRIPTION

The hike up Wheeler Mountain (2,371 feet) consists of two relatively easy legs, one at the base of the mountain and one across the top, separated by a short, steep climb in the middle. Once you gain the top of the cliff band at 0.7 mile, the views are frequent as the trail ducks in and out of the woods. Before hiking, check with Audubon Vermont (vt.audubon.org) for peregrine falcon activity here. The cliffs may be closed between March 15 and August 1 to protect falcon chicks.

White Trail begins just downhill from the parking lot, on the same side of the road. Descend through a narrow patch of woods, cross a small stream, and enter a meadow. The white-blazed trail stays along the right edge of the field. (At 0.1 mile, Red Trail departs to the right and ascends over several steeply angled bare ledges to rejoin White Trail on top of the cliffs. Descending Red Trail or going either direction in wet conditions is not recommended.) Continue straight on White Trail, leaving the meadow and walking along an old overgrown road through leafy recent tree growth that gradually gets more mature as you cross under Wheeler's steep hillside. Old sugar maples and an

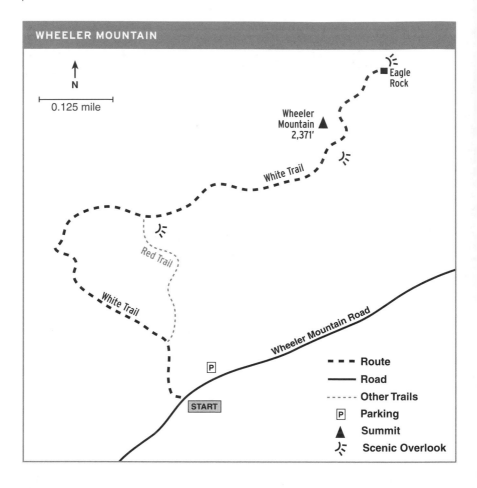

WHEELER MOUNTAIN

N

0.125 mile

Eagle Rock

Wheeler Mountain 2,371'

White Trail

Red Trail

White Trail

Wheeler Mountain Road

P

START

- - - Route
— Road
----- Other Trails
P Parking
▲ Summit
Scenic Overlook

abandoned heap of sugaring equipment appear alongside a stream. These streamside trees were once "tapped": Syrup makers inserted spouts to let some of the clear, watery sap run out during spring thaws. They then boiled the sap for hours to reduce its water content, making 1 gallon of maple syrup for every 35 to 50 gallons of sap collected.

Cross the stream on rocks and ascend next to it, following a smooth dirt trail as it switchbacks up the hill through a tall, older hardwood forest. A moderately pitched section of trail leads into the steepest part of this hike. The trail becomes eroded as it curves over roots and rocks. A couple of steep pitches lead to a more moderate rise along an eroded hillside, and then to a gradual incline as the forest changes primarily to spruce and fir. Crossing wooded, ledgy areas, White Trail exits the woods at 0.7 mile and meets the top of Red Trail at the first open vista. Wheeler Pond lies in the valley just below, and a

Wheeler Mountain's trail passes through sections of lovely, mossy, boreal forests between cliff-top outlooks with breathtaking views.

cluster of small local mountains, the largest of which is Granby (2,393 feet), rises due south.

Cross open ledges and reenter the woods, climbing gradually. Along this top part of Wheeler Mountain, the inconsistent blazes are at some points a red interior outlined with white, are at others just white, and occasionally aren't in evidence at all. Look for them on rocks as well as on trees as you weave through forests and over open areas.

At 1.0 mile, the trail emerges on open cliffs. Use extreme caution here. Scramble up a rock spine, with trees on the left and a drop on the right opening to wide views north, east, and south that get wider as you climb. From the panoramic views on top of the spine, head back into a thick, mossy, spruce/fir forest, edging around the summit proper. Descend gradually to the terminus of the hike at Eagle Rock, a ledge that feels like it's floating above the Northeast Kingdom landscape. Lake Willoughby shines beneath the cliffs of Mount Pisgah (2,751 feet). Beyond the lake, Bald Mountain (3,315 feet) is the noticeably conical peak. To the southeast, Burke Mountain (3,267 feet) is also distinct in its tall solitude.

Return to the trailhead the way you hiked up.

DID YOU KNOW?

Abenaki taught Vermont's early settlers how to make maple syrup and granulated maple sugar. Sap was collected in hollowed-out logs and either boiled (by heating rocks in a fire to a white-hot stage and then dropping them into the sap) or partially frozen (so that pure water could be removed in the form of ice).

MORE INFORMATION

Almost all of Wheeler Mountain is privately owned and is open to the public through the generosity of the landowners. Camping and fires are not allowed. Hikers are asked to leave by sunset, and not to hike April 1 to June 1, when the trail soils are wet and delicate. The final 0.3 mile of trail to Eagle Rock is within Willoughby State Forest, managed by the Vermont Department of Forests, Parks and Recreation, 1229 Portland Street, Suite 201, St. Johnsbury, VT 05819; 802-751-0123; vtfpr.org.

NEARBY

Food is available in Barton, 6.7 miles west. Crystal Lake State Park, also 6.7 miles west, is good for swimming and paddling. Closer by, Wheeler Pond (Trip 57) has a nice loop walk around it and the Green Mountain Club rents two cabins on its shore. The Fairbanks Museum has natural history exhibits and a planetarium in St. Johnsbury, 26 miles south.

TRIP 57
WHEELER POND AND GNOME STAIRS

Location: Sutton and Barton, VT
Rating: Easy
Distance: 1.6 miles round-trip
Elevation Gain: 175 feet
Estimated Time: 1 hour
Map: USGS Sutton

An easy ramble around Wheeler Pond leads to a series of magical little waterfalls tumbling through the woods.

DIRECTIONS
From the junction of VT 16 and US 5 in downtown Barton, head south on US 5 for 4.7 miles. Turn left onto the dirt Wheeler Mountain Road (Sutton Town Road 15). Go 1.2 miles to the trailhead parking area (space for 6 cars) on the right, which is shared with Moose Mountain Trail. *GPS coordinates:* 44° 43.03′ N, 72° 06.03′ W.

TRAIL DESCRIPTION
Wheeler Pond fills a shallow basin beneath Wheeler and Moose mountains. Wheeler Brook tumbles down from Wheeler Mountain, drifts through the pond, then continues steeply downhill over small waterfalls and stepped cascades called the Gnome Stairs. This short hike circles the east side of the pond, wanders a short distance downhill along the Gnome Stairs, then climbs back up to the pond and finishes the loop along a dirt road. With enough snow to cover the bulging rocks, the pond loop is a pleasant cross-country ski, but the steep, wet Gnome Stairs are better explored on snowshoes in winter. The loop around the pond is about 1.0 mile; Gnome Stairs is an additional 0.3 mile in each direction.

Wheeler Pond Trail begins in tandem with Moose Mountain Trail, immediately crossing a log bridge over the upper leg of Wheeler Brook. On the far bank, Moose Mountain Trail goes left. Go right, following Wheeler Pond Trail into a mixed hardwood forest. The understory is thick with ferns, lilies, tall hobblebush, and scraggly striped maple. In early summer, look for clusters of wispy white baneberry flowers on a tall spear (1 to 3 feet high);

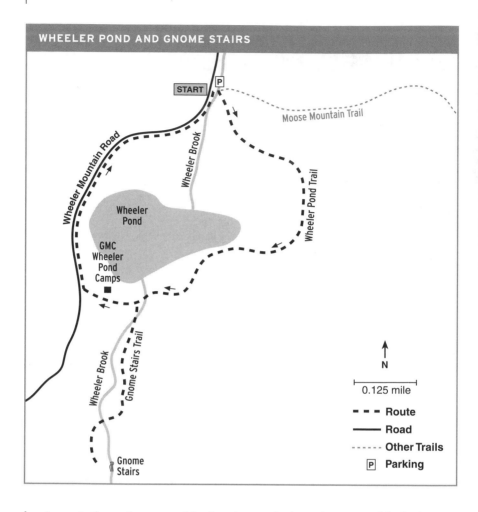

WHEELER POND AND GNOME STAIRS

START

P

Moose Mountain Trail

Wheeler Mountain Road

Wheeler Brook

Wheeler Pond

Wheeler Pond Trail

GMC
Wheeler
Pond
Camps

Wheeler Brook

Gnome Stairs Trail

Gnome
Stairs

N

0.125 mile

- - - Route
——— Road
----- Other Trails
P Parking

by August, the poisonous white berries, with their distinctive black dot, are noticeable against their red stalks.

At first, the blue-blazed trail wends high above the pond and the water is not visible unless the trees are bare. The route is rocky and undulating, crossing seeps and small streams. Mushrooms provide a splash of color in these moist, leaf-littered woods. The white stem and nodding flower of Indian pipe pokes up from the damp humus, relying on neighboring fungi for water and nutrients, as it has no chlorophyll to make its own food.

After about 0.4 mile, the trail descends and follows close to Wheeler Pond for a short distance. The shoreline is thick with shrubs and sometimes obscured from view by a screen of trees. Moose frequent this area—about half of the 70-odd pounds of plants moose need to eat each day are aquatic—so you are likely to see their cloven hoofprints along this muddy stretch.

Cascading water creates the Gnome Stairs as it spills out of Wheeler Pond.

The path then veers left, back into the woods, and continues to parallel the shore to the pond's outlet. The trail emerges at the water's edge, where a beaver dam bolsters the outlet, keeping placid water above and letting the white plumes of Wheeler Brook emerge from its base. From the dam, Wheeler Mountain's cliffy south side is visible.

Hop across Wheeler Brook on rocks about 40 feet below the beaver dam. Changes in water level and movement of rocks may alter the stream landscape; if the crossing seems too challenging, continue downstream to find alternate routes. On the far side, the trail forks. The Green Mountain Club's two rental camps are to the right. Go left, following Gnome Stairs Trail along the stream bank.

A short distance downhill, cross Wheeler Brook again and continue to descend along small waterfalls and cascades. A left turn leads the trail away from the water for a short distance before descending to the braided channels where the stream crosses a flat area. Pick your way across and follow the right bank down to the end of the trail 0.3 mile from the pond outlet. White curtains of water cascade down Gnome Stairs, a series of streamwide ledges beneath sheltering conifers.

White baneberry, also known as doll's eyes, grows in rich woods such as those above Wheeler Pond. Its starry, white flowers bloom in spring, and its poisonous berries on thick red stalks appear later in the summer.

Return uphill on the same trail, arriving at the junction by the pond outlet. Go left, passing the Green Mountain Club's camps to arrive on Wheeler Mountain Road. Turn right here and follow the dirt road 0.4 mile along the west shore of the pond to the trailhead parking area.

DID YOU KNOW?

From 1977 to 2003, AMC owned and operated Wheeler Pond Camps. AMC members built Wheeler Pond and Gnome Stairs trails, among other paths in this area.

MORE INFORMATION

The eastern half of Wheeler Pond is in Willoughby State Forest, managed by the Vermont Department of Forests, Parks and Recreation, 1229 Portland Street, Suite 201, St. Johnsbury, VT 05819; 802-751-0123; vtfpr.org. Wheeler Pond Camps are available for rent from the Green Mountain Club, 802-244-7037; greenmountainclub.org.

NEARBY

Barton, 6.7 miles west, has dining options and Crystal Lake State Park, with swimming and paddling. Lake Willoughby—with hiking, swimming, boating, and magnificent scenery—is close by, but the extension of Wheeler Mountain Road is very rough and may not be passable through to the lake's western shore. Go through Barton, 14 miles to the north shore, or through West Burke, 17 miles to the south shore.

TRIP 58
MONADNOCK MOUNTAIN

Location: Lemington, VT
Rating: Moderate to Strenuous
Distance: 5.0 miles round-trip
Elevation Gain: 2,108 feet
Estimated Time: 3 hours
Map: USGS Monadnock Mountain

This isolated peak combines a remote hiking experience with extensive views of far northern New Hampshire and Vermont.

DIRECTIONS

From the Lemington–Colebrook bridge across the Connecticut River, travel about 0.1 mile north on VT 102 to a gravel pit on the left. Hiker parking is on the far left side of the working quarry in an open lot; use caution and do not block access for trucks. *GPS coordinates:* 44° 54.06′ N, 71° 30.43′ W.

TRAIL DESCRIPTION

Monadnock Mountain (3,148 feet) is a true geologic monadnock—a peak standing alone because its rocks are more resistant to erosion than the surrounding landscape is. This hike ascends a rocky drainage between steep ridges on the mountain's east side. While rugged, the trail is well maintained and easily navigated, treating hikers to a journey through a remote and wild-feeling forest.

From the parking area, head 0.1 mile up a gravel road to a sign-in box in an open field. Following yellow markers, start along the left edge of the clearing, then turn right through a brushy meadow, popping over a low ridge halfway across. Departing the meadow, Monadnock Mountain Trail climbs into a recently reestablished forest of small fir, birch, and spruce. Along with the gravel pit, timber has long been harvested from Monadnock's slopes.

In a short distance, pass through an open, slightly older softwood plantation. Following a stream on your left and a tall, mossy ledge on your right, duck under a rock overhang and enter an older, mixed forest. A short, steep pitch leads to a stream crossing and the junction with the old fire road at 0.7 mile. Follow this road for the next steep 0.3 mile. (On your return trip, a loose pile of rocks resembling a cairn marks this junction.)

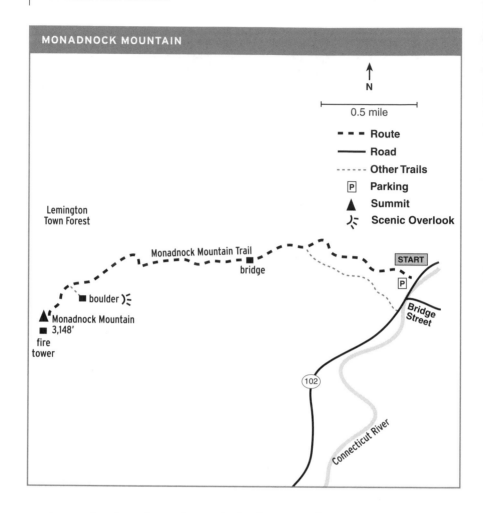

As you head up the rocky road, the footing will occasionally be difficult over loose rocks. When the road becomes more of a trail again, it crests a hill and swings right to cross the stream on a plank bridge at 1.0 mile. Be careful; algae and spray make the surface slippery. The mossy cascade beneath the bridge and a couple of seat-sized rocks make this a scenic place for a break.

From the bridge, the hike climbs steadily and moderately over ledges, rocks, and drainage gullies. Once in great disrepair, Monadnock Mountain Trail saw extensive reparation by NorthWoods Youth Conservation Corps during the summers of 2005 through 2007.

Climb through a stand of paper birch, then into the spruce/fir zone of the upper mountain. Red spruce, balsam fir, mountain ash, and paper birch are particularly suited to the thin, acidic soils and cold temperatures of mountaintops in New England. You can easily tell spruce and fir apart by shaking their

Old-man's beard lichen hangs from balsam fir branches in the dense forest on Monadnock Mountain's summit. A fire tower gives hikers views over the treetops.

hands: A spruce bough is spiny and sharp when you grip it, while a fir's is flat and friendly.

At 2.0 miles, a short dead-end spur trail on the left leads to a boulder with a view east. Staying right, ascend to the final, flat walk through a dense stand of conifers covered with old-man's beard and arrive at the base of the fire tower. Monadnock's height made it an obvious location for a lookout tower, which was built during the Great Depression by the Civilian Conservation Corps (see page 241). The foundation and chimney of the Monadnock fire warden's cabin remain just beyond the tower.

Over the pointed tips of Monadnock's thick summit forest, the Connecticut River meanders south through a glacially scoured valley, forming the Vermont–New Hampshire border. The White Mountains push up against the eastern shore of the river, most notably the Nash Stream mountains to the southeast. On a clear day, the tall ridge of the Presidential Range can be seen in the southeast, and Magalloway Mountain (3,350 feet) in the northeast. To the southwest, Nulhegan Basin is a sort of geologic opposite of Monadnock, in which the center of a high land eroded more quickly than its edges, leaving a 10-mile-wide depression surrounded by a ring of hills. To the northeast, Averill Mountain (2,240 feet) and Brousseau Mountain (2,723 feet; Trip 60) back the two Averill Lakes on the Quebec border.

Retrace your path to the trailhead.

DID YOU KNOW?

Gold has been mined in Vermont—but not very successfully. A reputed gold mine was on Monadnock Mountain, and small amounts of placer gold (pieces that have been eroded from their source) are present in many streams in Vermont. Hand-panning for gold is allowed on state and federal lands without a permit.

MORE INFORMATION

Monadnock Mountain Trail is partly on private land and partly on town forest land. Please respect the generosity of the landowners: Do not kindle fires, camp, or use motorized vehicles on the trail; carry out all trash. The trail is maintained by the NorthWoods Stewardship Center, P.O. Box 220, East Charleston, VT 05833; 802-723-6551; northwoodscenter.org.

NEARBY

The Connecticut River Paddlers Trail and Northern Forest Canoe Trail maintain access and campsites along the river. The Nulhegan Basin Division of the Silvio O. Conte National Fish and Wildlife Refuge has a visitor center and walking trails 18.5 miles southwest on VT 105. Food is along US 3 in Colebrook, New Hampshire, 0.8 mile east.

FROM THE CCC TO THE VYCC: CONSERVATION CORPS IN VERMONT

Vermont has almost as many trails as it has citizens. Okay, maybe that's an exaggeration, but think of not just the hiking trails that cobweb over the whole state but also the cross-country and alpine ski trails, the mountain-bike and paddling trails, the all-terrain-vehicle and snowmobile trails, the rail trails and horseback riding trails, and the birding trails and town park trails. How did one of this country's smallest states, with one of the smallest populations, come to be so covered with trails?

It would be too simple to say that the Civilian Conservation Corps (CCC) is responsible for all this, but in a way it's true. The Depression-era program—part of Franklin Delano Roosevelt's New Deal—harnessed the energies of unemployed young men to accomplish environmental conservation projects across the nation. The federal government originally allotted Vermont four CCC camps, but State Forester Perry Merrill had a long list of planned conservation projects, and he lobbied successfully for additional men and funding to complete them. Vermont hosted 30 CCC camps that supported more than 40,000 men as they constructed hiking and ski trails, state-park facilities, fire towers, and mountain roads. Their legacy is not only the physical infrastructure but also the promotion of a culture of outdoor recreation and conservation that today values all manner of trails.

Another CCC legacy is its many offspring. The first and one of the most successful descendants is the Student Conservation Association (SCA), which began in 1957 to save national parks from being "loved to death" and continues in a broader capacity today. In the 1970s, the federally funded Youth Conservation Corps followed SCA's lead and employed hundreds of thousands of young Americans. When federal funding was cut in 1981, many states, including Vermont, picked up the tab to keep these programs running. The Vermont Youth Conservation Corps (VYCC) was born in 1985.

Today, VYCC is a private, nonprofit organization that hires young people to complete conservation projects. The NorthWoods Conservation Corps, founded separately to serve the Northeast Kingdom region, hires young people as part of its mission "to help local youth become stewards of their natural and community resources."

If you come across a youth crew laboring on the trail, offer them some encouragement. The state's trails and recreation facilities depend on their hard work today—and on their attitudes and values in the decades to come.

TRIP 59
BLUFF MOUNTAIN

Location: Island Pond, VT
Rating: Moderate
Distance: 3.2 miles round-trip
Elevation Gain: 1,060 feet
Estimated Time: 2.5 hours
Map: USGS Island Pond

Steep rock outcrops provide exciting hiking and a bird's-eye view of the water and community of Island Pond.

DIRECTIONS

From the junction of VT 105 and VT 114 in the middle of Island Pond, go east on VT 105 for 0.2 mile and turn left onto South Street. Take the second right onto Mountain Street and drive 0.6 mile to the trailhead parking lot (space for about 6 cars) on the left. *GPS coordinates:* 44° 49.52′ N, 71° 52.57′ W.

TRAIL DESCRIPTION

Bluff Mountain (2,789 feet) is a north–south ridge with three high points, the middle being the proper summit. The Community Trail–Lookout Trail loop climbs the steep-sided southern summit (2,380 feet) overlooking Island Pond. Lookout Trail traverses a very steep pitch with the aid of iron handles affixed to the rock; children, dogs, and people who aren't comfortable with that level of exposure can use Bluff Mountain Community Trail to ascend as well as descend, and follow the gentle top section of Lookout Trail to the overlook. The steep section of Lookout Trail is best ascended, and best avoided altogether in wet or icy conditions. But for hikers who appreciate variety and challenge, Lookout Trail provides a fun, memorable experience.

Bluff Mountain Community Trail starts in a red-pine plantation, following blue blazes uphill through tidy rows of tall trees. At 0.1 mile, a register box marks the transition into a more natural forest of maple, birch, and fir. Ferns and the glossy, dark-green leaves of partridgeberry spread across the forest floor. Climbing moderately, cross an open swath at 0.2 mile, where blackberries and raspberries thrive. At 0.4 mile, cross an old, eroded two-track in the forest and continue snaking up the hill through a stand of big cedars.

A clearing on the southern end of Bluff Mountain gives hikers a perspective of the immense forests surrounding the lake and village of Island Pond.

For the first 0.8 mile, Bluff Mountain Community Trail climbs through Brighton Town Forest, and then, crossing onto private land, begins to cross the hill and descend. At 1.0 mile, it crosses a stream at the bottom of its descent and curves uphill to a junction. Community Trail goes right; this is your return route, or the alternate route uphill for hikers who want to avoid Lookout Trail. Go left onto the yellow-blazed Lookout Trail.

At first, Lookout Trail rises at a pleasant rate, crossing a couple of wet swaths filled with ferns, then crossing the hillside. A rock staircase begins the steep section of the trail. As you pick your way up the vertical pitch, notice how many birch trunks and branches lie on the hillside around you—debris from 1998's destructive ice storm. Steep becomes very steep, and for the final 0.1 mile of the climb you'll need your hands to help you ascend. At the top, a small view of the shining waters of Island Pond rewards your efforts. Continue a short distance up the trail to a grassy clearing with a bigger overlook and a more stable place to stand when viewing it.

The Village of Island Pond and its namesake lake are the highlights of this view. Island Pond is in an interesting position on a watershed divide. From the pond, the Clyde River flows northwest, descending to Lake Memphremagog,

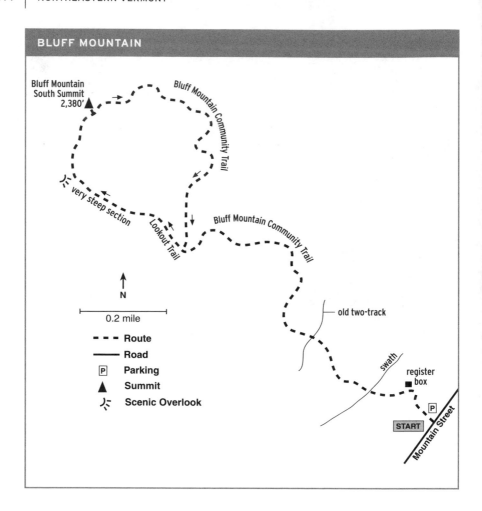

BLUFF MOUNTAIN

Bluff Mountain
South Summit
2,380'

Bluff Mountain Community Trail

very steep section

Lookout Trail

Bluff Mountain Community Trail

N

0.2 mile

- - - Route
—— Road
P Parking
▲ Summit
Scenic Overlook

old two-track

swath

register
box

P

START

Mountain Street

which drains north into the Saint Lawrence River. Just on the other side of Island Pond, the Nulhegan River rises from Nulhegan Pond and flows the opposite direction, southeast to the Connecticut River, which drains south into Long Island Sound.

Look closely at the ridge beyond Island Pond's waters to spot the blocky Cold War–era radar building on East Mountain (3,420 feet). The summit of Burke Mountain (3,267 feet) curves against the sky behind the Seneca Range to the south. New Hampshire's White Mountains are in the distant south, with the pointed summit of Mount Garfield (4,500 feet) east of the big hump of Mount Lafayette (5,260 feet).

Follow yellow blazes across the clearing and into the woods. A rolling, mossy path leads through a boreal forest to a short spur trail at 1.5 miles. The south, or lower-mountain summit, is here, on a large rock surrounded by

Steel handles aid hikers climbing the very steep slope of Lookout Trail. The Community Trail half of the loop provides an alternate route to the vista on top of Bluff Mountain.

trees. From the spur trail junction, the blue blazes of Bluff Mountain Community Trail lead through a damp, flat-bottomed ravine at 1.7 miles, and then into a smooth, gently sloping gully. The descent steepens for a short distance, then eases across the hill and zigzags down a rocky path, arriving at the Lookout Trail junction at 2.2 miles. From here, follow Bluff Mountain Community Trail out the way you hiked in.

DID YOU KNOW?
Paddlers on the Clyde River steer their boats through a tunnel under the Clyde River Hotel as they leave Island Pond.

MORE INFORMATION
Bluff Mountain's trails are maintained by the NorthWoods Stewardship Center, P.O. Box 220, East Charleston, VT 05833; 802-723-6551; northwoodscenter.org.

NEARBY
Northern Forest Canoe Trail's 740-mile route passes through Island Pond; a kiosk with more information is downtown in Pavilion Park, 1 mile south, which is also a nice place to picnic and swim. Camp, paddle, and swim at Brighton State Park, 3.5 miles east. Food and shops are in Island Pond, 1 mile south.

TRIP 60
BROUSSEAU MOUNTAIN

Location: Norton, VT
Rating: Easy to Moderate
Distance: 1.6 miles round-trip
Elevation Gain: 550 feet
Estimated Time: 1 hour
Map: USGS Averill

A short, pretty climb over the summit of this small peak leads to dramatic cliffs and a wide view south over lakes and mountains.

DIRECTIONS

From the junction of VT 114 and VT 147 in Norton, near the border-crossing station, follow VT 114 east for 3.0 miles. Turn right onto Brousseau Mountain Road and follow it 1.3 miles to its end at a gate. Park alongside the road (space for about 5 cars), being careful not to block the gate or driveways. (This road is not maintained in winter, so depending on the conditions, snowshoers may need to park at the bottom and add 2.6 miles round-trip to the hike.) *GPS coordinates: 44° 58.61′ N, 71° 44.47′ W.*

TRAIL DESCRIPTION

Brousseau Mountain (2,756 feet), just south of the Quebec border, is off the beaten path of most hikers; consequently, its incredible views and lovely forests are often quiet. Approaching this inconspicuous forested bump from the north, you don't see the dramatic cliffs on its south face until you arrive on top of them. Peregrine falcons have sometimes nested on these crags, and if they are there, the overlook may be closed to hikers between March 15 and August 1 to protect the chicks; check with Audubon Vermont (vt.audubon.org) for current information. The short, steady climb is appropriate for kids about ages 5 and older.

Go around the gate and follow the extension of Brousseau Mountain Road about 400 feet, where the trail goes left into the woods and passes a register box just inside the treeline. Climbing gradually through the thin trunks of a young forest, you will pass an old apple tree and brushy openings on both sides of the trail that hint at the land's recent history. After passing through a dim fir stand, the trail angles uphill more.

The mountains and immense forests of the Northeast Kingdom provide the backdrop to Little Averill Lake—the stunning view from the top of Brousseau Mountain.

At 0.4 mile, Brousseau Mountain Trail crosses a narrow swath cut across the mountain—the remains of a skid trail used to remove logs. After this, the forest becomes more boreal—a beautiful mix of fir, spruce, mountain ash, and paper birch. These trees are older than the ones below, and the thick trunks are spaced apart enough to give a view through the forest. The trail's treadway is often solid bedrock, lined with moss, blueberries, and ferns as the trail makes its way back and forth and sometimes directly up the slope. Occasional rock steps and bog bridges break up the long stripes of rock trail.

The pitch lessens as you enter a tunnel of tight saplings near the top of the mountain. Curving left, cross the forested summit at 0.7 mile. The trail drops to the right, descending through spruce and fir for 0.1 mile before arriving at the open rocks of the lookout. Leash dogs here, and keep children close by.

Little Averill Pond spreads across the valley beneath the cliffs, its inlet stream zigzagging through a marsh to the west. Sable Mountain (2,725 feet) is the little solo peak south of the pond, and Green (2,700 feet) and Black (2,800 feet) mountains form the high ground beyond the inlet marsh. Monadnock Mountain (3,148 feet; Trip 58) rises beyond ridges to the southeast, its fire tower discernible against the sky. Turbines visible on the ridges north and

BROUSSEAU MOUNTAIN

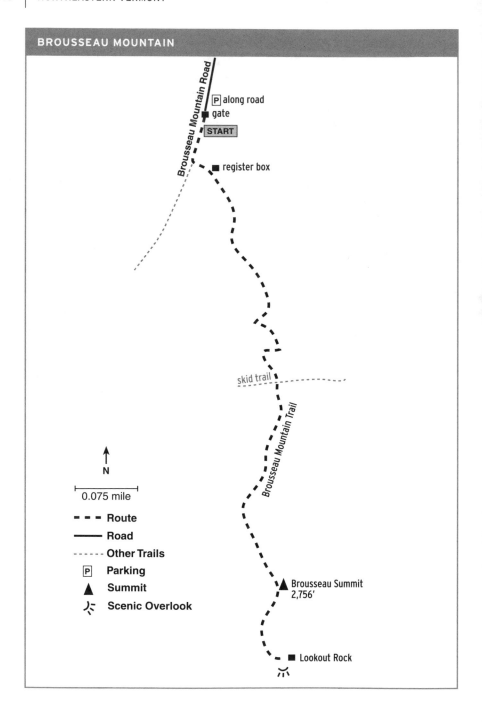

south of Monadnock are in New Hampshire, part of the 33-tower Granite Wind project. Beyond the wooded, watery lands of Kingdom and Victory state forests, New Hampshire's White Mountains spread across the southern horizon, including Mount Garfield (4,500 feet) and Mount Lafayette (5,260 feet). Jay Peak (3,858 feet) pokes above closer ridgelines to the west.

Return downhill the way you climbed up.

DID YOU KNOW?

Norton, Vermont, and Stanhope, Quebec, developed together, as did many other border towns in this rural area, where the lay of the land often influenced communities more than political lines did. A general store was situated on the international border for years, with doors on both sides, so residents of either country could enter to shop.

MORE INFORMATION

Brousseau Mountain Trail is maintained by the NorthWoods Stewardship Center, P.O. Box 220, East Charleston, VT 05833; 802-723-6551; northwoodscenter.org.

NEARBY

Little Averill and Great Averill ponds have placid paddling around the base of Brousseau Mountain. Mountain-bike at Hereford Mountain in East Hereford, Quebec, 19 miles northeast. Paddle, camp, and swim at Brighton State Park, 23 miles south. A general store in Norton provides some food; for more options, head to Island Pond, 20 miles south.

APPENDIX: MOUNTAIN BIKING

The popularity of mountain biking has grown rapidly in Vermont over the past decade, and so have the number of trails specifically for bikes. The Vermont Mountain Bike Association (VMBA) is a central organizer and promoter of mountain biking, with chapter organizations heading up trail work regionally. Some mountain-bike areas charge riders a fee to help defray maintenance expenses; other places are free to ride, with trail maintenance dependent on volunteers, memberships, and donations.

Here is a partial list of some of the best mountain biking in Vermont, with the caveat that more options exist than can be listed here, and more trails are being added each season, all across the state. For the most up-to-date information, consult local bike shops and VMBA chapters (vmba.org).

Kingdom Trails: The award-winning Kingdom Trails in East Burke have everything from beginner-friendly old farm roads to fast, flowing single-track to technical free-ride trails. With more than 100 miles of well-maintained, interconnected cross-country trails and a new lift-served downhill and free-ride area, this trail system is the leader in mountain biking not just in Vermont but in the Northeast. Website: kingdomtrails.com. Near: Burke Mountain (Trip 52).

Moosalamoo National Recreation Area: The U.S. Forest Service has joined forces with VMBA and various other groups to develop mountain biking in this diverse section of the northern Green Mountain National Forest. The trails range from dirt roads to technical single-track. Website: moosalamoo. org. Near: Rattlesnake Cliffs (Trip 20), Robert Frost Trail (Trip 21), and Mount Horrid's Great Cliff (Trip 31).

Vermont Ride Center: One of only five U.S. sites approved by the International Mountain Bike Association as a model in mountain-bike development, the Vermont Ride Center is a work-in-progress centered in the Waterbury–Stowe area and radiating to include trail systems in Bolton, Cambridge, and Jericho. All levels and all types of riding (cross-country, free-ride, and downhill) will be included by the time the project is complete. Website: vmba.org. Near: Camel's Hump (Trip 27) and Mount Hunger (Trip 41).

Trapp Family Lodge: High on the mountain above Stowe, this iconic resort's trail system offers 40 miles (and counting) of double- and single-track riding that connects into a network of local trails, accommodating all abilities of riders. Website: trappfamily.com. Near: Wiessner Woods (Trip 43), Stowe Pinnacle (Trip 44), and Sterling Pond (Trip 46).

Mad River Valley: This central Vermont area has long been a haven of steep technical riding, but recent developments at Blueberry Lake are increasing the miles of beginner and intermediate riding. Website: madriverriders.com. Near: Sunset Ledge (Trip 24), Mount Abraham (Trip 25), and Burnt Rock (Trip 26).

Millstone Hill: Circumnavigating scenic old granite quarries on the hill above Barre, more than 35 miles of trails provide tons of technical riding as well as loops for beginner and intermediate riders. Website: millstonetrails.com. Near: Spruce Mountain (Trip 28) and Owl's Head (Trip 29).

Chittenden County: With more than 100 miles of trails in a dozen locations not far from Burlington, Chittenden County offers options for all levels of riders. Consult local bike shops or vmba.org. Near: Colchester Pond (Trip 35) and Mount Mansfield (Trip 45).

Sleepy Hollow: This Huntington inn's 12 miles of intermediate and advanced single-track connect to a network of multiuse trails in Hinesburg Town Forest. Website: skisleepyhollow.com. Near: Camel's Hump (Trip 27).

Catamount Outdoor Family Center: These multiuse trails in Williston accommodate trail runners and hikers in addition to mountain bikers. Popular camps, races, and other events make the center a hub of local outdoor activity. Website: catamountoutdoor.com. Near: Mount Mansfield (Trip 45).

Norwich University Paine Mountain Outdoor Center: In 2011, Norwich University, in Northfield, began transforming its alpine ski hill into an outdoor center with a network of year-round multiuse trails. The mountain-bike trails that have been built have gotten rave reviews; work is ongoing. Website: norwich.edu. Near: Sunset Ledge (Trip 24), Mount Abraham (Trip 25), and Burnt Rock (Trip 26).

Green Mountain Trails: Twenty miles of multiuse single-track in Pittsfield, Stockbridge, and Chittenden offer all levels of riding on a variety of terrain. Website: greenmountaintrails.com. Near: Pico Peak (Trip 16), Deer Leap (Trip 18), and Mount Horrid's Great Cliff (Trip 31).

Pine Hill Park: Within the City of Rutland, a 300-acre preserve of wooded hills and ravines hosts 16 miles of multiuse single-track trails. The majority is intermediate level riding, but there are beginner-friendly routes and some more technical aspects for advanced riders. Website: pinehillpark.org. Near: White Rocks Ice Beds (Trip 12), Pico Peak (Trip 16), Deer Leap (Trip 18), and Buckner Preserve (Trip 19).

Sports Trails of the Ascutney Basin: The western flank of Mount Ascutney is covered with 30 miles of multiuse trails looping through woods and fields, accommodating all abilities. Website: stabvt.org. Near: Okemo Mountain (Trip 13), Mount Ascutney (Trip 14), and Mount Tom (Trip 15).

INDEX

A

Abenaki Indians, xviii
Addison, hikes near, 91–94
Allen Hill, 135–137
alpine areas, 99, 180–184
antecedent rivers, 162
Appalachian Trail, 29
  in central Vermont, 66, 72–73
  in southern Vermont, 2, 7–9, 27, 43–46,
    61–64

B

Barton, hikes near, 233–236
Big Muddy Pond, 197–200
Billings, Frederick, 60
bird-watching
  in central Vermont, 70, 82, 121
  in northeastern Vermont, 210
  in northwestern Vermont, 130, 134,
    139–140, 149–152
Black Mountain, 13–16
Blood Rock, 55–56
Bluff Mountain, 242–245
bogs, 117, 150–152
Bradford, hikes near, 118–121
Breadloaf Wilderness Area, 95–98
Brosseau Mountain, 246–249
Buckner Memorial Preserve, 75–78
Burke, hikes near, 211–214
Burke Mountain, 211–214
Burnt Mountain, 201–204
Burnt Rock, 103–105
Burton Island, 145–148

C

Cambridge, hikes near, 185–188
Camel's Hump, 106–109

catamounts, 175
Catamount Trail, 2
  in central Vermont, 66, 74
  in north-central Vermont, 153, 171–174,
    189
  in southern Vermont, 26, 50, 61
C. C. Putnam State Forest, 158–161, 163–166
central Vermont
  region description, 65–66
  trip descriptions, 67–126
  trip planner, x–xiii
Champion Lands conservation project, 209
Charlotte, hikes near, 127–134
child-friendly hikes
  in central Vermont, 67–98, 110–121
  in north-central Vermont, 154–157,
    167–174, 185–200
  in northeastern Vermont, 215–218,
    225–228, 233–236, 246–249
  in northwestern Vermont, 127–152
  in southern Vermont, 3–12, 17–33, 39–49,
    57–60
Civilian Conservation Corps (CCC), 241
clothing, xxiii
Colchester, hikes near, 138–141
Colchester Pond, 138–141
Connecticut River, xviii, 2
  hikes near, 237–240
conservation corps, 241
cross-country skiing, recommended trips,
    xxiv–xxv
  in central Vermont, 67–70, 83–90,
    118–121
  in north-central Vermont, 154–157,
    171–174
  in northeastern Vermont, 215–218,
    233–236
  in northwestern Vermont, 127–152

in southern Vermont, 10–12, 17–20,
    25–33, 39–46, 57–60

D
Darling State Park, 211–214
Deer Leap, 72–74
Devil's Gulch, 197–200
dog-friendly hikes
    in central Vermont, 67–74, 79–90, 95–124
    in north-central Vermont, 154–208
    in northeastern Vermont, 211–249
    in northwestern Vermont, 127–130,
        135–152
    in southern Vermont, 3–10, 17–20, 25–64
drinking water, 219
Dummerston, hikes near, 13–16
Duxbury, hikes near, 106–109

E
Eagle Mountain, 142–144
easy hikes
    in central Vermont, 67–74, 83–90, 95–98,
        113–121
    in north-central Vermont, 154–157,
        167–174, 193–196
    in northeastern Vermont, 215–218,
        225–236, 246–248
    in northwestern Vermont, 131–152
    in southern Vermont, 10–12, 17–24,
        43–49, 57–60
Eden, hikes near, 197–200
Elmore, hikes near, 189–192
Elmore Mountain, 189–192
Emmons, Ebenezer, 9

F
Falls of Lana, 79–82
Faulkner Park, 57–60
Fayston, hikes near, 103–105
fishing, 219
Frost, Robert, 74, 83–86

G
geocaching, 71
geology, 2, 9, 14, 162
Gile Mountain, 67–70
Gnome Stairs, 233–236
Gold Brook Covered Bridge, 179
gold mining, 240
Goshen, hikes near, 122–124
Great Cliff (Mount Horrid), 122–124
Green Mountain Club, xxv
Green Mountain National Forest, xxv, 2

hikes in, 7–9 , 25–28, 30–33, 43–49
Green Mountains, 1–2, 9
Groton State Forest, 110–116

H
Harmon Hill, 7–9
Haystack Mountain, 3–6
Helen W. Buckner Memorial Preserve, 75–78
hermit thrush, 163–164
Hubbard Park, 154–157
Hurricane Irene. *See* Tropical Storm Irene

I
invasive species, 141
Island Pond, hikes near, 242–245

J
Jay Peak, 205–208
jewelweed, 174
Johnson, hikes near, 193–196
Joseph Battell Wilderness, 122–124

K
Killington, hikes near, 61–64, 72–74

L
lady's slippers, 217
Lake Champlain, 65, 125, 152
    hikes along, 75–78, 87–90, 135–137,
        145–152
Lake Memphremagog, 208
Lake Willoughby, hikes near, 220–223,
    225–228
Leave No Trace principles, xxv–xxvi
Ledges Overlook, 21–24
Lemington, hikes near, 237–240
leopard frogs, 78
letterboxing, 71
Lincoln, hikes near, 95–102
Little Rock Pond, 43–46
Long Trail, xviii, 29
    in central Vermont, 66, 95–105, 108–109,
        122–124
    in northern Vermont, 185–188, 193–200,
        205–208
    in southern Vermont, 2, 7–9, 27–28,
        43–46, 61–64
lookout towers, 52
    in central Vermont, 67–69, 110–112
    in northern Vermont, 154–157, 189–192,
        214, 239–240
    in southern Vermont, 10–12, 50–56

loons, 215–218
L. R. Jones State Forest, 110–112
Ludlow Mountain. *See* Okemo Mountain
Lye Brook Falls, 30–33

M

Mad River Glen ski area, 105
Maidstone State Park, 215–219
Manchester, hikes near, 30–33, 35–38
maple syrup, 230, 232
Menden, hikes near, 61–64
Merck Forest and Farmland, 39–42
Middlesex, hikes near, 158–161
Milton, hikes near, 142–144
Missisquoi National Wildlife Refuge, 149–152
moderate hikes
    in central Vermont, 72–82, 87–94,
        103–105, 110–124
    in north-central Vermont, 154–166,
        176–179, 185–208
    in northeastern Vermont, 220–232,
        237–249
    in northwestern Vermont, 127–130,
        138–141
    in southern Vermont, 1–16, 25–33, 39–42,
        50–53, 57–60
Molly Stark State Park, 6, 10–12
Monadnock Mountain, 237–240
Montgomery, hikes near, 201–204
Montpelier, hikes near, 154–157
Moosalamoo National Recreation Area, 79–82
Moss Glen Falls, 167–171
Mount Abraham, 99–102
mountain biking, 251–253
mountain lions. *See* catamounts
Mount Antone, 39–42
Mount Ascutney, 54–56
Mount Equinox, 1, 35–38
Mount Holly, hikes near, 50–53
Mount Hor, 225–228
Mount Horrid, 122–124
Mount Hunger, 163–166
Mount Independence, 87–90
Mount Mansfield, 180–184
Mount Olga, 10–12
Mount Philo State Park, 127–130
Mount Pisgah, 220–223
Mount Tabor, hikes near, 43–46
Mount Tom, 57–60

N

natural history, 162, 195
New Discovery State Park, 113–116

north-central Vermont
    region description, 153
    trip descriptions, 154–210
    trip planner, xii–xv
northeastern Vermont
    region description, 209–210
    trip descriptions, 211–249
    trip planner, xiv–xv
northwestern Vermont
    region description, 125–126
    trip descriptions, 127–153
    trip planner, xii–xiii
Norton, hikes near, 246–249
Norwich, hikes near, 67–70

O

Okemo Mountain, 50–53
Orwell, hikes near, 87–90
Owl's Head, 113–116

P

paper birch, 204
Peacham, hikes near, 113–116
peregrine falcons, 228, 246
Pico Peak, 61–64
"pillows and cradles," 131–134
pitch pines, 16, 150–151
Plainfield, hikes near, 110–112
poison parsnip, 129
Prospect Rock, 193–196
Putney, hikes near, 17–20
Putney Mountain, 17–20

Q

questing, 71

R

Rattlesnake Cliffs, 79–82
rattlesnakes, 76
Ripton, hikes near, 83–86
Robert Frost Trail, 83–86
Robert T. Stafford White Rocks National
        Recreation Area, 47–49
Rupert, hikes near, 39–42

S

safety considerations, xxii–xxvi
Saint Albans, hikes near, 145–148
Salisbury, hikes near, 79–82
Searsburg Wind Farm, 12
Shelburne, hikes near, 135–137
Shelburne Bay Park, 135–137
Smuggler's Notch, 196

Snake Mountain, 91–94
snakes, 76
snowshoeing, xxiv–xxv
southern Vermont
    region description, 1–2
    trip descriptions, 3–66
    trip planner, viii–xi
Spruce Mountain, 110–112
Sterling Pond, 185–188
Stowe, hikes near, 167–174, 176–179
Stowe Pinnacle, 176–179
Stratton, hikes near, 25–28
Stratton Pond, 25–28
strenuous hikes
    in central Vermont, 99–109
    in north-central Vermont, 158–166,
        180–184
    in northeastern Vermont, 211–214,
        237–240
    in southern Vermont, 35–38, 50–56,
        61–64
striped maples, 193–194
Student Conservation Association (SCA), 241
Sunset Ledge, 95–98
Sutton, hikes near, 225–236
Swanton, hikes near, 149–152
swimming areas, 219
    in central Vermont, 78, 86, 94, 98, 112,
        116
    in north-central Vermont, 161, 166, 174,
        188–192, 196, 200
    in northeastern Vermont, 215–218, 223,
        232, 245
    in northwestern Vermont, 130, 135–137,
        140–141, 144–148
    in southern Vermont, 6, 9, 16, 21, 33, 38,
        42–46, 64

T
Taconic Mountains, 9, 38, 51, 65–66
thru-hiking, 29
Townshed, hikes near, 21–24
Townshed Lake Recreation Area, 21–24
trail maintenance, 224
trip locator map, iv
trip planner, viii–xv
trip planning, xxii–xxvi
Tropical Storm Irene, 34

U
Underhill, hikes near, 180–183

V
Valley of Vermont, 1–2, 9

W
Wallingford, hikes near, 47–49
Waterbury Center, hikes near, 163–166
waterfall hikes
    in central Vermont, 79–82
    in northern Vermont, 164–165, 167–170,
        188, 196, 233–236
    in southern Vermont, 30–33, 54–55
water pollution, 219
Westfield, hikes near, 205–208
West Haven, hikes near, 75–78
Westmore, hikes near, 220–223
wetlands, 117, 150–152
Wheeler Mountain, 229–232
Wheeler Pond, 233–236
White Rock Mountain, 158–161
White Rocks Ice Beds, 47–49
wilderness areas, 2, 122
Williams Woods, 131–134
Willoughby State Forest, 220–223, 225–228
Wilmington, hikes near, 3–6, 10–12
Windsor, hikes near, 54–56
winter hiking, xxiv–xxv. *See also* cross-
        country skiing
Woodford, hikes near, 7–9
Woodford State Park, 6, 9
Woodstock, hikes near, 57–60
Wright's Mountain, 118–121

ABOUT THE AUTHOR

JENNIFER LAMPHERE ROBERTS has spent most of her adult life on trails: hiking, skiing, biking, and paddling them; building them; and leading young people on them to learn about the backcountry.

Since earning her degree in education at the University of Vermont and attending the National Outdoor Leadership School, she has taught at outdoor-oriented schools in Oregon and Vermont; worked for the Appalachian Mountain Club in the White Mountains and the Berkshires; served on the Vermont Trails and Greenways Council; and worked for Northern Forest Canoe Trail in Vermont, helping to establish the 740-mile trail and edit its first official guidebook and map series.

Jennifer lives in Montpelier, Vermont, where she teaches backcountry skiing and mountain biking when she's not roaming the woods with her family.

Appalachian Mountain Club

Founded in 1876, AMC is the nation's oldest outdoor recreation and conservation organization. AMC promotes the protection, enjoyment, and understanding of the mountains, forests, waters, and trails of the Northeast outdoors.

People

We are more than 100,000 members, advocates, and supporters, including 12 local chapters, more than 16,000 volunteers, and over 450 full-time and seasonal staff. Our chapters reach from Maine to Washington, D.C.

Outdoor Adventure and Fun

We offer more than 8,000 trips each year, from local chapter activities to adventure travel worldwide, for every ability level and outdoor interest— from hiking and climbing to paddling, snowshoeing, and skiing.

Great Places to Stay

We host more than 150,000 guests each year at our AMC lodges, huts, camps, shelters, and campgrounds. Each AMC destination is a model for environmental education and stewardship.

Opportunities for Learning

We teach people skills to safely enjoy the outdoors and to care for the natural world around us through programs for children, teens, and adults, as well as outdoor leadership training.

Caring for Trails

We maintain more than 1,700 miles of trails throughout the Northeast, including nearly 350 miles of the Appalachian Trail in five states.

Protecting Wild Places

We advocate for land and riverway conservation, monitor air quality, research climate change, and work to protect alpine and forest ecosystems throughout the Northern Forest and Mid-Atlantic Highlands regions.

Engaging the Public

We seek to educate and inform our own members and an additional 2 million people annually through the media, AMC Books, our website, our White Mountain visitor centers, and AMC destinations.

Join Us!

Members meet other like-minded people and support our mission while enjoying great AMC programs, our award-winning AMC Outdoors magazine, and special discounts. Visit outdoors.org or call 800-372-1758 for more information.

APPALACHIAN MOUNTAIN CLUB
Recreation • Education • Conservation
outdoors.org

AMC BOOK UPDATES

AMC BOOKS STRIVES TO KEEP OUR GUIDEBOOKS AS UP-TO-DATE as possible to help you plan safe and enjoyable adventures.If after publishing a book we learn that trails have been relocated or route or contact information has changed, we will post the updated information online. Before you hit the trail, check for updates at outdoors.org/bookupdates.

While hiking, if you notice discrepancies with the trip description or map, or if you find any other errors in the book, please let us know by submitting them to amcbookupdates@outdoors.org or in writing to Books Editor, c/o AMC, 5 Joy Street, Boston, MA 02108. We will verify all submissions and post key updates each month. AMC Books is dedicated to being a recognized leader in outdoor publishing. Thank you for your participation.

AMC BOOKS & MAPS

EXPLORE THE POSSIBILITIES

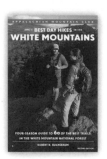